R. Gupta's®

RRB

Railway Recruitment Board

GROUP 'D'

(Posts in Level–1 of 7th CPC Pay Matrix)

Recruitment Exam

Previous Years' Papers

&

Practice Test Papers

(Solved)

2020
EDITION

Ramesh Publishing House, New Delhi

Published by
O.P. Gupta *for* Ramesh Publishing House

Admin. Office
12-H, New Daryaganj Road, Opp. Officers' Mess,
New Delhi-110002 ☎ 23261567, 23275224, 23275124

E-mail: info@rameshpublishinghouse.com
Website: www.rameshpublishinghouse.com

Showroom
● Balaji Market, Nai Sarak, Delhi-6 ☎ 23253720, 23282525
● 4457, Nai Sarak, Delhi-6, ☎ 23918938

Book Code: R-501

ISBN: 978-93-87604-62-9

HSN Code: 49011010

Contents

• • •

RAILWAY RECRUITMENT BOARD (RRB)
GROUP 'D' EXAM, 2018*

1. Which state cricket team has won the 2018 Vijay Hazare trophy?
  A. Saurashtra
  B. Rajasthan
  C. Odisha
  D. Karnataka

2. Given is a question followed by two arguments numbered I and II. Read the question and decide which of the arguments is strong with respect to the question.

  Question: Should shifting agriculture be practiced?

  Arguments: (*i*) No. It is not a worthy practice.

  (*ii*) Yes. When compared to modern methods of farming, it is less expensive.
  A. Only argument (*ii*) is strong
  B. Only argument (*i*) is strong
  C. Neither argument (*i*) nor (*ii*) is strong
  D. Either argument (*i*) or (*ii*) is strong

3. Read the given statement(s) and conclusions carefully and select which of the conclusions logically follow(s) from the statement(s).

  Statement: Recent research says listening to specific types of frequencies have a positive effect on human brain and it aids in healing.

  Conclusions: (*i*) Human brain responds to music.

  (*ii*) Certain frequencies are used to heal diseases in human body.
  A. Both the conclusions follow
  B. Neither conclusion follows
  C. Only conclusion (*i*) follows
  D. Only conclusion (*ii*) follows

4. What is the missing term in the series?

  YB25, WD23, ..., SH19
  A. UG21
  B. UF21
  C. UF20
  D. UG20

5. A solid metallic hemisphere with radius r is melted and cast into a solid right circular cone with the radius of the base $= r$. What is the ratio of their curved surface areas?
  A. $\dfrac{5}{\sqrt{2}}$
  B. $\dfrac{2}{\sqrt{5}}$
  C. $\dfrac{3}{2}$
  D. $\dfrac{5}{2}$

6. Four numbers, a, b, c and d are such that their overall average is 26.5. The average of a and b is 20. The average of c and d is:
  A. 35.5
  B. 31.5
  C. 33
  D. 32.5

7. Recently in 2018, assembly elections took place in which of the following states?
  A. Meghalaya
  B. Gujarat
  C. Assam
  D. West Bengal

8. Read the given statement and conclusions carefully and select which of the conclusions logically follow(s) from the statement.

  Statements: Some jaguars are cheetahs. Some cheetahs are leopards. All leopards are panthers.

  Conclusions: (*i*) All leopards are jaguars.

  (*ii*) Some panthers are cheetahs.
  A. Only conclusion (*ii*) follows
  B. Only conclusion (*i*) follows
  C. Either (*i*) or (*ii*) follows
  D. Both (*i*) and (*ii*) follow

9. Find the next term in the following series.

24XW23, 22VU21, ... ?

A. 20RT19   B. 20TS19
C. 20TR19   D. 20ST19

10. Who among the following approved the procurement of 111 utility helicopters for the Indian Navy at a cost of over ₹ 21,000 crores?

A. Defence Acquisition Council
B. Defence Procurement Commission
C. Defence Purchase Association
D. Defence Dealers Association

11. Genetic information is carried by long chains of molecules. What are these molecules called?

A. Phosphates   B. Nitrogenous Bases
C. RNA   D. Nucleotides

12. Astronauts in space communicate with each other by radio links because ....

A. sound waves can't travel in space
B. sound waves have low frequency
C. sound waves travel slowly in space
D. sound waves travel quickly in space

13. Choose the mirror image for the following figures:

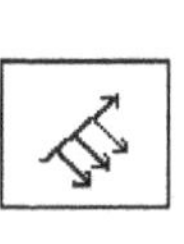
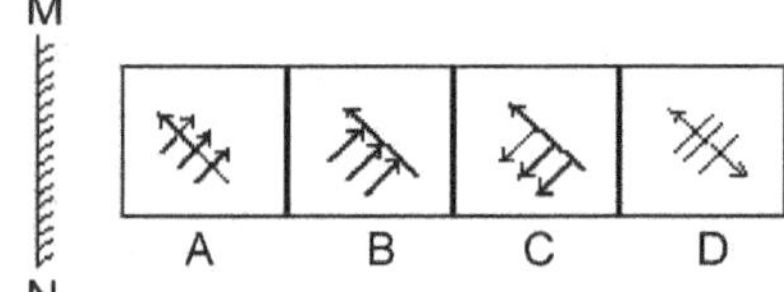

A. A   B. C
C. B   D. D

14. Who is termed as the 'Plastic Man of India', who has found a way to reuse plastic waste and make durable roads?

A. Rajagopalan Vasudevan
B. Rajagopalan Muruganantham
C. Arunachalam Muruganantham
D. Arunachalam Vasudevan

15. Starting from point O facing West a man walks 4 km to reach point A. He turns right, walks 4 km and reaches point B. Then, he turns right, walks 4 km and reaches point C. He turns right, walks 3 km and reaches point D. He turns left, walks 4 km and reaches point E. Then, he turns right, walks 5 km and reaches point F. At point F, the man is facing .... direction.

A. North   B. South
C. East   D. West

16. The kinetic energy acquired by a mass (m) in travelling distance starting from rest under the action of constant force is directly proportional to:

A. $\dfrac{1}{m}$ B. m^0

C. m D. $\dfrac{1}{\sqrt{m}}$

17. The royal city at Fatehpur Sikri, was built by Mughal Emperor .... in honour of Sufi saint Shaikh Salim Chishti.

A. Aurangzeb   B. Humayun
C. Shah Jahan   D. Akbar

18. Consider the following statement and decide which of the conclusions logically follows from the statements.

Statement: If you're a good computer programmer, then we definitely have a job for you.

Conclusions: (*i*) Good computer programmers are never jobless.

      (*ii*) We are in need of a good computer programmer.

A. Neither conclusion (*i*) nor (*ii*) follows
B. Only conclusion (*ii*) follows
C. Both conclusion (*i*) and (*ii*) follow
D. Only conclusion (*i*) follows

19. Find out the two signs that need to be switched for the equation to be equated.

$5 + 6 \times 3 - 4 \div 2 = (-1)$

A. × & +   B. − & ÷
C. ÷ & ×   D. + & −

20. Select the option that is related to the third term in the same way as the second term is related to the first term.

Alight : Descend :: House : .... ?

A. Pound   B. Home
C. Hug   D. Hen

21. Non-metals are generally more electronegative due to their:
A. large number of electrons
B. smaller atomic radii
C. smaller atomic number
D. smaller ionization energy

22. You are given a question and two statements. Identify which of the statements is/are necessary/sufficient to answer the question.

Question: There are 6 baskets in a supermarket that are used to load and unload commodity. All have been filled with tins of 2 different sizes and shapes. In total, how many tins have been loaded in the baskets?

Statements: (*i*) The shape of 6 tins is such that in one trolley, only 2 can fit.

(*ii*) The tins contain processed sauce.

A. The statements are not sufficient
B. Statement (*i*) alone is sufficient
C. Statement (*ii*) alone is sufficient
D. Statement (*i*) and (*ii*) together are necessary

23. Who has played the lead role in the movie 'Dangal' released in 2016?
A. Akshay Kumar
B. Shah Rukh Khan
C. Aamir Khan
D. Raj Kumar Rao

24. 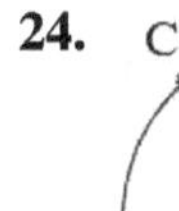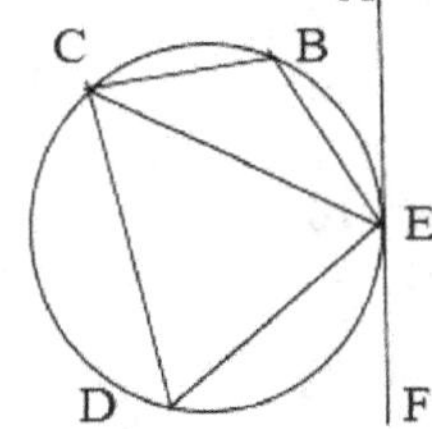

In the figure given above, AF is a tangent to the circle at E, $\angle CDE = 80°$ and $m\left(\overline{BC}\right) = m\left(\overline{BE}\right)$. What is the measure of $\angle BEA$?

A. 30°
B. 45°
C. 40°
D. 35°

25. The property of metals wherein they can be beaten into thin sheets is called:
A. expansion
B. malleability
C. ductility
D. conduction

26. Mass/Volume = ...
A. Pressure
B. Area
C. Density
D. Force

27. .... tissue is found beneath are skin, around the kidneys and between the internal organs.
A. Ligament
B. Areolar
C. Tendons
D. Adipose

28. Who among the following is known as 'The Guardian of Public Purse'?
A. Attorney General
B. Comptroller & Auditor General
C. Chief Minister
D. Prime Minister

29. Read the given statement(s) and conclusions carefully. Assuming that the information in the statement(s) is true, even if they appear to be at variance with commonly known facts, select which of the conclusions logically follow(s) from the statement(s) beyond reasonable doubt.

Statements: All crayons are pens.
All pens are nibs.

Conclusions: (*i*) All crayons are nibs.
(*ii*) All nibs are crayons.

A. Only (*ii*) follows
B. Only (*i*) follows
C. Both (*i*) and (*ii*) follow
D. Neither (*i*) nor (*ii*) follows

30. Which of the following numbers will have an even number of factors?
A. 16900
B. 52900
C. 30000
D. 36100

31. The SI unit of thrust is ....
A. Pascal
B. Ohm
C. Newton
D. Joule

32. The diagram shows the force field produced by a current-carrying wire. Name the force field.

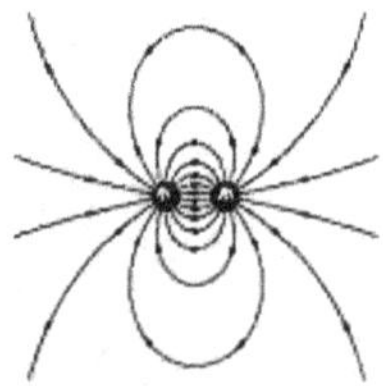

A. Electrostatic field
B. Magnetic field
C. Electromagnetic field
D. Static field

33. Ravi sold goods for ₹ 6250 and made a profit of 25% in the process. What would have been his profit percent if he had sold the same goods for ₹ 6000?
A. 10%   B. 15%
C. 20%   D. 5%

34. In .... tissue the cells are widely spaced.
A. Tendons   B. Cartilage
C. Bone   D. Ligament

35. The AIADMK party is a regional political party of which state?
A. Karnataka   B. Telangana
C. Tamil Nadu   D. Andhra Pradesh

36. Pressure × Area = ... ?
A. Thrust   B. Inertia
C. Momentum   D. Volume

37. Study the pattern in the following series and identify which figure from the answer figures will follow next.

Problem figure

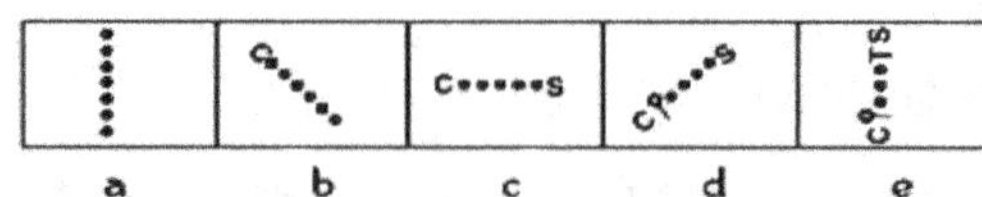

a   b   c   d   e

Answer figures

1   2   3   4   5

A. 5   B. 2
C. 3   D. 1

38. A hollow sphere with external and internal diameters as 24 cm and 16 cm, respectively, is melted into a cylinder with a base diameter of 32 cm. The height of the cylinder is closest to:
A. 7.33 cm   B. 5.56 cm
C. 5.16 cm   D. 6.33 cm

39. 

Using the above three shapes form a valid shape and identify your shape with the below options?

A. 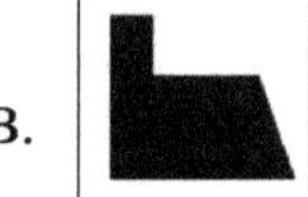   B. 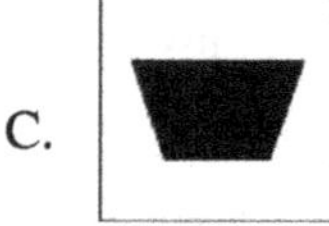

C. 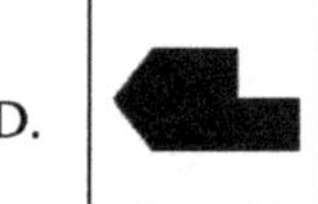   D.

40. Founded in 1927, Dr. Bhimrao Ambedkar University is a non-profit public higher education institution located in the urban setting of the large city of ....
A. Gorakhpur   B. Agra
C. Lucknow   D. Kanpur

41. Ratnagiri mines are found in which state?
A. Gujarat   B. Telangana
C. Maharashtra   D. Karnataka

42. How many groups are there in the modern periodic table?
A. 9   B. 18
C. 21   D. 8

43. The two roots of a quadratic equation are given as $x = \dfrac{5}{3}$ and $x = \dfrac{-3}{10}$. The equation can be written as:
A. $(10x - 3)(3x - 5) = 0$
B. $(10x + 3)(3x - 5) = 0$
C. $(10x + 3)(3x + 5) = 0$
D. $(10x - 3)(3x + 5) = 0$

44. Neela was sweeping the floor. When she was facing south-west, she moved the broom 90° along the floor to her right. In which direction is the broom facing with respect to its initial position?
A. North-West
B. South-West
C. North-East
D. South-East

45. Arjit's age is 3 years more than 1.5 times the age of Heera, whose age in turn is 10 years more than $\frac{2}{3}$ the age of Deepika. If 5 times the age of Deepika is equal to 3 times the age of Arjit, what is the sum of the present ages of the trio?
A. 99 years
B. 95 years
C. 100 years
D. 97 years

46. Select the option that is related to the third term in the same way as the second term is related to the first term.

Bird : Nest :: Lion : .... ?
A. Hive
B. Den
C. Igloo
D. Convent

47. Preeti tells Kajol, "Your mother's father's own son is my husband." How is Preeti related to Kajol?
A. Daughter
B. Cousin
C. Sister-in-law
D. Aunt

48. ₹ 10,000, invested at 30% rate of interest per annum, but compounded every four months, will give an amount of ₹ .... in one year.
A. 13270
B. 13000
C. 13300
D. 13310

49. Which of the numbers given below is NOT divisible by 4?
A. 89700
B. 76166
C. 43584
D. 74708

50. A body of mass m moving with velocity 4 km/h collides with a body of mass 3 m at rest. Now the coalesced mass starts to move with a velocity of:
A. 4 km/h
B. $\frac{4}{3}$ km/h
C. 1 km/h
D. 2 km/h

51. The square root of which of the numbers below will be rational?
A. 16848
B. 41872
C. 49883
D. 43264

52. Find the number of triangles in the given figure.

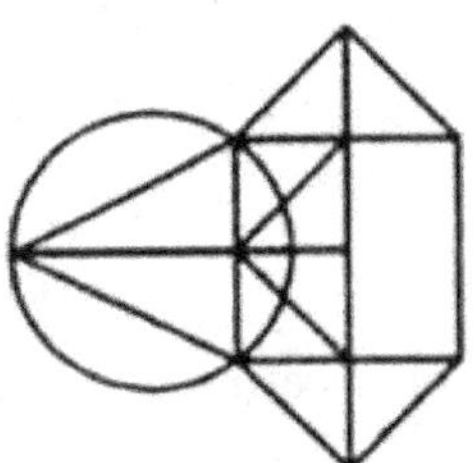

A. 14
B. 12
C. 10
D. 16

53. Atomic Power Station is located at *Rawatbhata*, in the state of ....
A. Maharashtra
B. Madhya Pradesh
C. Rajasthan
D. Gujarat

54. Which of the following numbers is a composite?
A. 263
B. 293
C. 283
D. 273

55. Find the next term in the following series.

48, 47, 50, 49, ... ?
A. 52
B. 58
C. 60
D. 57

56. As of February 2018, the Chairman of Central Board of Film Certification is:
A. Sujit Sircar
B. Prasoon Joshi
C. Swanand Kirkire
D. Pahlaj Nihalani

57. How many sectors are present in the below figure?

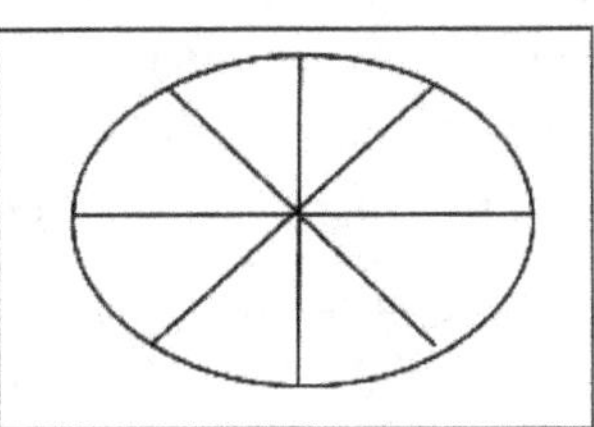

A. 64
B. 40
C. 48
D. 56

58. Oxides of non-metals are usually ....
  A. acidic
  B. neutral
  C. less reactive
  D. basic

59. .... describes pollination by the agency of ants.
  A. Emasculation
  B. Ficus Religiosa
  C. Dirmecophily
  D. Myrmecophily

60. Barkha Dutt is known for her role as which of the following?
  A. Politician
  B. Doctor
  C. Journalist
  D. Actor

61. The process of releasing of an egg from the ovary is called ....
  A. Fertilisation
  B. Reproduction
  C. Gestation
  D. Ovulation

62. The arithmetic mean of four distinct numbers is 90. If the greatest of the four numbers is 120, what is the maximum possible value of the range of the set of four numbers?
  A. 115
  B. 117
  C. 116
  D. 118

63. $105 \times 2 \div (3 \times 5) - 6 = ?$
  A. −70
  B. 5
  C. 8
  D. 35

64. Mohan's mother was four times as old as Mohan ten years ago. After 10 years, she will be twice as old as Mohan. How old is Mohan today?
  A. 20 years
  B. 15 years
  C. 22 years
  D. 32 years

65. A cube of 9 cm edge is immersed completely in a rectangular vessel containing water. If the base of the vessel is 12 cm × 15 cm, then find the rise in the level of water when the cube is immersed?
  A. 4.55 cm
  B. 6.05 cm
  C. 6.55 cm
  D. 4.05 cm

66. 4 W X Z 8 Q P O J 6 G T M V E U H 5 3 B

If the letters in the position 8, 12, 13 and 15 from the left are picked to form a meaningful word, then the third letter of the word would be:
  A. P
  B. O
  C. E
  D. M

67. The median of the first 25 whole numbers is:
  A. 10
  B. 12.5
  C. 15
  D. 12

68. Which of the following is NOT a difference between lenses and mirrors?
  A. Light reflects from a mirror. Light goes through and is refracted by a lens
  B. A concave mirror converges light to a focal point. For lenses, light converges to point for a convex lens
  C. A convex mirror converges light, as does a concave lens
  D. Lenses have two focal points, one on either side of the lens

69. 75% of the students passed in an examination. If 2 more students had passed the examination, 80% would have been successful. How many students are there in the class?
  A. 40
  B. 30
  C. 50
  D. 32

70. The Mission Olympic Cell (MOC) of the Union Ministry of Sports and Youth Affairs included the Men's .... team of India in the Target Olympic Podium Scheme.
  A. Hockey
  B. Shooting
  C. Football
  D. Badminton

71. What change will occur to the pH of a solution if its Hydrogen ion concentration is increased?
  A. The pH will decrease
  B. The pH will first increase and after some time, decrease
  C. The pH will remain the same
  D. The pH will increase

72. The square root of 19881 is:
  A. 149
  B. 129
  C. 141
  D. 131

73. The least reactive elements of the periodic table are:
  A. Transition elements
  B. Inner transition elements
  C. Alkali metals
  D. Noble gases

74. Newton's second law of motion ....
   A. is also called as law of conservation of momentum
   B. is also called as law of inertia
   C. describes the relationship between the forces on two interacting objects
   D. explains about change in momentum

75. What is the HCF of 132 and 176?
   A. 33
   B. 66
   C. 44
   D. 22

76. Shamim had to travel 420 km in 8 hours. If he travelled at an average speed of 60 km/h and took two breaks in between, the shorter break being one-third the duration of the longer. How many minutes was the longer break for?
   A. 45
   B. 30
   C. 40
   D. 35

77. An athlete in the Olympic games covers a distance of 100 m in 10s. His kinetic energy can be estimated to be in the range of:
   A. 200 J - 500 J
   B. 200000 J - 500000 J
   C. 20000 J - 50000 J
   D. 2000 J - 5000 J

78. A sum of money when invested for a year at the rate of 10% interest per annum compounded half-yearly becomes ₹ 44,100 at maturity. The sum invested was ....
   A. ₹ 40,000
   B. ₹ 40,500
   C. ₹ 39,800
   D. ₹ 40,250

79. Three out of the four options given below are related in a particular way. Choose the option that is different or odd from the others.
   A. Jhelum
   B. Betwa
   C. Chambal
   D. Yamuna

80. The .... has created National Highways Investment Promotion Cell (NHIPC) for attracting domestic and foreign investment for highways projects.
   A. NTPC
   B. SAIL
   C. TRAI
   D. NHAI

81. Read the statement and decide which of the conclusions logically follows from the statement.

Statement: This cup is filled with tea.

Conclusions: (*i*) The tea is too hot.
   (*ii*) The tea is sweet.
   A. Neither conclusion (*i*) nor (*ii*) follows
   B. Only conclusion (*i*) follows
   C. Both conclusions (*i*) and (*ii*) follow
   D. Only conclusion (*ii*) follows

82. Sravanthi is Varun's maternal grandmother. How is Varun's only sister's mother related to Sravanthi?
   A. Daughter
   B. Sister-in-law
   C. Aunt
   D. Sister

83. Which of the following Venn diagrams best illustrates the relation between the three given classes?

Professor, Student, Player

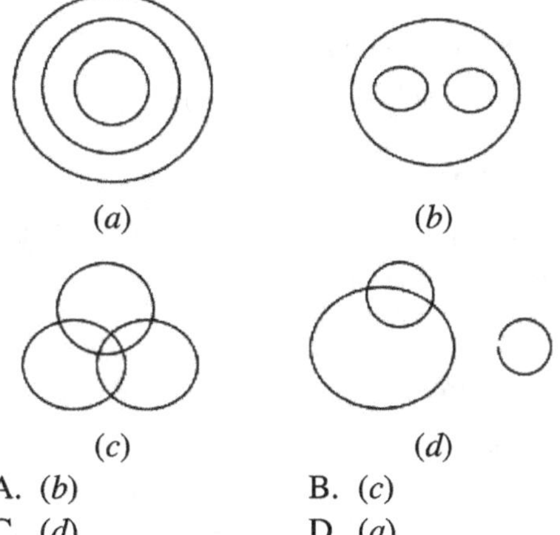

(*a*)   (*b*)

(*c*)   (*d*)

   A. (*b*)
   B. (*c*)
   C. (*d*)
   D. (*a*)

84. Shesh Anand Madhukar is a .... writer who was honoured with the Sahitya Academy Bhasha Samman Award in January, 2018.
   A. Maithili
   B. Kannada
   C. Magahi
   D. Sanskrit

85. Select the option that is related to the third term in the same way as the second term is related to the first term.

STEPS : SPETS :: CLOCK : .... ?
   A. KCOCL
   B. KCLOC
   C. KOCLC
   D. KCOLC

86. Find odd one out.
   A. VI
   B. 7
   C. IX
   D. VII

87. Sarthak can fill a sand-pit with sand in 36 days while Vivan takes 90 days to fill it. Ali can take the entire sand of a filled sand-pit out in 60 days. If all three start working when the pit is empty, in how many days will the sand-pit be full again?
   A. 45
   B. 54
   C. 48
   D. 50

88. The Godavari, Krishna, Kaveri and Vaigai are .... flowing rivers.
   A. north
   B. east
   C. west
   D. south

89. The sum of a rational and an irrational number is a/an ....
   A. Rational number
   B. Natural number
   C. Irrational number
   D. Complex number

90. Consider the following question and decide which of the statements is sufficient to answer the question.

Question: Find the value of z.

Statements: (*i*) $z^2 = 36 + a$

(*ii*) $a = x^2$ & $x = 8$

   A. Either (*i*) or (*ii*) is sufficient
   B. Both (*i*) and (*ii*) are sufficient
   C. Only (*i*) is sufficient
   D. Only (*ii*) is sufficient

91. Which of the following statements is NOT true?
   A. Bacteria present in the mouth produce acids by degradation of sugar and food particles remaining in the mouth
   B. When pH of the mouth is higher than 5.5, then tooth decay starts
   C. Tooth enamel made of calcium phosphate is the hardest substance in the body

   D. Using toothpaste, which are generally basic, helps neutralise the excess acid and prevent tooth decay

92. A and B can complete a task in 70 days, B and C can complete in 52.5 days while C and A can do the same task together in 42 days. How many days will each of A, B and C take to complete the task individually?
   A. 105, 210 and 70
   B. 56, 84 and 168
   C. 70, 210 and 105
   D. 84, 168 and 56

93. Which of the following is NOT an equation of motion?

   A. $s = ut + \dfrac{1}{2}at^3$

   B. $v = u + a$

   C. $s = ut + \dfrac{1}{2}at^2$

   D. $v^2 = u^2 + 2as$

94. Which children's movie features the famous song, "The Bare Necessities"?
   A. The Jungle Book
   B. Rockford
   C. Stanley's Tiffin Box
   D. The BFG

95. Consider the following question and decide which of the statements is sufficient to answer the question.

The simple interest on a sum of money is ₹ 100. What is the sum?

Statements: (*i*) The interest rate is 20% per annum.

(*ii*) The sum earned simple interest in 5 years.

   A. Both statements (*i*) and (*ii*) are sufficient
   B. Only statement (*i*) is sufficient
   C. Only statement (*ii*) is sufficient
   D. Either statement (*i*) or (*ii*) is sufficient

96. Which of the following statements is correct?
- A. Two or more resistors are said to be connected in series if different current flows through them
- B. Two or more resistors are said to be connected in series if the same current flows through them
- C. Two or more resistors are said to be connected in parallel if the same current flows through them
- D. Two or more resistors are said to be connected in parallel if different current flows through them

97. The atomic number of the atom that becomes stable by gaining 3 electrons in 5th shell is:
- A. 57
- B. 51
- C. 55
- D. 59

98. Find the odd one out:
- A. Quadratic Equation
- B. Cubic Equation
- C. Linear Equation
- D. Real Numbers

99. Which of the following cup/tournament is NOT associated with Cricket?
- A. Irani trophy
- B. Ranji trophy
- C. Begum Hazrat Mahal trophy
- D. Vijay Hazare trophy

100. Raja Ravi Verma was a painter and sculptor from the state of ....
- A. Uttar Pradesh
- B. Kerala
- C. Tamil Nadu
- D. Assam

ANSWERS

1	2	3	4	5	6	7	8	9	10
*	A	D	B	B	C	A	A	B	A

11	12	13	14	15	16	17	18	19	20
D	A	B	A	B	B	D	B	C	B

21	22	23	24	25	26	27	28	29	30
B	A	C	C	B	C	D	B	B	C

31	32	33	34	35	36	37	38	39	40
C	*	C	B	C	A	*	D	A	B

41	42	43	44	45	46	47	48	49	50
C	B	B	A	C	B	D	D	B	C

51	52	53	54	55	56	57	58	59	60
D	A	C	D	A	B	D	A	D	C

61	62	63	64	65	66	67	68	69	70
D	B	C	A	D	D	D	C	A	A

71	72	73	74	75	76	77	78	79	80
A	C	D	D	C	A	D	A	A	D

81	82	83	84	85	86	87	88	89	90
A	A	C	C	D	B	A	B	C	B

91	92	93	94	95	96	97	98	99	100
B	A	*	A	A	B	B	D	C	B

For this question, discrepancy is found in question/answer. So, this question is ignored for all candidates.

EXPLANATORY ANSWERS

4. 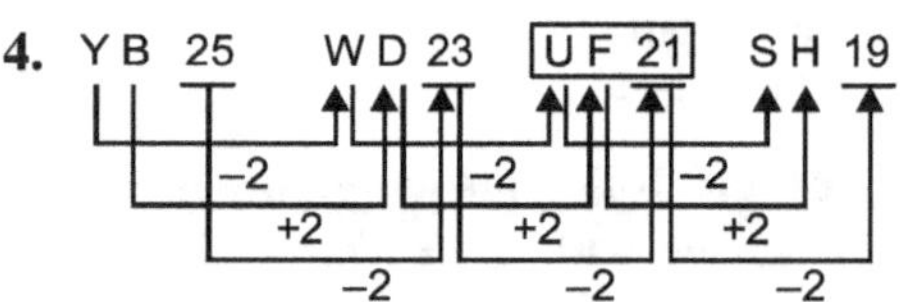

5. $\because$ Volume of Hemisphere

= Volume of solid right circular cone

$$\frac{2}{3}\pi r^3 = \frac{1}{3}\times \pi r^2 h$$

$$h = 2r$$

Required Ratio of their curved surface area

$$= \frac{2\pi r^2}{\pi r l} = \frac{2r}{l} = \frac{2r}{\sqrt{5}r} = \frac{2}{\sqrt{5}}$$

$$\left[\because l = \sqrt{r^2 + h^2} = \sqrt{r^2 + (2r)^2} = \sqrt{5}r\right]$$

6. We have,

$$\frac{a+b+c+d}{4} = 26.5$$

$$a + b + c + d = 106 \qquad ...(i)$$

and, $$\frac{a+b}{2} = 20$$

$$a + b = 40 \qquad ...(ii)$$

From (i) and (ii)

$$c + d = 106 - 40$$

$$= 66$$

$$\text{Average} = \frac{66}{2}$$

$$= 33.$$

8. 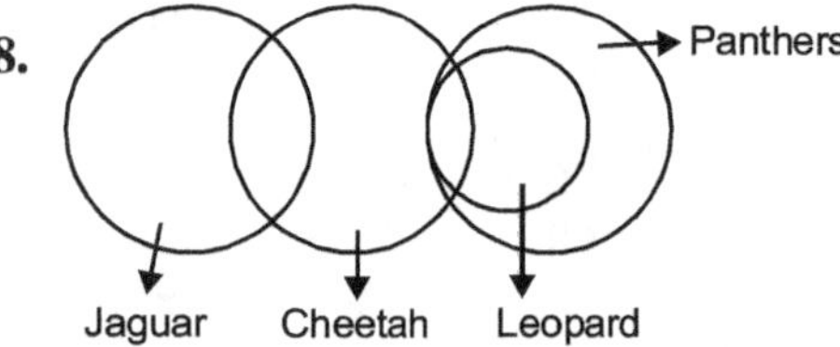

Hence, only conclusion (ii) follows.

9. 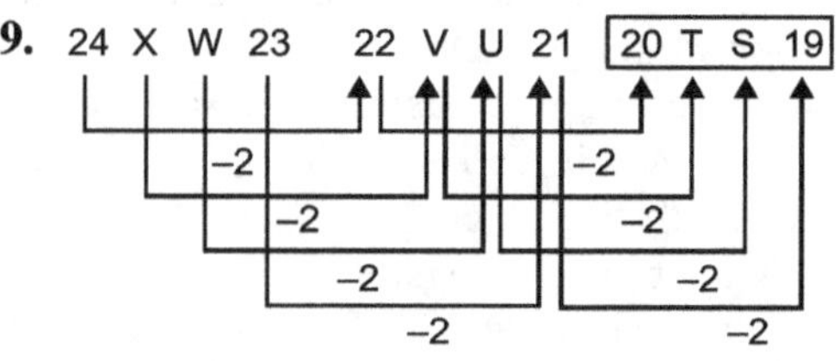

15. 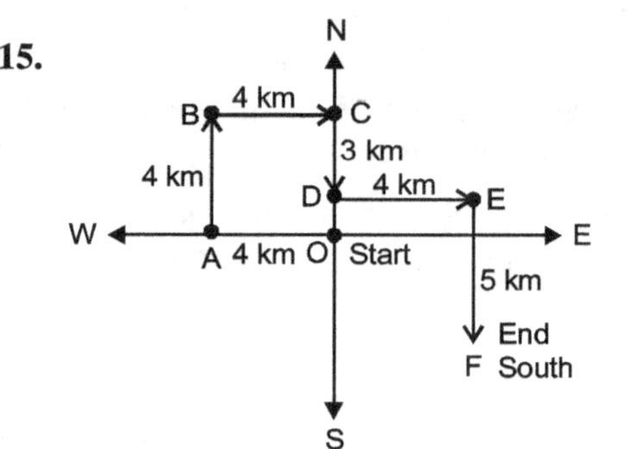

The man is facing south direction.

19. $5 + 6 \times 3 - 4 \div 2 = (-1)$

After checking the options, we get

A. $\times$ & +

$$= 5 \times 6 + 3 - 4 \div 2$$
$$= 5 \times 6 + 3 - 2$$
$$= 30 + 3 - 2$$
$$= 31$$

B. $-$ & $\div$

$$= 5 + 6 \times 3 \div 4 - 2$$
$$= 5 + 6 \times \frac{3}{4} - 2$$
$$= 5 + \frac{9}{2} - 2$$
$$= 3\frac{3}{2}$$

C. $\div$ & $\times$

$$= 5 + 6 \div 3 - 4 \times 2$$
$$= 5 + 2 - 4 \times 2$$
$$= 5 + 2 - 8$$
$$= 7 - 8$$
$$= (-1)$$

Hence option C is correct.

24. $\angle CBE = 180° - 80° = 100°$

$\because \quad m\left(\overline{BC}\right) = m\left(\overline{BE}\right)$

$\therefore \qquad \angle BCE = \angle BEC$

$$= \frac{180 - 100}{2}$$

$$= \frac{80}{2}$$

$$= 40°$$

$\angle BEA = \angle BCE = 40°$

(Alternate Segment Angle)

29.

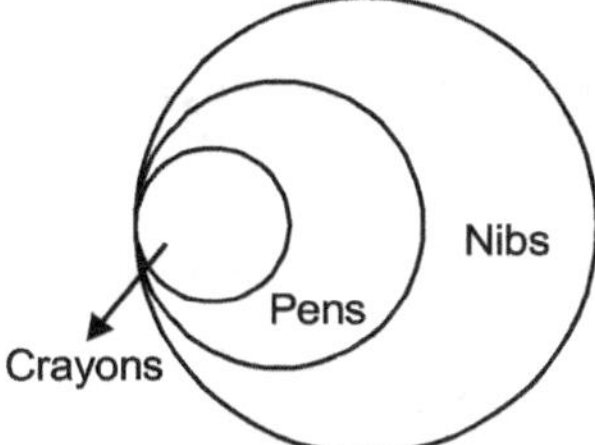

Hence, only conclusion (*i*) follows.

30. A.

2	16900
2	8450
5	4225
5	845
13	169
13	13
	1

$16900 = 2 \times 2 \times 5 \times 5 \times 13 \times 13$

$\qquad = (2)^2 \times (5)^2 \times (13)^2$

Total factor

$\qquad = (2 + 1)\ (2 + 1)\ (2 + 1)$

$\qquad = 3 \times 3 \times 3$

$\qquad = 27$

B.

2	52900
2	26450
5	13225
5	2645
23	529
23	23
	1

$52900 = 2 \times 2 \times 5 \times 5 \times 23 \times 23$

$\qquad = (2)^2 \times (5)^2 \times (23)^2$

Total factor

$\qquad = (2 + 1)\ (2 + 1)\ (2 + 1)$

$\qquad = 3 \times 3 \times 3$

$\qquad = 27$

C.

2	30000
2	15000
2	7500
3	3750
5	1875
5	375
5	75
5	15
3	3
	1

$30000 = 2 \times 2 \times 2 \times 2 \times 5 \times 5 \times 5 \times 5 \times 3$

$\qquad = (2)^4 \times (5)^4 \times (3)^1$

Total factor

$\qquad = (4 + 1)\ (4 + 1)\ (1 + 1)$

$\qquad = 5 \times 5 \times 2$

$\qquad = 50$

D.

2	36100
2	18050
5	9025
5	1805
19	361
19	19
	1

$36100 = 2 \times 2 \times 5 \times 5 \times 19 \times 19$

$\qquad = (2)^2 \times (5)^2 \times (19)^2$

Total factor

$\qquad = (2 + 1)\ (2 + 1)\ (2 + 1)$

$\qquad = 3 \times 3 \times 3$

$\qquad = 27$

Hence, 30000 will have even No. of factors.

33. $\because$

$$\frac{SP_1}{100 \pm P/L\%} = \frac{SP_2}{100 \pm P/L\%}$$

$$\frac{6250}{100 + 25} = \frac{6000}{100 + P}$$

$$\frac{6250}{125} = \frac{6000}{100 + P}$$

$$\frac{50}{1} = \frac{6000}{100 + P}$$

$$5000 + 50\,P = 6000$$

$$50\,P = 1000$$

$$P = 20\%.$$

38. Let, the height of cylinder = h cm

External radius (r_2) = $\dfrac{24}{2}$ = 12 cm

Internal radius (r_1) = $\dfrac{16}{2}$ = 8 cm

Radius of cylinder (r) = $\dfrac{32}{2}$ = 16 cm

Volume of hollow sphere
$$= \text{Volume of cylinder}$$

$$\frac{4}{3}\pi\left(r_2^3 - r_1^3\right) = \pi r^2 h$$

$$\frac{4}{3}\left((12)^3 - (8)^3\right) = (16)^2 \times h$$

$$\frac{4}{3}(1728 - 512) = 256 \times h$$

$$\frac{4}{3} \times 1216 = 256 \times h$$

$$h = \frac{4 \times 1216}{3 \times 256}$$

$$= \frac{4864}{768}$$

$$= 6.33 \text{ cm.}$$

43. If a quadratic equation has roots α and β, then quadratic equation $(x - \alpha)(x - \beta) = 0$

$$\left(x - \frac{5}{3}\right)\left(x + \frac{3}{10}\right) = 0$$

$$(3x - 5)(10x + 3) = 0.$$

44.

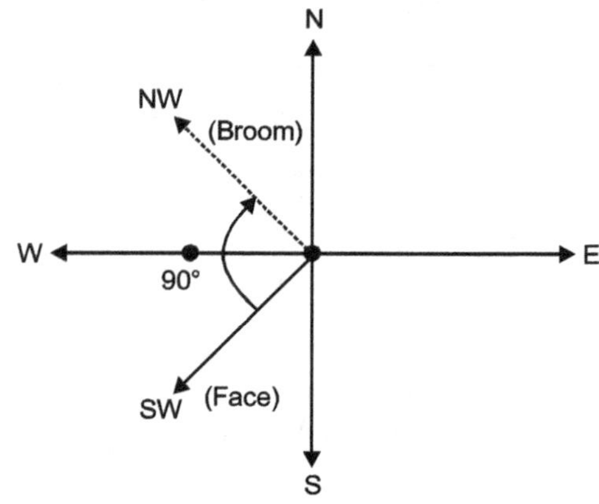

Broom will be in North-West direction.

45. We have,

Arjit's age = 1.5 × Heera's age + 3 ...(i)

Heera's age = $\dfrac{2}{3}$ × Deepika's age + 10 ...(ii)

5 × Deepika's age = 3 × Arjit's age

Deepika's age = $\dfrac{3}{5}$ × Arjit's age ...(iii)

From eq (ii)

Heera's age = $\dfrac{2}{3} \times \dfrac{3}{5}$ × Arjit's age + 10

$$= \frac{2}{5} \times \text{Arjit's age} + 10$$

From eq (i)

Arjit's age = $1.5 \times \left(\dfrac{2}{5}\text{Arjit's age} + 10\right) + 3$

Arjit's age = $\dfrac{3}{5}$ Arjit's age + 15 + 3

$\dfrac{2}{5}$ Arjit's age = 18

Arjit's age = 45 years

From eq (iii)

Deepika's age = $\dfrac{3}{5} \times 45$ = 27 years

From eq (*ii*)

Heera's age = $\dfrac{2}{3} \times 27 + 10$ = 28 years

Required sum of their ages
= 45 + 27 + 28
= 100.

46. As Bird lives in Nest, similarly Lion lives in Den.

47. 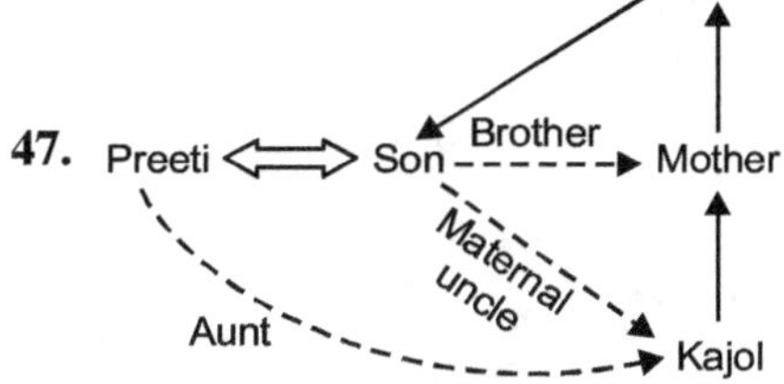

48. Principal (P) = ₹ 10,000

$\because$ Compounded every four month

$\therefore$ $\qquad t = 3$ years

$$r = \dfrac{30\%}{3}$$

$$= 10\%$$

$\therefore$ $\qquad$ Interest $= P\left(1 + \dfrac{r}{100}\right)^t$

$$= 10000\left(1 + \dfrac{10}{100}\right)^3$$

$$= 10000\left(\dfrac{11}{10}\right)^3$$

$$= 10000 \times \dfrac{1331}{1000}$$

$$= 13310.$$

49. A number is divisible by 4, if the last two digit is divisible by 4.

51. A. $\sqrt{16848}$ = 129.79 (Irrational)

B. $\sqrt{41872}$ = 204.62 (Irrational)

C. $\sqrt{49883}$ = 223.35 (Irrational)

D. $\sqrt{43624}$ = 208 (Rational)

52. 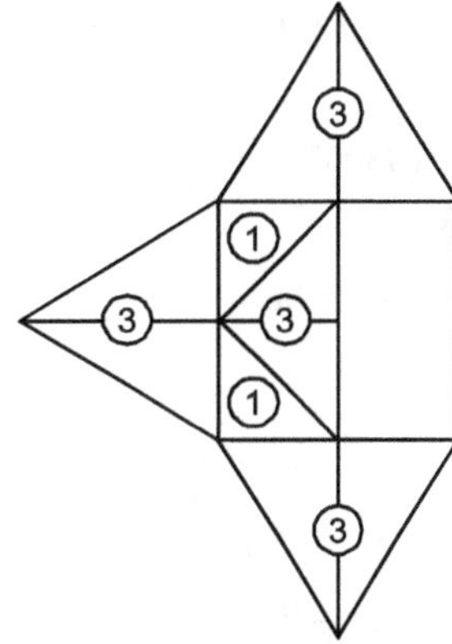

$\therefore$ Total Triangles = 3 + 3 + 3 + 3 + 1 + 1 = 14.

54. A No. is a composite number, if it is not a prime No.

Since 273 is not a prime No. So this is a composite number.

54.

62. Sum of four distinct no. $(a + b + c + d)$
$= 4 \times 90 = 360$
We have, Greatest number $(d) = 120$
$\qquad a + b + c = 360 - 120 = 240$
Then, smallest possible number = 3
$\qquad\qquad$ Range = Max − Min
$$= 120 - 3$$
$$= 117.$$

64. Let, Mohan's today age $= x$ years
Mohan's mother age $= 4(x - 10)$
After 10 years,
$\qquad 4(x - 10) + 10 + 10 = 2(x + 10)$
$\qquad\qquad 4x - 40 + 20 = 2x + 20$
$\qquad\qquad\qquad 2x = 40$
$\qquad\qquad\qquad x = 20$ years.

65. Let, the rise in the level of water $= x$ cm
$$(9)^3 = 12 \times 15 \times x$$
$$x = \dfrac{729}{12 \times 15}$$
$$= 4.05 \text{ cm.}$$

66. 8, 12, 13 and 15 letter from the left are

O, T, M, E

Meaningful word is TOME

∴ Third letter = M.

69. Let, the total students in the class = x

$$80\%x - 75\%x = 2$$
$$5\%x = 2$$
$$x = \frac{2 \times 100}{5}$$
$$= 40.$$

72. $\sqrt{19881} = 141$

```
            141
        ┌─────────
      1 │ 1 98 81
      1 │ 1
     ───┼────────
     24 │  98
      4 │  96
    ────┼────────
    281 │    281
      1 │    281
    ────┼────────
        │     ×
```

75. HCF (132, 176) = 44

```
   132 ) 176 ( 1
         132
        ─────
      44 ) 132 ( 3
           132
          ─────
            ×
```

76. Time $= \dfrac{420}{60} = 7h$

Shorter Break + Longer Break $= 8 - 7 = 1h$

$$...(i)$$

Given, Shorter Break $= \dfrac{\text{Longer Break}}{3}$ $...(ii)$

From eq (i) and (ii)

$$\frac{4}{3} \times \text{Longer Break} = 1h$$

$$\text{Longer Break} = \frac{3}{4}h$$

$$= \frac{3}{4} \times 60 \text{ min}$$

$$= 45 \text{ min}.$$

78. Let, sum $= ₹\, x$

∵ Compounded Half-yearly

∴ $\quad r = \dfrac{10\%}{2} = 5\%$

$t = 2$ years

∵ $\quad A = P\left(1 + \dfrac{r}{100}\right)^t$

$$44100 = x\left(1 + \frac{5}{100}\right)^2$$

$$44100 = x\left(\frac{21}{20}\right)^2$$

$$44100 = x \times \frac{441}{400}$$

$$x = ₹\, 40,000$$

∴ Sum was ₹ 40,000.

82.

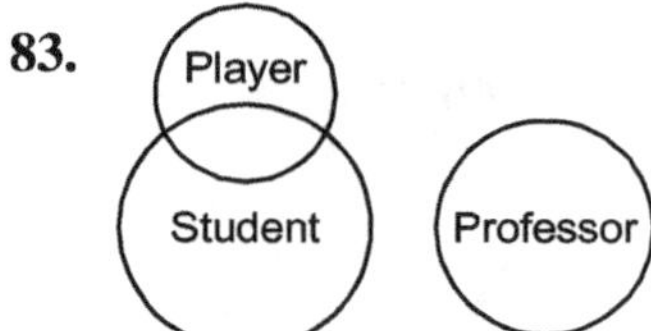

83.

85. As STEPS : SPETS

Reverse order

Similarly,

CLOCK : KCOLC

Reverse order

86. Except 7, all others are Roman Numbers.

87. By all three the sand pit filled with sand in one day

$$= \frac{1}{36} + \frac{1}{90} - \frac{1}{60}$$

$$= \frac{5+2-3}{180}$$

$$= \frac{4}{180}$$

$\therefore$ Required no. of days $= \dfrac{180}{4} = 45$ days.

90. (*i*) $z^2 = 36 + 9$

(*ii*) $a = x^2$ & $x = 8$

$\therefore a = (8)^2 = 64$

$\therefore z^2 = 36 + 64$

$z^2 = 100$

$z = \pm 10$

$\therefore$ Both (*i*) and (*ii*) are sufficient.

92. (A + B), one day's work $= \dfrac{1}{70}$

(B + C), one day's work $= \dfrac{1}{52.5} = \dfrac{2}{105}$

(C + A), one day's work $= \dfrac{1}{42}$

$2(A+B+C)$, one day's work $= \dfrac{1}{70} + \dfrac{2}{105} + \dfrac{1}{42}$

$$= \frac{3+4+5}{210} = \frac{12}{210}$$

(A + B + C), one day's work $= \dfrac{6}{210} = \dfrac{2}{70}$

A's one day's work $= \dfrac{2}{70} - \dfrac{2}{105}$

$$= \frac{6-4}{210}$$

$$= \frac{2}{210}$$

$$= \frac{1}{105}$$

$\therefore$ A can complete the task in 105 days

B's one day's work $= \dfrac{2}{70} - \dfrac{1}{42}$

$$= \frac{6-5}{210}$$

$$= \frac{1}{210}$$

$\therefore$ B can complete the task in 210 days

C's one day's work $= \dfrac{2}{70} - \dfrac{1}{70} = \dfrac{1}{70}$

$\therefore$ C can complete the task in 70 days.

95. Sum (P) = ₹ 100

(*i*) Interest Rate (*r*) = 20% per annum

(*ii*) Time (*t*) = 5 years

$$SI = \frac{p \times r \times t}{100}$$

$$= \frac{100 \times 20 \times 5}{100}$$

$$= ₹ \, 100$$

$\therefore$ Both statements (*i*) and (*ii*) are sufficient.

RAILWAY RECRUITMENT BOARD (RRB)
GROUP-'D' EXAM, 2014

1. Huen Tsang, famous Chinese traveller to India memorial is located at?
   A. Gaya
   B. Rajgir
   C. Pavapuri
   D. Nalanda

2. In which landmark judgement did the Supreme Court of India lay down guidelines against sexual harassment of women at workplace?
   A. Nilabati Behera vs. State of Odisha
   B. Vishakha vs. State of Rajasthan
   C. Maneka Gandhi vs. Union of India
   D. Hussainara Khatoon vs. State of Bihar

3. Which monument was built to commemorate the visit of King George V and Queen Mary to Bombay?
   A. India Gate
   B. Gateway of India
   C. Victoria Terminus
   D. Elephanta Caves

4. Next to Delhi, which is the most populated Union Territory in India?
   A. Chandigarh
   B. Puducherry
   C. Daman and Diu
   D. Andaman and Nicobar

5. Termination of sitting of a House without any definite date being fixed for the next sitting is called:
   A. Adjournment, Sine die
   B. Porogation
   C. Expunction
   D. Question Hour

6. In which country FIFA World Cup–2018 will be played?
   A. Sao Paulo
   B. Brazil
   C. Argentina
   D. Russia

7. Buenos Aires is the Capital of which country?
   A. Argentina
   B. Brazil
   C. Costa Rica
   D. Jamaica

8. Shri Narendra Modi assumed Office of PM on:
   A. 16 May, 2014
   B. 22 May, 2014
   C. 26 May, 2014
   D. 28 May, 2014

9. A programme to augment power supply to rural areas as announced in the Budget speech 2014-15 is named after:
   A. Deen Dayal Upadhyay
   B. Shyama Prasad Mukherji
   C. Madan Mohan Malviya
   D. Pradhan Mantri

10. Joint Parliamentary Sessions are chaired by the:
    A. Prime Minister of India
    B. Speaker of the Lok Sabha
    C. President of India
    D. Vice President of India who is the Chairman of the Rajya Sabha

11. How many non-permanent members are there in the Security Council?
    A. 10
    B. 12
    C. 15
    D. 8

12. The minimum age to qualify for election to the Lok Sabha is:
    A. 18 years
    B. 21 years
    C. 35 years
    D. 25 years

13. The National Integration Council (NIC) is chaired by the:
    A. Prime Minister
    B. President
    C. Finance Minister
    D. Home Minister

14. Sargasso Sea is found in which Ocean?
    A. Arctic Ocean
    B. Atlantic Ocean
    C. Indian Ocean
    D. Antarctic Ocean

15. October 2, the birthday of Mahatma Gandhi is internationally observed as:
    A. Non-violence Day
    B. Vegetarians Day

C. Martyrs' Day
D. Communal Harmony Day

16. Bhagat Singh and B.K. Dutt threw bombs in the Legislative Assembly as a protest against:
A. Passage of Public Safety bill
B. Death of Lala Lajpat Rai
C. Jallianwalla Bagh massacre
D. Visit of Simon Commission

17. Which of the following cities has been chosen to be the headquarters of the new development bank to be established by BRICS countries?
A. Macau
B. Beijing
C. Hong Kong
D. Shanghai

18. .... of the Constitution of India lays down provision for power of the Supreme Court to review its own judgements.
A. Article 134
B. Article 135
C. Article 136
D. Article 137

19. Surajkund Crafts Mela is celebrated in the month of:
A. January
B. December
C. February
D. March

20. Sonepur, the venue of one of the largest cattle fairs is located in which of the following States?
A. Gujarat
B. Rajasthan
C. Bihar
D. Uttarakhand

21. Who is NOT a Cabinet Minister in the GOI as on 15 Oct., 2014?
A. Shri Kalraj Mishra
B. Shri Ashok Gajapathi Raju Pusapati
C. Smt. Harsimrat Kaur Badal
D. Shri Piyush Goyal

22. Who is a Cabinet Minister in GOI as on 15 Oct., 2014?
A. Smt. Nirmala Sitharaman
B. Shri Prakash Javadekar
C. Shri Thaawar Chand Gehlot
D. General V.K. Singh

23. 'Rani-ki-vav', an eleventh century step well which was included in the World Heritage Sites list is located in ...... district of Gujarat.
A. Patan
B. Mehsana
C. Banaskantha
D. Sabarkantha

24. 'Gariphema', which has been declared India's first tobacco free village is located in:
A. Nagaland
B. Mizoram
C. Manipur
D. Assam

25. Cancer is a disease where we find uncontrolled:
A. Cell division
B. Cell swelling
C. Cell inflammation
D. Cell deformity

26. If the lens of eye becomes opaque, the disease is called:
A. Myopia
B. Astigmatism
C. Glaucoma
D. Cataract

27. In which city is the Indian Institute of Petroleum (IIP) located?
A. Digboi (Assam)
B. Mumbai (Maharashtra)
C. Ankaleshwar (Gujarat)
D. Dehradun (Uttarakhand)

28. Jalandhar in Punjab is famous for which industry?
A. Diamond
B. Fire works
C. Petrochemicals
D. Sports goods

29. The Governor of a State can be removed by:
A. Chief Minister
B. Union Home Minister
C. Prime Minister
D. President

30. Who among the following advises the President to impose the President's Rule in the State?
A. Chief Justice of High Court
B. Speaker of the Legislative Assembly of the State
C. Chief Minister
D. Governor

31. National Rural Livelihood Scheme has been launched:
A. to help SHG for gainful employment
B. for fighting diseases
C. for increasing agricultural supply
D. for fighting draught and floods

32. B.K.S. Iyengar, who was awarded Padma Vibhushan in 2014 died in August, 2014. He was associated with:
A. Bharat Natyam   B. Kathakali
C. Ayurveda   D. Yoga

33. What is the minimum broadband speed prescribed by Telecom Regulatory Authority of India?
A. 256 kbps   B. 512 kbps
C. 1 gbps   D. 2 gbps

34. Between which stations did the first train run in India?
A. Bombay to Delhi
B. Kolkata to Patna
C. Delhi to Agra
D. Boribunder to Thane

35. Which is a Paramilitary Force?
A. Assam Rifles   B. Sikh light infantry
C. The Garhwal Rifles D. Gorkha Rifles

36. The change of state directly from solid to gas called:
A. Evaporation   B. Sublimation
C. Condensation   D. Deposition

37. Which of the following is used for measurement of high temperatures?
A. Vapour thermometer
B. Energy meter
C. Resistance thermometer
D. Pyrometer

38. What is H_2O commonly known as?
A. Hydrogen
B. Oxygen
C. Hydrogen and Oxygen
D. Water

39. Which one of the following elements is used in the manufacture of fertilizers?
A. Flourine   B. Lead
C. Potassium   D. Aluminium

40. UIDAI stands for:
A. Universal Identification Authority of India
B. Unique Identity Authority of India
C. Unique Identification Application of India
D. Unique Identification Authority of India

41. The salary of a worker is first increased by 5% and then it is decreased by 5%. What is the change in his salary?
A. .26   B. .25
C. .20   D. .21

42. If $0 < k < 1$, then the greatest among the following is:
A. k B. k^2
C. $\sqrt{k}$ D. $k\sqrt{k}$

43. Present ages of Sameer and Anand are in the ratio of $5 : 4$ respectively. Three years hence, the ratio of their ages will become $11 : 9$ respectively. What is Anand's present age in years?
A. 24
B. 27
C. 40
D. Cannot be determined

44. Some students planned a picnic. The budget for food was ₹ 500. But, 5 of them failed to go and thus the cost of food for each member increased by ₹ 5. How many students attended the picnic?
A. 15   B. 20
C. 25   D. 30

45. If 16% of $x = 128$, then 125% of x equals:
A. 1000   B. 128
C. 100   D. 150

46. A man took loan from a bank at the rate of 12% p.a. simple interest. After 3 years he had to pay ₹ 5,400 interest only for the period. The principal amount borrowed by him was:
A. ₹ 2,000   B. ₹ 10,000
C. ₹ 15,000   D. ₹ 20,000

47. All of the following are examples of real security and privacy risks except:
A. Viruses   B. Identity theft
C. Hackers   D. Spam

48. The set of instructions that tells the computer what to do is __________.
A. Soft copy   B. Software
C. Hardware   D. Hard copy

49. .... is the heart of the computer and this is where all the computing is done.
A. Keyboard
B. Monitor
C. Central Processing Unit
D. Printer

50. Name the African country that will use India-made Electronic Voting Machines (EVMs) in the Presidential Election, scheduled in November 2014.
A. Namibia   B. Mauritius
C. Burundi   D. Nigeria

51. Name the Indian Navy Ship that was dedicated to the nation by Prime Minister Narendra Modi on 14 June, 2014?
A. INS Vikramaditya   B. INS Arihant
C. INS Chakra Akula   D. INS Shardul

52. Which party of South Africa won the national elections for the fifth time in a row on 9 May, 2014?
A. Democratic Alliance
B. United Democratic Movement
C. National Freedom Party
D. African National Congress

53. Telangana became the 29th State of Union India on:
A. 1 June, 2014   B. 2 June, 2014
C. 3 June, 2014   D. 4 June, 2014

54. Who was appointed as the Chief Executive Officer of Infosys on 11 June, 2014?
A. K.V. Kamath   B. S. Gopalakrishna
C. Vishal Sikka   D. U.B. Pravin Rao

55. National Song 'Vande Mataram' has been taken from:
A. Gitanjali   B. Constitution
C. Anand Math   D. Train to Pakistan

56. Where is 'Statue of Liberty' located?
A. London   B. New York
C. Ahmedabad   D. Bonn

57. Who is the Sanskrit poet called as the Indian Shakespeare?
A. Tulsidas   B. Kalidas
C. Kautilya   D. Sudraka

58. Which of the following books has been written by Vikram Seth?
A. Islamic Bomb
B. My God Died Young
C. A Suitable Boy
D. Look Back in Anger

59. Name the Opinion Poll which gave closest prediction of election results in the recently concluded general elections?
A. NDTV-Hansa research
B. CNN-IBN-Lokniti
C. Times Now-ORG
D. News 24-Chanakya

60. As a prince where was Ashoka sent to suppress the revolt?
A. Taxila   B. Kalinga
C. Ujjain   D. Deccan

61. Umesh directly went from P to Q which is 9 feet distant. Then he turned to the right and walked 4 feet. After this he turned to the right and walked a distance which is equal from P to Q. Finally he turned to the right and walked 3 feet. How far is he now from P?
A. 6 feet   B. 5 feet
C. 1 foot   D. 0 foot

62. Shyam walks 5 km towards East and then turns left and walks 6 km. Again he turns right and walks 9 km. Finally he turns to his right and walks 6 km. How far is he from the starting point?
A. 26 km   B. 21 km
C. 14 km   D. 9 km

63. A man bought an article and sold it at a gain of 5%. If he had bought it at 5% less and sold it for ₹ 1 less, he would have made a profit of 10%. The C.P. of the article was:
A. ₹ 100   B. ₹ 150
C. ₹ 200   D. ₹ 250

64. An auto rickshaw is moving at a speed of 40 km/hr for 2 hours 30 minutes. If he reaches the destination in another 1 hour then the total distance covered by the auto will be:
A. 140 km   B. 120 km
C. 160 km   D. 200 km

65. $\sqrt{0.0169} \times B = 1.3$. What is the value of B?
A. 100
B. 10
C. 1000
D. None of these

66. What is the cube root of .000216?
A. 0.6
B. 0.06
C. 77
D. 87

67. Deepak said to Nitin, "That boy playing with the football is the younger of the two brothers of the daughter of my father's wife." How is the boy playing football related to Deepak?
A. Son
B. Brother
C. Cousin
D. Brother-in-law

68. Pointing to a woman, Abhijit said, "Her grand-daughter is the only daughter of my brother." How is the woman related to Abhijit?
A. Sister
B. Grand-mother
C. Mother-in-law
D. Mother

69. If the word POTTER can be coded as MBNZQN, how can REPORT be written?
A. NQMNBZ
B. NQMBNZ
C. NBQMNZ
D. NQBMNZ

70. If in a code language, STARK is written as LBFMG and MOBILE is written as TNRSPJ, how is BLAME written in that code?
A. TSFRJ
B. RPFTJ
C. NJFTP
D. TSFGJ

71. Find the relationship as expressed in the given pair:
GOOD : BAD : : ROOF : ?
A. Window
B. Floor
C. Walls
D. Pillars

72. Find the relationship as expressed in the given pair:
Man : Biography : : Nation : ?
A. Leader
B. People
C. Geography
D. History

73. Find the relationship as expressed in the given pair:
Fog : Visibility : : Aids : ?
A. Cancer
B. Resistance
C. Virus
D. Death

74. Find the relationship as expressed in the given pair:
Scissors : Lever : : Toothed wheel : ?
A. Wedge
B. Gear
C. Press
D. Pulley

75. One term in the number series is wrong. Find out the wrong term:
125, 126, 124, 127, 123, 129
A. 126
B. 124
C. 123
D. 129

76. One term in the number series is wrong. Find out the wrong term:
105, 85, 60, 30, 0, –45, –90
A. 105
B. 60
C. 0
D. –45

77. In each of the following questions, a word has been given, followed by four other words, one of which cannot be formed using the letters of the given word. Find that word.
CONSTRUCTION
A. Suction
B. Coins
C. Caution
D. Notion

78. In each of the following questions, a word has been given, followed by four other words, one of which cannot be formed using the letters of the given word. Find that word.
OBSTETRICIAN
A. Sober
B. Termite
C. Retain
D. Siren

79. The speed of a bus is 72 km/h. The distance covered by the bus in 5 seconds is:
A. 50 m
B. 74.5 m
C. 100 m
D. 60 m

80. If a student can read 15 pages in 24 minutes, then the time taken to read a book of 60 pages is:
A. 90 minutes
B. 1 hour 36 minutes
C. 85 minutes
D. 1 hour 24 minutes

81. The theory of economic drain of India during British imperialism was propounded by:
A. M.K. Gandhi
B. Jawaharlal Nehru
C. Dadabhai Naoroji
D. R.C. Dutt

82. Which one of the following areas of India produces largest amount of cotton?
A. North Western India and Gangetic West Bengal
B. North Western and Western India
C. Western and Southern India
D. Plains of Northern India

83. Consider the following rivers:
1. Kishenganga   2. Ganga
3. Wainganga   4. Penganga
The correct sequence of these rivers when arranged in the north-south direction is:
A. 1, 2, 3, 4   B. 2, 1, 3, 4
C. 2, 1, 4, 3   D. 1, 2, 4, 3

84. Alamatti Dam is situated on which river?
A. Godavari   B. Kavery
C. Krishna   D. Mahanadi

85. Gandhi Sagar Dam is a part of which one of the following?
A. Chambal Project
B. Kosi Project
C. Damodar Valley Project
D. Bhakra Nangal Project

86. Which among the following books was authored by a lady of the Mughal Royal House?
A. Babur Namah   B. Akbar Namah
C. Humayun Namah   D. Badshah Namah

87. The planets on either side of the earth are:
A. Mercury and Venus   B. Mars and Jupiter
C. Mars and Venus   D. Venus and Saturn

88. Which Bank has the largest number of branches in India?
A. P.N.B.   B. Central Bank
C. SBI   D. HDFC

89. State Bank of India Financial Headquarters is located at:
A. Kolkata   B. Delhi
C. Mumbai   D. Gurgaon

90. .... increases levels of bilirubin in the blood.
A. Malaria   B. Cancer
C. Tuberculosis   D. Jaundice

91. Which country or countries will host World Cup Cricket in 2015?
A. England
B. Australia-Newzealand
C. West Indies
D. India-Pakistan

92. Who won the Arjuna Award for cricket in the year 2014?
A. Ravindra Jadeja   B. R. Ashwin
C. Virat Kohli   D. Shikhar Dhawan

93. Where did Gautam Buddha attain Parinirvana?
A. Bodh Gaya   B. Kushinagara
C. Rajgriha   D. Vaishali

94. Lord Mahavira died at:
A. Pava Puri   B. Sanchi
C. Vaishali   D. Varanasi

95. First Indian to win an Oscar Award:
A. Bhanu Athaiya   B. A.R. Rahman
C. Rasul Pookutty   D. None of these

96. Who is called the "Father of Indian Cinema"?
A. A.K. Hangal
B. Amitabh Bachhan
C. Alok Nath
D. Dada Saheb Phalke

97. Universal receivers can receive blood from:
A. Group AB only
B. Group O only
C. Groups A, AB
D. Groups O, A, B, AB

98. What is the instrument for measuring blood pressure called?
A. Electrocardiogram
B. Anemometer
C. Stethoscope
D. Sphygmanometer

99. Name the continent where 'Tundra' type of climate is found:
A. Europe   B. Asia
C. Africa   D. Australia

100. Which is NOT a Greenhouse Gas?
A. Nitrous oxide   B. Ozone
C. Sulphur dioxide   D. Carbon dioxide

ANSWERS

1	2	3	4	5	6	7	8	9	10
D	B	B	B	A	D	A	C	A	B

11	12	13	14	15	16	17	18	19	20
A	D	A	B	A	C	D	D	C	C

21	22	23	24	25	26	27	28	29	30
D	C	A	A	B	D	D	D	D	D

31	32	33	34	35	36	37	38	39	40
A	D	B	D	A	B	D	D	C	D

41	42	43	44	45	46	47	48	49	50
B	C	A	B	A	C	D	D	C	A

51	52	53	54	55	56	57	58	59	60
A	D	B	C	C	B	B	C	D	A

61	62	63	64	65	66	67	68	69	70
C	C	C	A	B	B	B	D	B	B

71	72	73	74	75	76	77	78	79	80
B	C	B	D	D	C	C	B	C	B

81	82	83	84	85	86	87	88	89	90
C	C	A	C	A	C	A	C	C	D

91	92	93	94	95	96	97	98	99	100
B	B	A	A	A	D	B	D	A	C

EXPLANATORY ANSWERS

41. Let salary of worker = ₹ 100

When salary increased 5%, then new salary

$$= 100 + 100 \times \frac{5}{100} = 105$$

When salary decreased 5%, then new salary

$$= 105 - 105 \times \frac{5}{100} = 99.75$$

∴ Change in resultant salary

$$= 100 - 99.75 = 0.25.$$

42. As, $k < 1$ and > 0

∴ Number of minimum power of $k >$ no. of maximum power of k.

k^1 — Power 1 k^2 — Power 2

$\sqrt{k}$ — Power ½ $k\sqrt{k}$ — Power ³⁄₂

Numbers are written in ascending order is

$$\sqrt{k} > k > k\sqrt{k} > k^2$$

43. Let present age of Sameer and Anand be $5x$ and $4x$ years

After 3 years their ages will be $(5x + 3)$ and $(4x + 3)$ years respectively.

According to the question,

$$\frac{5x+3}{4x+3} = \frac{11}{9}$$

$$9(5x + 3) = 11(4x + 3)$$

$$45x + 27 = 44x + 33 \Rightarrow x = 6$$

∴ Present age of Anand

$$4x = 4 \times 6 = 24 \text{ years.}$$

44. Let no. of students went to make a picnic = n

Amount paid by each student $= \dfrac{500}{n}$

Amount paid by each student when 5 students did not go to picnic $= \dfrac{500}{n-5}$

According to the question,

$$\frac{500}{n-5}-\frac{500}{n}=5 \Rightarrow \frac{100}{n-5}-\frac{100}{n}=1$$

$$\frac{100n-100(n-5)}{n(n-5)}=1$$

$$\Rightarrow \qquad n(n-5)=500$$

$$n^2-5n-500=0$$

$$n=\frac{5\pm\sqrt{25+2000}}{2}$$

$$n=\frac{5\pm45}{2}=25$$

$\therefore$ Number of students who went to picnic

$$n-5=25-5=20$$

45. $x\times\dfrac{16}{100}=128 \Rightarrow x=\dfrac{128\times100}{16}=800$

$$800\times\frac{125}{100}=1000 \ .$$

46. $P=\dfrac{SI\times100}{t\times r}=\dfrac{5400\times100}{12\times3}=15000$

61. 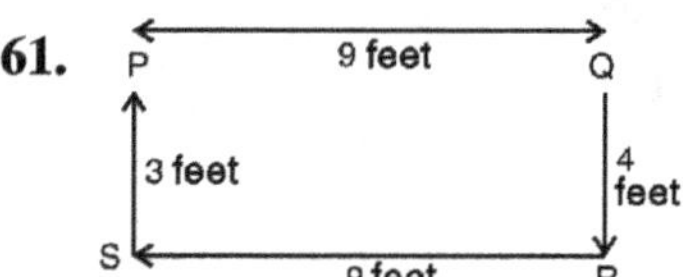

Hence required distance $=4-3=1$ foot

62.

Hence, distance from the starting point
$=5+9=14$ km.

63. Let C.P. of the article be $\xcancel{} x$

After 5% increase C.P.

$$=x+x\times\frac{5}{100}=\frac{21x}{20}$$

After 5% decrease C.P.

$$=x-x\times\frac{5}{100}=\frac{19x}{20}$$

According to the question,

$$\frac{\left\{\left(\frac{21x}{20}-1\right)-\frac{19x}{20}\right\}\times100}{\frac{19x}{20}}=10$$

$$\left(\frac{x}{10}-1\right)\times100=\frac{19x}{2}$$

$$\Rightarrow \qquad 10x-\frac{19x}{2}=100$$

$$x=\text{₹ }200$$

64. Distance $=$ speed $\times$ time

$$=40\times3.5=140 \text{ km.}$$

65. $\sqrt{0.0169}\times B=1.3$

$$\sqrt{(0.13)^2}\times B=1.3$$

$$0.13\times B=1.3$$

$$B=\frac{1.3}{0.13}=10$$

66. $\sqrt[3]{0.000216}=\sqrt[3]{(0.06)^3}=0.06$

69. Word: | P | O | T | T | E | R |

Code: | M | B | N | Z | Q | N |

Hence REPORT is coded as NQMBNZ.

70. STARK is coded as MOBILE
and LBFMG is coded as TNRSPJ
Hence, BLAME is coded as RPFTJ.

75. 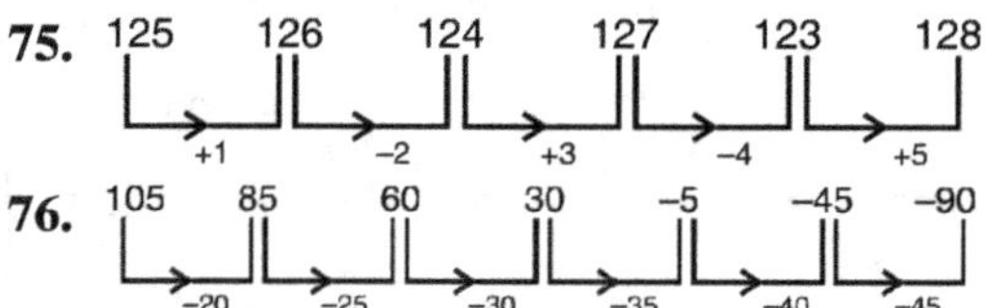

76.

79. 72 km/hr $=72\times\dfrac{5}{18}$ m/s $=20$ m/s

Distance covered in 5 seconds

$$=5\times20=100 \text{ m.}$$

80. $\because$ Time taken to read 15 pages $=24$ minutes

$\therefore$ Time taken to read 60 pages

$$=\frac{24}{15}\times60=96 \text{ minutes}$$

$$=1 \text{ hour } 36 \text{ minutes}$$

RAILWAY RECRUITMENT BOARD (RRB)
GROUP-'D' EXAM, 2013

1. Sound waves cannot pass through:
   A. a solid-liquid mixture
   B. a liquid-gas mixture
   C. an ideal gas
   D. a perfect vacuum

2. On account of its numerous temples, which city is also known as the 'Cathedral City of India'?
   A. Madurai
   B. Bhubaneswar
   C. Varanasi
   D. None of the above

3. Who was appointed as ambassador to China during the time of Mohammad bin Tughlaq?
   A. Ibn Batutah   B. Barbosa
   C. Barani   D. Abdur Razzak

4. A two digit number is such that the product of the digits is 8. When 18 is added to the number, then the number is reversed. The number is:
   A. 18   B. 42
   C. 81   D. 24

5. The Securities Market is governed by the rules which are framed by:
   A. IRDA   B. SEBI
   C. NSE   D. RBI

6. The court which has jurisdiction over election disputes under Section 80 of the representation of people Act, 1951 is:
   A. Supreme Court
   B. High Court
   C. Election Commission
   D. Administrative Tribunal

7. Water stored in a Dam possesses:
   A. No energy   B. Electrical energy
   C. Kinetic energy   D. Potential energy

8. A man sells 200 mangoes at the cost price of 250 mangoes. His profit per cent is:
   A. 12.5%   B. 25%
   C. 20%   D. None of the above

9. The ratio of the incomes of A and B is 5 : 4 and the ratio of their expenditure is 3 : 2. If at the end of year each saves ₹ 1600, then the income of A is:
   A. ₹ 3400   B. ₹ 3600
   C. ₹ 4000   D. None of the above

10. Sarkaria Commission was set up for the review of relations between:
    A. Legislature and Executive
    B. The Prime Minister and the President
    C. Centre and States
    D. Executive and Judiciary

11. Under the PIN Code System, the number of postal zones in India is:
    A. 6   B. 4
    C. 5   D. 9

12. Where was the first cotton mill in India set up?
    A. Surat
    B. Bombay (Mumbai)
    C. Ahmedabad
    D. Coimbatore

13. Name the first indigenously developed Rotavirus Vaccine of India:
    A. Rotomid   B. Ratavac
    C. Rotacid   D. Rotovac

14. When two drops of Iodine solution are put on a food substance, we get blue-black colour. This indicates the presence of:
    A. Proteins   B. Fats
    C. Vitamins   D. Starch

15. Which Indian region is the only place in the world where the Asiatic wild ass is found?
A. The Sunderbans
B. Leh and Ladakh
C. Coromandel
D. Rann of Kutch

16. GR, IP, KN, ML, ...
A. OJ, RI
B. QG, SF
C. OJ, QH
D. OJ, QS

17. 5 m/s = ?
A. 8 km/hour
B. 12 km/hour
C. 15 km/hour
D. 18 km/hour

18. Who was the winner of prestigious Jnanpith award for the year 2012?
A. Amar Kant (Hindi)
B. Dr. Ravuri Bharadwaja (Telugu)
C. Pratibha Ray (Odia)
D. Shrilal Shukla (Hindi)

19. Find the area of a square if the sum of the diagonals is 100 cm.
A. $1000 \ cm^2$
B. $1250 \ cm^2$
C. $5000 \ cm^2$
D. None of the above

20. The International Bank for Reconstruction and Development is located at:
A. Geneva
B. Washington
C. New York
D. Hague

21. What is the name of first indigenously developed super computer of India?
A. Tejas
B. Anupam
C. Aryabhatta
D. Param

22. If 20 men take 30 days to complete a job, in how many days can 25 men complete the same job?
A. 22
B. 24
C. 25
D. None of the above

23. NTPC will set up Simhadri Super Thermal Power Station in which state?
A. Uttar Pradesh
B. Goa
C. Assam
D. Andhra Pradesh

24. Which type of root is found in grass?
A. Tap Root
B. Fibrous Root
C. Lateral Root
D. Modified Root

25. The profit earned after selling an article for ₹ 1,754 is the same as the loss made after selling the article for ₹ 1,492. The cost price of the article is:
A. ₹ 1,623
B. ₹ 1,523
C. ₹ 1,689
D. None of the above

26. In the human body, the basic building blocks are:
A. Bones
B. Muscles
C. Nerves
D. Cells

27. In the first battle of Panipat, Babur defeated which Lodhi ruler to establish Mughal empire in India?
A. Ibrahim Lodhi
B. Sikandar Lodhi
C. Bahlul Lodhi
D. Daulat Lodhi

28. Which of the following is **not** a permanent member of the UN Security Council?
A. France
B. UK
C. China
D. Japan

29. Which out of the following was not one of the purposes of "Sarais" built during Sher Shah?
A. Warehouse for arms and ammunition
B. For officers
C. For travellers
D. Post-house

30. When a body falls freely towards the earth, its total energy:
A. Increases
B. Decreases
C. Remains Constant
D. First increases then decreases

31. Yuki Bhambri is associated with which sport?
A. Tennis
B. Badminton
C. Squash
D. Golf

32. Palace : Hut : : Elephant : ?
A. Cow
B. Car
C. Rat
D. Bus

33. Saffron is obtained from which part of the plant?
A. Stigma
B. Anther
C. Stamen
D. Pollen

34. The Railway Budget 2013-14 has proposed to introduce a new hyper luxury class to be called:
A. Udaan
B. Anand
C. Apoorva
D. Anubhuti

35. Hawaiian Islands are located in:
A. South Atlantic Ocean
B. North Pacific Ocean
C. North Atlantic Ocean
D. South Pacific Ocean

36. "SIP" in Mutual Fund business means:
A. Salaried Individuals and Plans
B. Systemised Insurance Plan
C. Systematic Investment Plan
D. None of the above

37. Quick Silver is the other name of:
A. Silver
B. Quartz
C. Mercury
D. Copper

38. Work done is measured by:
A. mass × velocity
B. mass × acceleration
C. force × distance
D. force × time

39. What is the National Tree of India?
A. Peepal
B. Banyan
C. Mango
D. Neem

40. The greatest five digit number exactly divisible by 9 and 13 is:
A. 99945
B. 99918
C. 99964
D. 99972

41. Krishnadevaraya belonged to:
A. Saluva Dynasty
B. Satvahana Dynasty
C. Tuluva Dynasty
D. None of the above

42. Which is the First Railway Station in India?
A. New Delhi Station
B. Howrah Station
C. Victoria Terminal (Chhatrapati Shivaji Terminal)
D. None of the above

43. Who won the Golden Ball in Champions Trophy 2013?
A. Shikhar Dhawan
B. Virat Kohli
C. Ravindra Jadeja
D. Suresh Raina

44. Which one of the following is not a part of the Scheduled Banking structure in India?
A. Moneylenders
B. Public Sector Banks
C. State Co-operative Banks
D. Private Sector Banks

45. Who among the following was the Chairman of the Sixth Pay Commission?
A. Justice A.K. Majumdar
B. Justice R.C. Lahoti
C. Justice A.R. Lakshmanan
D. Justice B.N. Srikrishna

46. The greatest number of 5 digits which starts from 8 and ends with 7 is:
A. 89997
B. 88997
C. 88887
D. 87987

47. The writer of 'Brihatkatha' was:
A. Dattamitra
B. Gudadhya
C. Bhadrabahu
D. Sarvavarman

48. What number should be added to 2714 to make it a perfect cube?
A. 10
B. 15
C. 30
D. None of the above

49. Who among the following attended all the three Round Table Conferences?
A. Madan Mohan Malviya
B. Dadabhai Naoroji
C. Mahatma Gandhi
D. B.R. Ambedkar

50. What does COBOL stand for?
A. Computer Business Oriented Language
B. Common Business Oriented Language
C. Common British Oriented Language
D. None of the above

51. ABC : ZYX : : CBA : _? a_
A. BCA
B. XYZ
C. YZX
D. ZXY

52. The Article of the Indian Constitution which automatically becomes suspended on Proclamation of Emergency is:
A. Article 19
B. Article 21
C. Article 14
D. None of the above

53. Twenty men can lay a road of 50 km long in 10 days. In how many days can 15 men lay a road of 75 km long?
- A. 10 days
- B. 20 days
- C. 30 days
- D. 40 days

54. The Fifth Summit of BRICS was held on March 26-27, 2013 in:
- A. New Delhi
- B. Moscow
- C. Rio de Janeiro
- D. Durban

55. The climate region with high temperature, throughout the year and heavy rainfall is:
- A. Monsoon
- B. Mediterranean
- C. Equatorial
- D. Savannas

56. Which one of the following indicates the correct chronological order of era in India?
- A. Vikram-Shaka-Gupta-Harsha
- B. Gupta-Harsha-Vikram-Shaka
- C. Gupta-Shaka-Vikram-Harsha
- D. Vikram-Harsha-Gupta-Shaka

57. Cost of two pencils and three erasers is ₹ 18, while the cost of one pencil and two erasers is ₹ 11. The cost of each pencil is:
- A. ₹ 4
- B. ₹ 3
- C. ₹ 6
- D. ₹ 8

58. A hereditary disease in which the blood does not clot and the affected person may bleed to death even from a small cut, is called:
- A. Haemophilia
- B. Leukaemia
- C. Haemorrhage
- D. None of the above

59. Who gave the slogan "Go Back to the Vedas"?
- A. Ramakrishna Paramhans
- B. Raja Rammohan Roy
- C. Swami Dayanand Saraswati
- D. Swami Vivekanand

60. Curd is sour due to presence of:
- A. Acetic acid
- B. Tartaric acid
- C. Lactic acid
- D. None of the above

61. What is the distance of running in a marathon race?
- A. 24 miles 105 yards
- B. 26 miles 385 yards
- C. 28 miles 405 yards
- D. 26 miles

62. Which among the following is in liquid state at normal room temperature?
- A. Sodium
- B. Mercury
- C. Copper
- D. Phosphorus

63. In National Film Awards 2013, the Best actress award was conferred on:
- A. Usha Jadhav for Marathi film Dhag
- B. Aarti Anklekar Tikekar for Marathi film Samhita
- C. Namrata Rao for Kahaani
- D. Rituporno Ghosh for Chitrangada

64. Which of the following pairs is correct?
- A. Surya Sen : Chittagong Uprising Case
- B. Ramprasad Bismil : Second Lahore Conspiracy Case
- C. Bhagat Singh : Kakori Conspiracy Case
- D. Chandrashekhar Azad : Delhi Bomb Case

65. Which Cruise ship sank last year in Mediterranean Sea, was salvaged recently?
- A. Costa Pacifica
- B. Costa Favolosa
- C. Costa Columbia
- D. Costa Concordia

66. The first talkie film of India was
- A. Alam Ara
- B. Harish Chandra
- C. Kismat
- D. None of the above

67. Guru Govind Singh was killed in 1708 at:
- A. Nanded
- B. Amritsar
- C. Kiratpur
- D. Anandpur

68. What will be the compound interest on ₹ 15625 for 3 years at 8% per anum, if the interest is compounded annually?
- A. ₹ 4805
- B. ₹ 4508
- C. ₹ 4580
- D. ₹ 4058

69. Which country was known as Abyssinia?
- A. Liberia
- B. Somalia
- C. Ethiopia
- D. Zambia

70. If a car travels 20 km in 2 hours and another 10 km in 3 hours, the average speed of the car is:
- A. 6 km/h
- B. 8 km/h
- C. 10 km/h
- D. None of the above

71. Which layer of the atmosphere is closest to the earth?
- A. Stratosphere
- B. Troposphere
- C. Mesosphere
- D. Thermosphere

72. The battle of Wandiwash was fought between:
A. English and Hyder Ali
B. English and the French
C. English and the Marathas
D. None of the above

73. In which of the following cities, the first women post office in the country was established in March 2013?
A. New Delhi   B. Mumbai
C. Kolkata   D. None of the above

74. Who is the head of the 'State Executive'?
A. Governor   B. Chief Minister
C. State Cabinet D. None of the above

75. Who built Charminar in Hyderabad?
A. Ibrahim Qutub Shah
B. Mohammed Quli Qutub Shah
C. Ali Adil Shah
D. Ibrahim Adil Shah

76. Who came to India after Portuguese?
A. French   B. Dutch
C. British   D. None of the above

77. What is Panchayati Raj?
A. It is a community development programme
B. It is a Co-operative movement
C. It is a scheme of self-governance
D. None of the above

78. What is the most common element in the Universe?
A. Oxygen   B. Hydrogen
C. Helium   D. Iron

79. Shravanabelagola is associated with:
A. Buddhism   B. Jainism
C. Hinduism   D. All of the above

80. In Uttrakhand legislative assembly one member is nominated from:
A. Christian Community
B. Parsi Community
C. Anglo-Indian Community
D. Muslim Community

81. Mahatma Gandhi returned to India, leaving South Africa for ever in:
A. 1910   B. 1914
C. 1905   D. None of the above

82. Who was the first Bangladeshi cricketer to score a double century in test cricket?
A. Mohammad Ashraful
B. Mashrafe Mortaza
C. Mushfiqur Rahim
D. None of the above

83. Which Indian state would you be in if you were watching birds at Ranganathittu Birds Sanctuary, situated on an island in the Kaveri River?
A. Andhra Pradesh   B. Karnataka
C. Tamil Nadu   D. Kerala

84. Which of the following countries has the same colours in its National Flag as India?
A. Nepal   B. Bangladesh
C. Italy   D. Spain

85. If 60% of K is 30 less than 75% of K, the value of K is:
A. 500   B. 400
C. 300   D. 200

86. The biggest Public Sector Undertaking in the country is:
A. Railways   B. Roadways
C. Airways   D. None of the above

87. 114, 225, 336, 447, 558, _?_
A. 569   B. 789
C. 779   D. 669

88. $74 + 12 \times 0.75 - 6 = ?$
A. 72   B. 67
C. 62   D. 77

89. Which one of the following rebellions is associated with Sidhu and Kanhu?
A. Kole Rebellion   B. Munda Rebellion
C. Bhil Rebellion   D. Santhal Rebellion

90. When an object is thrown up, the force of gravity:
A. Acts in the direction of the motion
B. Acts in the direction opposite to the motion
C. Remains constant as the body moves up
D. Increases as the body moves up

91. Which is the first element in Periodic Table?
A. Helium   B. Hydrogen
C. Carbon   D. Neon

92. Germination of seed is known as:
A. Sapling
B. Sprouts
C. Vegetation
D. None of the above

93. Internal forces:
A. Are always balanced forces
B. Are never balanced forces
C. May or may not be balanced
D. None of the above

94. "Half a life" is a novel by which of the following authors?
A. Salman Rushdie
B. V.S. Naipaul
C. Anita Desai
D. Chetan Bhagat

95. The battle between Alexander and Porus took place on the bank of the river:
A. Ravi
B. Beas
C. Sutlej
D. Jhelum

96. Human rights day is observed on:
A. 24th January
B. 16th March
C. 10th December
D. None of the above

97. 1, 3, 4, 5, 7, 9, 11, ?
A. 12
B. 18
C. 14
D. 15

98. Where is Centre for Cellular and Molecular Biology located?
A. New Delhi
B. Pune
C. Bangalore
D. Hyderabad

99. What will remain after subtracting 11 ten times from 121?
A. 0
B. 11
C. 22
D. 10

100. What is the main function of IMF?
A. Finance investment loans to developing countries
B. Acts as private sector lending arm of World Bank
C. Helps to solve Balance of Payment problems of member countries
D. None of the above

ANSWERS

1	2	3	4	5	6	7	8	9	10
D	B	A	D	B	B	D	C	C	C
11	12	13	14	15	16	17	18	19	20
D	B	B	D	D	C	D	B	B	B
21	22	23	24	25	26	27	28	29	30
D	B	D	B	A	D	A	D	A	A
31	32	33	34	35	36	37	38	39	40
A	C	A	D	B	C	C	C	B	B
41	42	43	44	45	46	47	48	49	50
C	C	C	A	D	A	B	C	B	B
51	52	53	54	55	56	57	58	59	60
B	A	B	D	C	B	B	A	C	C
61	62	63	64	65	66	67	68	69	70
B	B	A	A	D	A	A	D	C	A
71	72	73	74	75	76	77	78	79	80
B	B	A	A	B	B	C	B	B	C
81	82	83	84	85	86	87	88	89	90
B	C	B	*	D	A	D	D	D	B
91	92	93	94	95	96	97	98	99	100
B	B	A	B	D	C	A	D	B	A

* = No correct option

15

EXPLANATORY ANSWERS

1. Sound is produced in a material medium by a vibrating source. As the vibrating source moves forward, it compresses the medium past it, increasing the density locally. This part of medium compresses the layer next to it by collisions. It's speed depends on the elastic and inertia properties of the medium. Thus medium is necessary to travel sound wave.

4. Let, number be $(10x + y)$
   According to the question,
   $$xy = 8$$
   and
   $$(10x + y) + 18 = 10y + x$$
   or, $\qquad y - x = 2$
   $$y = 2 + x$$
   Now, $\quad x \cdot (2 + x) = 8$
   $$2x + x^2 = 8$$
   $$x^2 + 2x - 8 = 0$$
   $$(x + 4)(x - 2) = 0$$
   $$x = -4 \text{ and } 2$$
   $\qquad\qquad$ {Neglecting –ve value}
   When, $\qquad x = 2$
   $$y = 2 + 2 = 4$$
   Required number $= 10 \times 2 + 4$
   $$= 24.$$

7. All material which is confeded in a region at rest, contains potential energy.

8. Let cost price of each mango = ₹ 1
   Sell price of 200 mangoes = ₹ 250
   Cost price of 200 mangoes = ₹ 200
   $\qquad$ Profit $= 250 - 200 = ₹ 50$
   $$\text{Profit \%} = \frac{50}{250} \times 100 = 20\%.$$

9. x is an identity which is present in all ratios.
   Income ratio of A and B
   $$= 5x : 4x$$
   Expenditure ratio of A and B
   $$= 3x : 2x$$

Saving ratio of A and B
$$= 5x - 3x : 4x - 2x$$
$$= 2x : 2x$$
Given that,
$$2x = 1600$$
$\therefore \qquad\qquad x = 800$
$\therefore$ Income of A $= 5x = ₹ 4000.$

16.

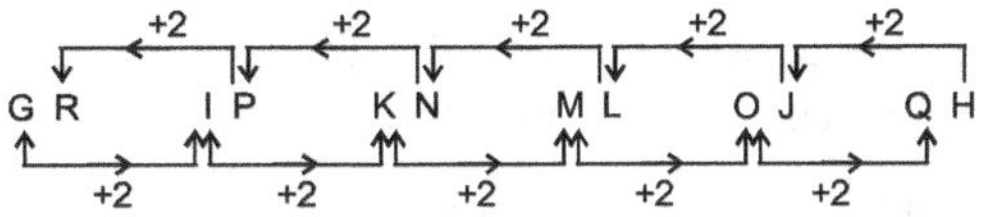

+2   +2   +2   +2   +2
G R   I P   K N   M L   O J   Q H
+2   +2   +2   +2   +2

17. $\qquad 5\dfrac{m}{s} = 5 \times \dfrac{18}{5} \text{ km/hr}$
    $$= 18 \text{ km/hr.}$$

19. In a square two diagonals are equal. So, length of each diagonal
    $$= \frac{100}{2} = 50 \text{ cm}$$
    Area of square $= \dfrac{1}{2} \{\text{diagonal}\}^2$
    $$= \frac{1}{2}\{50\}^2 = 1250 \text{ cm}^2.$$

22. 20 men complete a job in 30 days
    So, 1 man complete a job in 30×20 days
    $\therefore$ 25 men complete same job in
    $$\frac{30 \times 20}{25} = 24 \text{ days.}$$

25. Let cost price of the article = ₹ x.
    According to the question,
    $$1754 - x = x - 1492$$
    Or, $\qquad 2x = 1754 + 1492 = 3246$
    $\therefore \qquad\qquad x = ₹ 1623.$

30. Total energy of freely falling body remains constant.

37. Mercury which is only element found in liquid form also called as quick silver.

38. The work done on a particle by the resultant force is equal to the change in its kinetic energy.

The quantity $\vec{F}.\vec{dr} = F.dr \cos\theta$ is called the work done by the force $\vec{F}$ on the particle during the small displacement $\vec{dr}$.

40. L.C.M. of 9 and 13 = 117.
Least number among given four number which is divisible by 117 is 99918.

46. The greatest number of 5 digits starts from 8 and ends with 7 is 89997.

48. $(14)^3 = 14 \times 14 \times 14$
$$= 2744$$
$$= 2714 + 30.$$

50. COBOL is a computer language which is acronym for 'Common Business Oriented Language'.

51. ABC : ZYX : : CBA : XYZ.

53. 20 men can lay a road of 50 km long in 10 days.
So, 1 men can lay a road of 50 km long in 10 × 20 days

1 men can lay a road of 1 km long in $\dfrac{10 \times 20}{50}$ days

∴ 15 men can lay a road of 75 km long in

$$\dfrac{10 \times 20}{50} \times \dfrac{75}{15} = 20 \text{ days.}$$

57. Let the cost of 1 pencil and 1 eraser be x and y respectively.
According to the question,
$$2x + 3y = 18 \qquad ..(i)$$
$$\text{And} \quad x + 2y = 11 \qquad ...(ii)$$
From (i) and (ii), we get cost of each pencil = $x = ₹\ 3$.

62. Mercury is the only element which is found in liquid state.

68. Compound interest

$$\text{C.I.} = P\left[\left(1+\dfrac{r}{100}\right)^{t} - 1\right]$$

$$= 15625\left[\left(1+\dfrac{8}{100}\right)^{3} - 1\right]$$

$$= 15625\left[\dfrac{27 \times 27 \times 27}{25 \times 25 \times 25} - 1\right]$$

$$= 15625\left[\dfrac{19683 - 15625}{15625}\right]$$

$$= ₹\ 4058.$$

70. Average speed

$$= \dfrac{\text{Total distance travelled}}{\text{Total time taken}}$$

$$= \dfrac{20 + 10}{3 + 2}$$

$$= 6 \text{ km/hr.}$$

85. According to the question,

$$K \times \dfrac{60}{100} = K \times \dfrac{75}{100} - 30$$
$$\text{or, } 75K - 60K = 30 \times 100$$
$$15K = 3000$$
$$K = 200.$$

87.

114	225	336	447	558	669
+111	+111	+111	+111	+111	

88. $74 + 12 \times 0.75 - 6$
$$= 74 + 9 - 6 = 77.$$

91. Modern Periodic table is based on atomic number. Hydrogen with atomic number 1, occupied first place in the table.

97. 1, 3, 4, 5, 7, 9, 11, 12 .

99. $121 - 110 = 11.$

RAILWAY RECRUITMENT BOARD (RRB)
GROUP-'D' EXAM, 2008

1. The compound interest of ₹ 4000 for 2 years at 10 per cent per annum is—
   A. ₹ 1000   B. ₹ 804
   C. ₹ 800   D. ₹ 840

2. Expression $a^3 + b^3 + c^3 - 3\,abc$ is equal to the following—
   A. $(a + b + c)(a^2 + b^2 + c^2 + ab + bc + ca)$
   B. $(a + b + c)(a^2 + b^2 + c^2 - ab - bc - ca)$
   C. $(a - b - c)(a^2 + b^2 + c^2 - ab - bc - ca)$
   D. $(a + b + c)(a^2 - b^2 - c^2 + ab + bc + ca)$

3. The factors of $9x^2 - 22xy + 8y^2$ are—
   A. $(3x - 8y)(3x - y)$ B. $(9x - 4y)(x - 2y)$
   C. $(x + 4y)(9x - y)$ D. $(9x - 2y)(x - 4y)$

4. A 90 metre long train runs at the speed of 72 km/h. It crosses a bridge in 10 seconds then the length of bridge is—
   A. 200 m   B. 100 m
   C. 90 m   D. 150 m

5. The simplification of $\left(\dfrac{3}{8}\right)^{-2} \times \left(\dfrac{4}{5}\right)^{-3}$ is–
   A. $\dfrac{9}{125}$ B. $\dfrac{64}{125}$
   C. $\dfrac{125}{64}$ D. $\dfrac{125}{9}$

6. 12 men finish a piece of work in 10 days working 8 hours daily. How many men are required to finish the same work in 8 days working 15 hours?
   A. 4   B. 5
   C. 6   D. 8

7. Simplify $\left[\dfrac{\sqrt{50} \times \sqrt{20} \times \sqrt{54}}{\sqrt{200} \times \sqrt{135}}\right]$ and choose the correct answer from the following options—
   A. 1   B. $\sqrt{2}$
   C. 2   D. 4

8. Simplify $5\dfrac{1}{4} + 3\dfrac{1}{2} \div 1\dfrac{1}{4} - 1\dfrac{1}{4}$ and choose the correct answer—
   A. $3\dfrac{1}{4}$ B. $2\dfrac{2}{5}$
   C. $6\dfrac{4}{5}$ D. $8\dfrac{3}{4}$

9. If $x + \dfrac{1}{8} = 8$, then the value of $x^2 + \dfrac{1}{x^2}$ is—
   A. 64   B. 62
   C. 66   D. 16

10. A student was said to multiply by $\dfrac{8}{17}$ to a number but he multiplied by $\dfrac{8}{17}$. The result was 225 more than the real result. Then the number was—
   A. 450   B. 136
   C. 272   D. 189

11. $\dfrac{2}{7}$ part of students in a class are girls. If the total number of boys is 560, then what is the number of girls?
   A. 112   B. 224
   C. 336   D. 56

12. There is sufficient food for 300 men for 90 days in a barrack. After 20 days 50 men left the barrack. The remaining food will be sufficient for how many days?
   A. 90 days   B. 70 days
   C. 84 days   D. 105 days

13. A family expends $\frac{1}{3}$ on food, $\frac{1}{4}$ on education $\frac{1}{5}$ on recreation of their incomes and saves the rest amount. If the monthly saving is ₹ 260 the monthly income of the family is—
- A. ₹ 1200
- B. ₹ 1800
- C. ₹ 2400
- D. ₹ 1000

14. If $x = -3$ and $y = 2$, the value of expression $16x^2 + 40xy + 25y^2$ is—
- A. –288
- B. –388
- C. 288
- D. 4

15. If the parallel sides of a trapezium are 57 cm and 39 cm respectively and if the distance between those sides is 28 cm, then area of trapezium is—
- A. 2016 cm^2
- B. 672 cm^2
- C. 2688 cm^2
- D. 1344 cm^2

16. If $\dfrac{16-x}{x} = \dfrac{22}{10}$, then value of x is—
- A. 5
- B. 6
- C. 10
- D. 11

17. A shopkeeper buys an almirah for ₹ 6250 and spends ₹ 375 to repair it. Then he sells it for ₹ 6890. Percentage profit/loss to the shopkeeper is—
- A. 8% loss
- B. 4% gain
- C. 2.8% gain
- D. 5.6% gain

18. The cube root of $2\dfrac{10}{27}$ is—
- A. $1\dfrac{1}{3}$
- B. $\dfrac{64}{27}$
- C. $\dfrac{8}{9}$
- D. $1\dfrac{4}{9}$

19. The value of
$$\dfrac{2x^4 + x^3 - 27x^2 + 36x - 15}{2x - 5}$$ is—
- A. $x^3 + 3x^2 - 6x + 3$
- B. $2x^3 - x^2 + 3x - 3$
- C. $x^3 - 5x^2 + 10x + 3$
- D. $2x^3 - 5x^2 + 7x - 1$

20. The area of square field is 676 m^2. What will be the expenditure to fence around the field with thorny wire? The price of the thorny wire is ₹ 10 per metre.
- A. ₹ 1040
- B. ₹ 1000
- C. ₹ 260
- D. ₹ 520

21. If the radius of a sector is 16 cm and the length of the arc is 18.5 cm, then area of the sector is—
- A. 148 cm^2
- B. 296 cm^2
- C. 74 cm^2
- D. 222 cm^2

22. If the price of $\dfrac{3}{4}$ part of an article is ₹ 90, then the price of $\dfrac{2}{3}$ part of the article is—
- A. ₹ 45
- B. ₹ 80
- C. ₹ 120
- D. ₹ 60

23. The value of
$$\dfrac{1.81 \times 1.81 \times 1.81 + 1.19 \times 1.19 \times 1.19}{1.81 \times 1.81 - 1.81 \times 1.19 + 1.19 \times 1.19}$$ is—
- A. 2.15
- B. 2
- C. 3.75
- D. 3

24. A steamer covers a distance between two harbours with downstream in 4 hours. While with upstream it covers distance in 5 hours. If the speed of stream is 2 km/h what will be the distance between two harbours?
- A. 60 km
- B. 75 km
- C. 100 km
- D. 80 km

25. The ratio of milk and water in a mixture is 5 : 3. How much water should be mixed to get reverse ratio?
- A. 32 litre
- B. 24 litre
- C. 40 litre
- D. 50 litre

26. Which number should be subtracted from 4000; so that the remaining number should be divided by 19?
- A. 5
- B. 18
- C. 15
- D. 10

27. The LCM of 15, 18, 36 and 144 is—
- A. 144
- B. 360
- C. 1440
- D. 720

28. If $a + b = 7$, then the value of $(a - b)^2 + 4ab + 1$ is—
A. 49
B. 50
C. 51
D. Can not be determined.

29. $5^4 \times 5^8$ is equal to—
A. 5^{20}
B. 5^{32}
C. 5^{12}
D. 15^{12}

30. A dealer buys a washing machine. He gets 10% profit in spite of giving 20% discount at the labelled price. The labelled price is—
A. 9575
B. 10325
C. 8500
D. 8750

31. If the difference of $\frac{1}{7}$ part and $\frac{1}{8}$ part of a number is 2, then sum of digits of the number is—
A. 4
B. 6
C. 7
D. None of these

32. Average salary of 20 employees in an office is ₹ 1900. If the salary of manager is also added, then average salary becomes ₹ 2000. The manager's salary is—
A. ₹ 4,400
B. ₹ 4,000
C. ₹ 2,400
D. ₹ 2,000

33. If $(x - y) = 6$ and $xy = 1$, then find the value of $(x^3 - y^3)$ from the given options—
A. 217
B. 216
C. 234
D. 236

34. Simplifying $\sqrt{64} + \sqrt{0.64} + \sqrt{0.0064}$, we get—
A. 64.64
B. 4.444
C. 8.888
D. 70.12

35. If number $34\boxed{}151$ is fully divided by 9, then value of $\boxed{}$ is—
A. 8
B. 4
C. 0
D. 5

36. Two–digit number is 4 times the sum of its digits. If 18 is added in this number, then the places of digits are changed. The number is—
A. 36
B. 24
C. 16
D. 48

37. A clerk goes to his office at the speed of 4 km/h then he arrives 5 minutes late. If he goes at 5 km/h, then he arrives $2\frac{1}{2}$ minutes before. What is the distance between his house and office?
A. 2 km
B. 2.5 km
C. 3 km
D. 3.5 km

38. Anil purchased two chairs for ₹ 1500 each. He sold one at 6% gain and another at 4% loss. Loss/Gain percent in total transaction is—
A. 2% gain
B. 1% gain
C. 2% loss
D. 1% loss

39. The diameter of 21 cm long iron pipe is 8 cm. If thickness of the pipe is 1 cm and density of iron is 7 gram/cm^3, then weight of the pipe is—
A. 3.696 kg
B. 3.234 kg
C. 4.158 kg
D. 5.256 kg

40. A and B are working together to finish a work in 12 days, while B alone finishes the work in 30 days. In how many days A alone will finish the same work?
A. 20 days
B. 15 days
C. 10 days
D. 12 days

41. Which is odd in the following?
A. Red
B. Black
C. Yellow
D. Colour

42. In a bus for first 1.6 km 40 P, for next 1.4 km 35 P and for every next 3 km 25 P is charged. How much distance a man can travel in ₹ 4?
A. 42 km
B. 43 km
C. 45 km
D. 39 km

43. The correct order of the dynasties (from begining) is—
A. Khilji, Ghulam, Tughlaq, Mughal
B. Ghulam, Khilji, Tughlaq, Mughal
C. Ghulam, Khilji, Mughal, Tughlaq
D. Tughlaq, Ghulam, Khilji, Mughal

44. Ice floats on water, because—
A. Ice absorves some water and floats
B. Due to chemical reaction between ice and water

C. Density of ice is less than density of water
D. None of these

45. Which is odd one in the following?
A. March
B. April
C. June
D. September

46. Panini is related to which area?
A. Painting
B. Sanskrit grammar
C. Dancing
D. Medical education

47. Which city is not situated on the bank of the river Ganga?
A. Kanpur
B. Dhanbad
C. Patna
D. Haridwar

48. The first Guru of 'Sikhs' was—
A. Guru Arjundev
B. Guru Angad
C. Guru Nanakdev
D. Guru Gobind Singh

49. It is three in my wrist watch. If the hand of hour indicates towards east, then the hand of minute indicates—
A. Towards North
B. Towards South
C. Towards West
D. Towards North-east

50. The border of which state does not touch the neighbouring country?
A. Bihar
B. Jharkhand
C. West Bengal
D. Uttar Pradesh

51. Which will be the correct order if these fractions are arranged in increasing order?
$$\frac{2}{5}, \frac{1}{2}, \frac{3}{7}, \frac{2}{3}, \frac{1}{4}$$
A. $\frac{1}{4}, \frac{3}{7}, \frac{2}{5}, \frac{1}{2}, \frac{2}{3}$
B. $\frac{1}{4}, \frac{2}{5}, \frac{3}{7}, \frac{1}{2}, \frac{2}{3}$
C. $\frac{1}{4}, \frac{1}{2}, \frac{2}{5}, \frac{3}{7}, \frac{2}{3}$
D. $\frac{2}{5}, \frac{1}{4}, \frac{1}{2}, \frac{3}{7}, \frac{2}{3}$

52. Angle between hour and minute at evening half past 8 will be—
A. 90°
B. 75°
C. 60°
D. 85°

53. Deepak moves 40 metres north, then he turns right and moves 50 metres. Again he turns right and goes 40 metres. How far away is he from his starting point?
A. 0 m
B. 50 m
C. 40 m
D. 10 m

54. Who founded the Ram Krishna Mission?
A. Ram Krishna Paramhansa
B. Swami Vivekananda
C. Dayanand Saraswati
D. Raja Ram Mohan Roy

55. Which has the major participation in power generation in India?
A. Thermo-electric Power
B. Hydro-electric Power
C. Nuclear-Power
D. Wind-Power

56. Correct order of the three presidents of India according to their tenure is—
A. Dr. Rajendra Prasad; Dr. Zakir Hussain; Dr. S Radhakrishnan.
B. Dr. Rajendra Prasad; Dr. S. Radhakrishnan; Dr. Zakir Hussain
C. Dr. S. Radhakrishnan; Dr. Rajendra Prasad; Dr. Zakir Hussain
D. None of these

57. How many colours are seen when the sun rays pass through a prism?
A. 5
B. 6
C. 7
D. 8

58. Rajendra was born on 3rd March 1978. Manoj is 4 days elder than Rajendra. If Republic day fell on Saturday on that year, on which day was Manoj born?
A. Wednesday
B. Friday
C. Tuesday
D. Thursday

59. How many edges are there in a cube?
A. 6
B. 12
C. 8
D. 16

60. In a computer language CPU means—
A. Computerized Power Unit
B. Central Processing Unit
C. Central Power Unit
D. Central Periferal Unit

61. Which of the following works as fuel in human body?
A. Protein   B. Vitamin
C. Carbohydrate   D. Water

62. Carrot is the main source of vitamin—
A. A   B. B
C. C   D. D

63. Which one is not matched correctly?

Countries	Capitals
A. Russia	Moscow
B. Nepal	Kathmandu
C. China	Tokyo
D. Afghanistan	Kabul

64. Who Which had discovered marine route from Europe to India?
A. Columbus
B. Vasco-da-gama
C. East India Company
D. Magalon

65. Two flat mirrors are inclined at 90°. Then the number of formed images is—
A. 1   B. 2
C. 3   D. 4

Directions (Q.No. 66 to 70): *Which number/word will come at (?) in the given series/questions?*

66. 1, 3, 7, 15, (?)
A. 16   B. 31
C. 46   D. 30

67. 81, 27, 9, 3, (?)
A. 3   B. 9
C. 1   D. 27

68. Drama : Director : : Team : (?)
A. Spectators   B. Captain
C. Players   D. Play-ground

69. 1, 9, 25, 49, 81, (?)
A. 144   B. 169
C. 100   D. 121

70. Daughter : Mother : : Mars : (?)
A. Earth   B. Girl
C. Sister   D. Sun

71. After which battle Ashoka adopted Buddhism?
A. Battle of Kalinga
B. Battle of Peshawar
C. Battle of South India
D. Battle of Khanwa

72. Which of the following is not a metal?
A. Carbon   B. Sulphur
C. Aluminium   D. Nitrogen

73. Which one of the following is not matched correctly?
A. Tajmahal   -   Agra
B. Golghar   -   Patna
C. Buland Darwaja   -   Fatehpur Sikri
D. Qutub Minar   -   Lucknow

74. Sun temple is situated at—
A. Tanjaur   B. Khajuraho
C. Wapi   D. Konark

75. How many teams have participated in recently finished Indian Premier League (IPL) Cricket tournament?
A. 6   B. 7
C. 8   D. 9

76. Which will come at (?) in the series pqrs, rspq, qpsr, (?)
A. rpsq   B. srpq
C. rsqp   D. srqp

77. Which river does not pass through Bihar?
A. Kosi   B. Yamuna
C. Baghmati   D. Sone

78. Mahendra Singh Dhoni plays for which IPL cricket team?
A. Kolkata   B. Mumbai
C. Hyderabad   D. Chennai

79. Which Indian cricketer scored maximum run in an innings of a test match?
A. Sunil Gawaskar   B. Sachin Tendulkar
C. Virendar Sehwag   D. VVS Laxman

80. Category of state can not be provided to national territory of Delhi because—
A. Its legislature is not bicameral
B. It is national capital region, its legislature and council of ministers have limited powers
C. Here is no high-court
D. It has no language

81. Some cards are distributed among A, B, C, and D. A gets one less than B, while C gets 5 more than D. B and D, get equal number of cards. Who gets the minimum number of cards?
A. A   B. B
C. C   D. D

82. Who had united the princely states?
A. C. Rajgopalachari
B. Dr. Rajendra Prasad
C. Sardar Patel
D. Netaji Subhash Chandra Bose

83. Gopal is taller than Mohan but smaller than Ram. Mohan is taller than Sohan but smaller than Ram. Who is the tallest?
A. Gopal   B. Mohan
C. Ram   D. Sohan

84. Ex-officio Chairman of Planning Commission is—
A. President of India
B. Prime Minister of India
C. Leader of Opposition
D. Finance Minister

85. Census in India is held after the period of—
A. 5 years   B. 7 years
C. 10 years   D. 20 years

86. Which among the following does not participate in the election of the president of India?
A. Rajya Sabha
B. Lok Sabha
C. Legislative assembly
D. Legislative council

87. The largest alive mammal is—
A. Elephant   B. Blue Whale
C. Camel   D. Giraffe

88. Match List I and List II and choose the correct answer from the code given.

List-I	List-II
(a) Establishment of Mughal empire	1. Sir Saiyed Ahmed Khan
(b) Organisation of Indian National Army	2. Akbar
(c) Foundation of Muslim University	3. Babur
(d) Din-e-Ilahi	4. Subhash Chandra Bose

Code:

	(a)	(b)	(c)	(d)
A.	3	4	1	2
B.	3	4	2	1
C.	3	1	4	2
D.	2	4	1	3

89. pH value of pure water is—
A. 6   B. 7
C. 8   D. 9

90. What is the name of the official residence of the president of United States of America?
A. White House
B. Pentagon
C. Downing street
D. Bakingham Palace

91. Term of the members of Rajya Sabha is—
A. 4 years   B. 5 years
C. 6 years   D. 10 years

92. Which of the following is Leap year?
A. 1986   B. 1906
C. 1980   D. 1998

93. Where I am standing, a river is flowing from my back side. Something is floating in the river from my left to right. If the river is flowing from west to east then which direction I am facing?
A. East   B. West
C. North   D. South

94. Indian Railway is mainly—
A. Metre gauge   B. Narrow gauge
C. Broad gauge   D. Standard gauge

95. Sardar Sarovar Dam is being built on the river—
A. Narmada   B. Mahanadi
C. Godawari   D. Tapti

96. Match List-I and List-II and choose the correct answer from the given code.

List-I	List-II
(a) Acceleration	1. Fahrenheight
(b) Force	2. Joule

(*c*) Finished work   3. Newton
(*d*) Temperature   4. Metre/Second^2
Code:

	(*a*)	(*b*)	(*c*)	(*d*)
A.	4	2	3	1
B.	2	4	3	1
C.	4	3	2	1
D.	3	4	2	1

97. Match List-I and List-II and choose the correct answer from the given code.

List-I		**List-II**
(Epics)		**(Religion)**
(*a*) Quran	1.	Christian
(*b*) Bible	2.	Islam
(*c*) Jataka	3.	Sikh
(*d*) Guru Granth Sahib	4.	Buddhist

Code:

	(*a*)	(*b*)	(*c*)	(*d*)
A.	1	2	4	3
B.	2	1	3	4
C.	2	3	1	4
D.	2	1	4	3

98. Name the house whose chairman is not the member of the house—
A. Lok Sabha
B. Rajya Sabha
C. Legislative Assembly
D. Legislative Council

99. Match List-I and List-II and choose the correct answer from the given code.

List-I		**List-II**
(*a*) Thailand	1.	South America
(*b*) Ghana	2.	Asia
(*c*) Argentina	3.	Europe
(*d*) Spain	4.	Africa

Code:

	(*a*)	(*b*)	(*c*)	(*d*)
A.	2	4	1	3
B.	2	4	3	1
C.	4	2	1	3
D.	2	1	4	3

100. Leader of 'Bhudan Movement' was—
A. Binoba Bhave   B. Mahatma Gandhi
C. Sardar Patel   D. Rajgopalachari

101. Which among the following is correct?
A. East Central Railway — Hajipur
B. Eastern Railway — Kolkata
C. Northern Railway — New Delhi
D. Central Railway — Allahabad

102. Students in a class are sitting in a row to take photo. Shailendra is fourth from the end and 27th from the other end. Total number of students in the class is—
A. 32   B. 29
C. 31   D. 30

103. Who is the president of Bhartiya Janta Party?
A. Lal Krishna Advani   B. Atal Behari Vajpai
C. Rajnath Singh   D. Venkaiya Naidu

104. Which of the following emperors had changed his capital from Delhi to Daulatabad?
A. Firoz Tughlaq
B. Muhammad Tughlaq
C. Alauddin Khilji
D. Qutubuddin Aibak

105. Four friends are sitting in a row. Raju is right to Pankaj and Virendra is right to Raju. Sanjay is left to Virendra and Raju. But he is not at the end of the row. Who is sitting on the right end of the row?
A. Raju   B. Virendra
C. Sanjay   D. Pankaj

106. Which is measured with decibel?
A. Intensity of sound
B. Quantity of sugar in blood
C. Density of air
D. Altitude of aeroplane during light

107. India ranks in population—
A. 1   B. 2
C. 3   D. 4

108. Who had discovered the United States of America?
A. Vasco-da-gama   B. Columbus
C. Magalon   D. Captain Cook

109. Which writ is required to present prisoner before the court?
A. Mandamus   B. Habeas corpus
C. Quo Warranto   D. Certiorari

110. Founder of 'Gadar Party' was—
A. Lala Lajpat Ray
B. Sohan Singh Bhakha
C. Lala Hardayal
D. Jagatpal Singh

111. Which of the following can not change in nitrogenic compound from atmospharic nitrogen?
A. Soyabean   B. Wheat
C. Ground nut   D. Beans

112. Which of the following gases is not available at normal temperature?
A. Hydrogen   B. Iodine
C. Florine   D. Helium

113. Which of the following pairs is wrong?
A. Ram Charit Manas......... Tulsidas
B. Kamayani .... Jai Shankar Prasad
C. Madhushala .... Sumitra Nandan Pant
D. My Experiment with Truth .... M.K. Gandhi

114. Author of 'Satanic Verses' is—
A. Salman Rusdie   B. Vikram Seth
C. R.K. Narayan   D. Mulkraj Anand

115. Indian Constitution came in force on—
A. 15th August 1947   B. 26th January 1950
C. 26th January 1947   D. 15th August 1950

116. Which of the following places is related to an ancient university?
A. Rajgir   B. Nalanda
C. Sarnath   D. Vaishali

117. By which article of the Consitution of India the president rule can be imposed?
A. Article 356   B. Article 352
C. Article 370   D. Article 324

118. If length and breadth are increased by 20% then the increase in area will be—
A. 40%   B. 20%
C. 44%   D. 36%

119. Which of the following is Vitamin C defficiency desease?
A. Scurvy   B. Night blindness
C. Ricket   D. Beri-Beri

120. Who is the chief of Maharashtra Navnirman Sena?
A. Uddhav Thakre   B. Raj Thakre
C. Bala Sahab Thakre   D. None of these

121. The leader of Pakistan Peoples Party who was killed in bomb explosion—
A. Zulfikar Ali Bhutto   B. Benazir Bhutto
C. Saddam Hussain   D. Fidel Castro

122. A rod magnet is hanged with a sting, which direction will it face?
A. North-South
B. East-West
C. No particular direction
D. Depends on the length of magnet

123. 'Sati' was abolished by—
A. Cornwalis   B. Warren Hastings
C. Dalhousie   D. William Bentinck

124. Kanishka was an emperor of which dynasty?
A. Maurya   B. Gupta
C. Kushan   D. Chalukya

125. If the fourth day of a month falls after two days of Monday then which day will be on 19th of the month?
A. Monday   B. Wednesday
C. Friday   D. Thursday

126. The value of gravitation of accelaration 'g' is—
A. 9.8 m/s^2 B. 98 m/s^2
C. 0.98 m/s^2 D. 0.098 m/s^2

127. Which metal is produced at Kolar?
A. Copper   B. Aluminium
C. Silver   D. Gold

128. The Olympic sports of 2008 were organised in—
A. Beijing   B. Atlanta
C. Melbourn   D. Seoul

129. On which place 'Kumbha Fair' is not held?
A. Allahabad   B. Bhopal
C. Haridwar   D. Nasik

130. Which of the following is nuclear fuel?
A. Thorium   B. Graphite
C. Diamond   D. Silicon

131. Which pair is not correctly matched?

Folk dance		States
A. Bihu	—	Andhra Pradesh
B. Bhangra	—	Punjab
C. Dandiya	—	Gujarat
D. Nautanki	—	Uttar Pradesh

132. If Ram gives one mango to Shyam their number becomes same. But if Shyam gives one mango to Ram, Ram has three times of mango of Shyam. How many mangoes do they have?
A. 4 and 2
B. 5 and 7
C. 5 and 3
D. 6 and 4

133. In which of the following festivals Sun is worshipped?
A. Buddha Purnima
B. Holi
C. Chhath
D. Diwali

134. 'Durand cup' is related to—
A. Hockey
B. Cricket
C. Tennis
D. Football

135. Which of the following pairs is not correct?

A. Kolkata	— West Bengal
B. Cochin	— Karnataka
C. Kandla	— Gujarat
D. Vishakhapattnam	— Andhra Pradesh

136. 'Freedom is my birth right' is a slogan given by—
A. Bal Gangadhar Tilak
B. Jawaharlal Nehru
C. Lala Lajpat Roy
D. Netaji Subhash Chandra Bose

137. Match List-I and List-II and choose the correct answer from the given code.

List-I	List-II
(a) Uttar Pradesh	1. Chennai
(b) Bihar	2. Jaipur
(c) Rajsthan	3. Patna
(d) TamilNadu	4. Lucknow

Code:

	(a)	(b)	(c)	(d)
A.	1	3	2	4
B.	4	3	1	2
C.	4	3	2	1
D.	1	3	4	2

138. Which of the following is a kharif crop?
A. Wheat
B. Rice
C. Beans
D. Mustard

139. Which of the following is used to make the bread soft?
A. Alcohol
B. Clorella
C. Agar
D. Yeast

140. Work of dynamo is—
A. To change the electrical energy in heat
B. To change the mechanical energy in electricity.
C. To change the electrical energy in mechanical energy
D. To change the chemical energy in electrical energy

141. Name the head of the political party which won maximum seats in recently held constitution assembly elections, in Nepal.
A. Gyanendra
B. Prachanda
C. Veer Vikram Shah
D. None of these

142. Which of the following is related to green revolution?
A. Albert Einstein
B. Norman Borloug
C. Benzamin Franklin
D. Kapildev

143. Animia is a deficiency desease of—
A. Copper
B. Calcium
C. Zink
D. Iron

144. Diabetes is caused by the deficiency of—
A. Testa staron
B. Insulin
C. Vitamin 'D'
D. Calcium

145. $\dfrac{3}{4} + \dfrac{2}{5} + \dfrac{3}{7} = ?$
A. $\dfrac{23}{20}$
B. $\dfrac{41}{35}$
C. $\dfrac{161}{140}$
D. $\dfrac{221}{140}$

146. Nuclear deal with which country is in news recently?
A. Britain
B. China
C. Australia
D. USA

147. Alexander invaded India in—
A. 320 BC   B. 326 BC
C. 261 AD   D. 256 AD

148. Chief minister of Maharashtra is—
A. Ashok Chavhan   B. Manohar Joshi
C. Gopinath Munde   D. SM Krishna

149. Match List-I with List-II and choose the correct answer from the given code.

List-I	List-II
(a) Thermometer	1. Voltage
(b) Barometer	2. Purity of milk
(c) Voltmeter	3. Pressure
(d) Lactometer	4. Temperature quotient

Code:

	(a)	(b)	(c)	(d)
A.	4	2	1	3
B.	3	4	2	1
C.	3	4	1	2
D.	4	3	1	2

150. Which of the following blood groups is universal recepter?
A. A   B. B
C. AB   D. O

ANSWERS

1	2	3	4	5	6	7	8	9	10
D	B	B	B	D	D	B	C	B	B

11	12	13	14	15	16	17	18	19	20
B	C	A	D	D	A	B	A	A	A

21	22	23	24	25	26	27	28	29	30
A	B	D	D	A	D	D	B	C	A

31	32	33	34	35	36	37	38	39	40
A	B	C	C	B	B	B	B	B	A

41	42	43	44	45	46	47	48	49	50
D	A	B	C	A	B	B	C	A	B

51	52	53	54	55	56	57	58	59	60
B	B	B	B	A	B	C	A	B	B

61	62	63	64	65	66	67	68	69	70
C	A	C	B	C	B	C	B	D	D

71	72	73	74	75	76	77	78	79	80
A	C	D	D	C	B	B	D	C	B

81	82	83	84	85	86	87	88	89	90
A	C	C	B	C	D	B	A	B	A

91	92	93	94	95	96	97	98	99	100
C	C	C	C	A	C	D	B	A	A

101	102	103	104	105	106	107	108	109	110
D	D	C	B	B	A	B	B	B	C

111	112	113	114	115	116	117	118	119	120
B	B	C	A	B	B	A	C	A	B

121	122	123	124	125	126	127	128	129	130
B	A	D	C	D	A	D	A	B	A

131	132	133	134	135	136	137	138	139	140
A	C	C	D	B	A	C	B	D	B

141	142	143	144	145	146	147	148	149	150
B	B	D	B	D	D	B	A	D	C

27

EXPLANATORY ANSWERS

1. Compound interest

$$= 4000\left[\left(1+\frac{10}{100}\right)^2 - 1\right] = 4000\left[\frac{121}{100} - 1\right]$$

$$= 4000 \times \frac{21}{100} = ₹\ 840$$

3. $9x^2 - 22xy + 8y^2 = 9x^2 - 18xy - 4xy + 8y^2$
$= 9x(x - 2y) - 4y(x - 2y) = (x - 2y)(9x - 4y)$

5. $\left(\dfrac{3}{8}\right)^{-2} \times \left(\dfrac{4}{5}\right)^{-3} = \left(\dfrac{8}{3}\right)^2 \times \left(\dfrac{5}{4}\right)^3$

$$= \frac{8\times 8}{3\times 3} \times \frac{5\times 5\times 5}{4\times 4\times 4} = \frac{125}{9}$$

6.

Men	Days	Hours
12 ↑	10 ↓	8 ↓
x ↑	8 ↓	15 ↓

So that,
$$\frac{x}{12} = \frac{10}{8} \times \frac{8}{15}$$

$$\therefore \quad x = \frac{10\times 8}{8\times 15} \times 12 = 8 \ \text{men}$$

9. $x + \dfrac{1}{x} = 8$

$$x^2 + \frac{1}{x^2} = \left(x + \frac{1}{x}\right)^2 - 2 \times x \times \frac{1}{x}$$

$$= (8)^2 - 2 = 62$$

10. Let the required number be x, then

$$\frac{8}{17}x + 225 = x \div \frac{8}{17} \Rightarrow \frac{17}{8}x - \frac{8}{17}x = 225$$

$$\Rightarrow \frac{289x - 64x}{136} = 225 \Rightarrow \frac{225x}{136} = 225$$

$$\therefore x = 136$$

11. Part of boys $= 1 - \dfrac{2}{7} = \dfrac{5}{7}$

Now, $\dfrac{5}{7}$ part $= 560$

Then $\dfrac{2}{7}$ part $= \dfrac{560}{5} \times 2 = 224$

Number of girls $= 224$.

12. Number of remaining days
$$= 90 - 20 = 70$$
Number of remaining men
$$= 300 - 50 = 250$$

men	days
300 ↑	70 ↓
250 ↑	x ↓

So that,
$$\frac{x}{70} = \frac{300}{250}$$

$$\Rightarrow \quad x = \frac{6}{5} \times 70 = 84 \ \text{days}$$

13. Remaining part of income

$$= 1 - \left(\frac{1}{3} + \frac{1}{4} + \frac{1}{5}\right) = 1 - \frac{47}{60} = \frac{13}{60}$$

Now, $\dfrac{13}{60}$ part $= ₹\ 260$

Then, monthly income of family

$$= \frac{260 \times 60}{13} = ₹\ 1200$$

14. $16x^2 + 40xy + 25y^2$
$= (4x)^2 + 2 \times 4x \times 5y + (5y)^2$
$= (4x + 5y)^2$
$= (4x - 3 + 5 \times 2)^2$ [Here $x = -3$ and $y = 2$]
$= (2^2) = 4$

18. $\sqrt[3]{2\dfrac{10}{27}} = \sqrt[3]{\dfrac{64}{27}} = \sqrt[3]{\dfrac{4\times 4\times 4}{3\times 3\times 3}} = \dfrac{4}{3} = 1\dfrac{1}{3}$

20. One side of a square field $= \sqrt{626} = 26$ m
then its perimeter $= 4 \times 26 = 104$ m
Cost of thorny wire $= 104 \times 10 = ₹\ 1040$

21. Here, $18.5 = \dfrac{\theta}{360} \times 2\pi \times 16$

$$\Rightarrow \frac{\theta}{360} = \frac{18.5}{2\pi \times 16} \qquad ...(i)$$

Then area of sector $= \dfrac{\theta}{360} \times \pi r^2$

$$= \frac{18.5}{2\pi \times 16} \times \pi \times 16 \times 16$$

$$\text{(From eq. }(i))$$

$$= 148 \text{ cm}^2$$

22. Cost of $\dfrac{3}{4}$ part = ₹ 90

then cost of $\dfrac{2}{3}$ part = $90 \times \dfrac{4}{3} \times \dfrac{2}{3}$ = ₹ 80

24. Speed of steamer in calm water = x km/h

then, $(x + 2) \times 4 = (x - 2) \times 5$

$\Rightarrow \qquad 4x + 8 = 5x - 10$

$\Rightarrow \qquad x = 18$ km/h

Distance between two harbours

$$= (18 + 2) \times 4 = 80 \text{ km}$$

25. Let x litre water be mixed in the mixture

$$\frac{3}{8} \times 48 + x = \frac{5}{8}(48 + x)$$

$\Rightarrow \qquad 144 + 8x = 240 + 5x$

$\Rightarrow \qquad 3x = 96$ litre

$\therefore \qquad x = 32$ litre

26. $4000 = 19 \times 210 + 10$

Now, subtracting 10 from 4000 it will be divided by 19.

27.
$$15 = 3 \times 5$$
$$18 = 2 \times 3 \times 3$$
$$36 = 2 \times 2 \times 3 \times 3$$
$$144 = 2 \times 2 \times 2 \times 2 \times 3 \times 3$$
$$\text{Then LCM} = 2 \times 2 \times 2 \times 2 \times 3 \times 3 \times 5$$
$$= 720$$

30. SP of washing machine

$$= \frac{110}{100} \times 7660 = ₹ 8426$$

Then its labelled price

$$= \frac{100}{88} \times 8426 = ₹ 9575$$

31. Let the number is = x, then

$$\frac{x}{7} - \frac{x}{8} = 2 \Rightarrow \frac{x}{56} = 2$$

$\therefore \qquad x = 112$

Sum of the digits of number

$$= 1 + 1 + 2 = 4$$

36. Let the number is = $10x + y$, then

$$10x + y = 4(x + y)$$

$\Rightarrow \qquad 6x = 3y$

$\Rightarrow \qquad y = 2x \qquad\qquad ...(i)$

Again $10x + y + 18 = 10y + x$

$\Rightarrow \qquad 9x - 9y = -18$

$\Rightarrow \qquad x - y = -2$

$\Rightarrow \qquad x - 2x = -2$

$\Rightarrow \qquad x = -2$

And, $\qquad y = 2x = 2 \times 2 = 4$

$$\text{Number} = 10x + y = 10 \times 2 + 4$$
$$= 24$$

40. Work of A for 1 day

$$= \frac{1}{12} - \frac{1}{30} = \frac{5-2}{60} = \frac{3}{60} = \frac{1}{20}$$

Now, A will do the work alone in 20 days.

42. From question,

(40 + 35) paise for (1.6 + 1.4) km

75 paise for 3 km.

$\qquad$ Rest amount = 400 − 75 = 325 paise

Distance covered in 325 paise

$$= \frac{325}{25} \times 3 = 39 \text{ km.}$$

Hence, he will travel (3 + 39)

$$= 42 \text{ km in } ₹ 4$$

58. Date of birth of Rajendra = 3rd March, 1978

Date of birth of Manoj = 27th February, 1978

Republic day = 26 January, 1978 = Saturday

It would be Saturday on 2nd, 9th, 16th and 23rd February

Hence birth day of Manoj would be on Wednesday.

81. Let $(x - 1)$ and x be the number of cards got by A and B and $(y + 5)$ and y be the number of cards got by C and D

Now $x = y$.

Hence A got the minimum number of cards.

125. From question,

4th of the month = Wednesday

So that, 11th and 18th are also Wednesday

$\therefore$ 19th of the month = Thursday.

RAILWAY RECRUITMENT BOARD (RRB)
GROUP-'D' EXAM, 2007

1. Recently the Mittal group acquired the steel company ____
   A. Arcellor
   B. Chorus
   C. Posco
   D. Jindal

2. Where is the headquarters of UNESCO located?
   A. Paris
   B. Oslo
   C. Rome
   D. Istanbul

3. Which of the following locations is known for missile test?
   A. Chandipur
   B. Pokharan
   C. Sri Harikota
   D. The Sunderbans

4. When the rate of interest is decreased to 12.5% p.a. from 13%, there is a loss of ₹ 104 in the annual income. What is the principal?
   A. ₹ 20800
   B. ₹ 21200
   C. ₹ 22400
   D. ₹ 23200

5. The Kalinga battle was fought near which of the following places?
   A. Barabati
   B. Balasore
   C. Dhouli
   D. Udaygiri

6. Which least number when added to 2000 makes it exactly divisible by 19?
   A. 7
   B. 11
   C. 14
   D. 17

7. Which kind of energy is there in a stretched rubber band?
   A. Kinetic
   B. Magnetic
   C. Potential
   D. Constant

8. Which of the following places is known for path figurine painting?
   A. Painting
   B. Raghurajpur
   C. Pipili
   D. Jajpur

9. A car covers the 1/3rd of its total distance at 60 kmph, next 1/3rd at 30 kmph and the remaining distance at 10 kmph, then what is the average speed of the whole journey?
   A. 33 kmph
   B. 25 kmph
   C. 20 kmph
   D. 15 kmph

10. Who is the present captain of Indian National Hockey team?
    A. Dhanraj Pillai
    B. Probodh Tirki
    C. Gaganjit Singh
    D. Dilip Tirki

11. Who built the famous Jagannath temple?
    A. Ashoka
    B. Kharvel
    C. Jajati Keshari
    D. Chola Gangdev

12. What will be the compound interest on a sum of ₹ 6000 for 2 years at the rate of 12% per annum?
    A. ₹ 1526
    B. ₹ 1772
    C. ₹ 1886
    D. ₹ 2072

13. Indicating towards a picture Rita tells her daughter. "He is the only son of my mother's mother." How is Rita related to that man?
    A. Sister
    B. Nephew/Niece
    C. Aunt/Maternal mother
    D. Mother

14. Hindustan Zinc Plant is located at:
    A. Engule
    B. Paradip
    C. Kakinanda
    D. Vishakhapatnam

15. Which is the longest river of India?
    A. Godavari
    C. Sindhu
    B. Krishna
    D. Ganges

16. At which of the following places was located an important village of old Kalinga?
    A. Puri
    B. Baripada
    C. Tosali
    D. Kyonjhar

17. Who was awarded first with Prime Minister Prize for significant work in public administration?
A. Y.V. Reddy
B. Bimal Jalan
C. N. Gopalaswamy
D. Rajiv Chawla

18. Which part of the body is affected by Pneumonia?
A. Brain   B. Heart
C. Lungs   D. Kidney

19. The average weight of A, B and C is 70 kg but the average weight of A and B is 90 kg. What is the weight of C?
A. 30 kg   B. 35 kg
C. 40 kg   D. 45 kg

20. Which river originates from Odisha and merges with Godavari?
A. Brahmani   B. Rushikulya
C. Nagawali   D. Indravati

21. The Chilka lake is in:
A. Punjab   B. Chhattisgarh
C. Odisha   D. Haryana

22. Light, radiowaves and X-rays are ____waves.
A. Electro magnetic
B. Nuclear
C. Magnetic resonance
D. Seismic

23. Which of the following is a red planet?
A. Jupiter   B. Mars
C. Mercury   D. Sun

24. The ratio of A and B is 5 : 7. The value of A is 185, then B is equal to:
A. 129   B. 239
C. 259   D. 3.79

25. The headquarters of World Health Organisation is located at:
A. Geneva   B. Paris
C. Berlin   D. Washington

26. In Odisha, Mig is built at
A. Cuttak   B. Sambalpur
C. Berhampur   D. Sunaveda

27. Which of the following is the first college of Odisha?
A. Orissa Veterinary College
B. Revanshaw College
C. Wurla Engineering College
D. Government Arts College

28. Which of the following is a Hockey player?
A. Dilip Tirki   B. V.V.S. Lakshman
C. B. Bhutia   D. Pravin Thipse

29. The square root of 24649 is:
A. 127   B. 137
C. 157   D. 247

30. Which of the following is a chief Kharif crop in Odisha?
A. Jawar   B. Bajara
C. Rice   D. Wheat

31. Eager : Interest : : Sharp : ?
A. Desire   B. Height
C. Smile   D. Intelligence

32. The ratio of 50 ml and 2 litres is:
A. 1 : 20   B. 1 : 25
C. 1 : 40   D. 1 : 80

33. Who worte My Experiments with Truth?
A. Jawaharlal Nehru
B. Rabindranath Tagore
C. M.K. Gandhi
D. Jai Prakash Narayan

34. The deficiency of vitamin 'C' causes
A. Paralysis   B. Scurvey
C. T.B.   D. Jaundice

35. What will come in place of the question mark in the following number series?
16, 21 , 7, 13, 18, 6, 19, ?, ?
A. 22 and 6   B. 24 and 8
C. 22 and 8   D. 24 and 6

36. If one side of a square is decreased by 5%, its area decreases by
A. 6.75%   B. 9.75%
C. 12.50%   D. 25%

37. Which of the following states is the most densely covered with forests?
A. Odisha   B. Madhya Pradesh
C. Asom   D. Arunachal Pradesh

38. Who among the following was awarded Nobel Prize in Physics?
A. J.C. Bose
B. Hargobind Khurana
C. S. Chandra Shekhar
D. Amartya Sen

39. The 'Gateway of India' is situated in:
A. Delhi   B. Mumbai
C. Chennai   D. Kolkata

40. Sultan Azlan Sah Hockey Tournament, 2007 was won by:
A. India   B. Pakistan
C. South Korea   D. Australia

41. Winter crop season is known in India as:
A. Rabi   B. Winter
C. Kharif   D. Poddu

42. $1 \div \dfrac{3}{7}$ of $\dfrac{49}{10} + \dfrac{1}{7} - \dfrac{2}{7} = ?$
A. $\dfrac{1}{5}$ B. $\dfrac{1}{2}$
C. $\dfrac{1}{3}$ D. $\dfrac{1}{21}$

43. Which Indian player has taken the highest number of wickets in Test Cricket?
A. B.S. Bedi   B. Kapil Dev
C. Sri Nath   D. Anil Kumble

44. The population of a city is 70000. It increases at 10% in the first year and at 20% in the following year. What will be the population after 2 years?
A. 77000   B. 84000
C. 92400   D. 104000

45. Which river flows in India through Tibbet?
A. Ravi   B. Beas
C. Brahmaputra   D. Ganges

46. The decimal equivalent of 7 gm of a kilogram is:
A. 0.7   B. 0.07
C. 0.007   D. 0.0007

47. Hyderabad was earlier known as:
A. Bhagyanagar   B. Nizamabad
C. Secunderabad   D. Golconda

48. Kullu Valley is situated in:
A. Punjab   B. Himachal Pradesh
C. Kashmir   D. Uttarakhand

49. Muchkund power project is situated in the state of:
A. Andhra Pradesh   B. Odisha
C. Gujarat   D. Karnataka

50. Which mountain range divides India into north and south?
A. Nilgiris   B. Satpura
C. Vindhyas   D. Aravali

51. The telegraphic code was invented by:
A. S.F.B. Morse   B. Arcwright
C. Thomas Addison   D. G. Marconi

52. In a sum of ₹ 11.70, the coins of one rupee, 50 paise and 5 paise are in the ratio 3 : 5 : 7. Find the number of 50 paise coins
A. 6   B. 10
C. 14   D. 20

53. Which place is famous for Jain caves?
A. Ellora   B. Khandgiri
C. Kapilash   D. Sarnath

54. The first successful synchronous satellite of India is:
A. SLV   B. APPLE
C. ROHINI   D. INSAT

55. Find the missing number in the following matrix.

2	5	?
10	5	2
5	4	25

A. 10   B. 15
C. 20   D. 25

56. Which of the following places is famous for thermal power plant?
A. Hirakud   B. Manipal
C. Polavaram   D. Talcher

57. Indira Gandhi Zoological park is located in:
A. Vishakhapatnam   B. Hyderabad
C. Puri   D. Bhubaneshwar

58. The universal blood donor is:
A. Group 'A'　　　B. Group 'B'
C. Group 'AB'　　D. Group 'O'

59. Which state is the biggest producer of cotton?
A. Kerala　　　　B. Karnataka
C. Andhra Pradesh　D. Maharashtra

60. The VIBGYOR spectrum is related to
A. Light　　　　B. Sound
C. Motion　　　D. Energy

61. Who invented telephone?
A. Graham Bell　　B. K.G. Gillette
C. Wright brothers　D. E. Torricelli

62. A man sells an article for ₹ 3550 and loses 19%. The cost price of the article is:
A. ₹ 4283　　　　B. ₹ 4350
C. ₹ 4383　　　　D. ₹ 4450

63. The largest number which divides 411, 752 and 1031 leaving remainder 8 in each case, is:
A. 8　　　　　　B. 11
C. 21　　　　　D. 31

64. The pilotless aircraft developed by DRDO which is targetted, is:
A. Tejas　　　　B. Vijay
C. Lakshya　　　D. Varun

65. The first Indian woman justice of Supreme Court of India is:
A. Kiran Bedi　　　B. Brinda Karat
C. Fatima Bibi　　D. Mohini Giri

66. The instrument used to measure the intensity of earthquake is:
A. Dynamometer　　B. Seismograph
C. Fathometer　　D. Magnetometer

67. The LCM of $\dfrac{2}{3}, \dfrac{4}{9}, \dfrac{5}{6}$ and $\dfrac{7}{12}$ is:
A. $\dfrac{1}{18}$　　　　B. $\dfrac{1}{36}$
C. $\dfrac{35}{9}$　　　　D. $\dfrac{140}{3}$

68. The first train in India was inaugurated in:
A. 1753　　　　B. 1784
C. 1853　　　　D. 1857

69. The calculating machine was invented by:
A. Pascal　　　　B. Bill Gates
C. Issac Newton　　D. Goodyear

70. A man travels for 4 hours. The half of the journey is covered with bus at 40 kmph and the remaining at 30 kmph by scooter. What distance did he cover?
A. 17.5 km　　　　B. 37.14 km
C. 137.14 km　　　D. 117.5 km

71. Who is the Chairman of National Human Rights Commisssion in India?
A. S. Rajendra Babu　B. V.N. Kaul
C. U.S. Mishra　　D. R.C. Lahouti

72. The urban population is most in:
A. Tamil Nadu　　B. West Bengal
C. Karnataka　　　D. Maharashtra

73. Who wrote 'Abhigyan Shakuntalam'?
A. Charak　　　　B. Harisen
C. Bann Bhatta　　D. Kalidas

74. A man buys 8 mangoes for ₹ 9 and sells them at 9 mangoes for ₹ 8. His gain or loss per cent is
A. 10.18% loss　　B. 10.18% gain
C. 20.98% loss　　D. 20.98% gain

75. Which is understood best for conducting electricity?
A. Radiators　　　B. Conductors
C. Vectors　　　　D. Regulators

76. The other name of evergreen forests is:
A. Deciduous forests　B. Tropical forests
C. Alpine forests　　D. None of these

77. 7, 8, 10, 13, 17,?
A. 18　　　　　　B. 20
C. 22　　　　　　D. 24

78. Lignite is found in abundance in:
A. Odisha　　　　B. Andhra Pradesh
C. Tamil Nadu　　D. Karnataka

79. The western seacoast in India is known as:
A. Coromandal　　B. Malabar
C. Palk Strait　　D. Konkan

80. The river called China's sorrow is:
A. Yang te　　　　B. Hwang Ho
C. Three Gorges　　D. Shinago

81. Fraction 3/2 is equivalent to what per cent?
    A. 55%   B. 75%
    C. 150%   D. 175%

82. On January 26, 1950, India became:
    A. Independent   B. Democratic
    C. Republic   D. Non-aligned

83. A car moves at 120 kmph, the distance covered by it in 15 minutes is:
    A. 20 km   B. 30 km
    C. 40 km   D. 50 km

84. Who invented the cholera vaccine?
    A. Joseph Lister   B. Louis Pasteur
    C. Edward Jenner   D. Roger Beacon

85. The smallest fraction in the following is:
    A. $\dfrac{7}{9}$ B. $\dfrac{5}{9}$
    C. $\dfrac{8}{9}$ D. $\dfrac{5}{7}$

86. The two nuclear explosions took place in:
    A. Kutch   B. Andaman
    C. Pokharan   D. Sunderban

87. In a group, the grandfather and his wife, father, mother, their three sons and their wives and two daughters of each son are included. The number of women in the group is:
    A. 11   B. 13
    C. 15   D. 17

88. A cricketer scored at an average of 52 runs in 8 matches. The average of first 5 matches was 50, the average of the last 3 matches is:
    A. 51.5   B. 52.3
    C. 53.5   D. 55.5

89. The missile fired from ground to air is:
    A. Agni   B. Trishul
    C. Naag   D. Prithvi

90. The Railway Coach factory is situated in:
    A. Varanasi   B. Kapurthala
    C. Chittaranjan   D. Perambur

91. If a bus covers 135 km in 3 hours, then time taken to cover 200 km at the same speed is:
    A. 3.22 hrs   B. 3.44 hrs
    C. 4.22 hrs   D. 4.44 hrs

92. The vegetation has life. Who researched on it?
    A. Hargobind Khurana
    B. Hippocratus
    C. Edward Jenner
    D. J.C. Bose

93. Which is an ice fed river?
    A. The Ganges   B. The Mahanadi
    C. The Tapti   D. The Godavari

94. The largest among the following is:
    A. $\dfrac{7}{19}$ B. $\dfrac{12}{16}$
    C. $\dfrac{11}{17}$ D. $\dfrac{13}{18}$

95. The Runn of Kutch is known for:
    A. Lions   B. Tigers
    C. Herbivores   D. Wild asses

96. The first commercial non-civilian aircraft is:
    A. Tejas   B. Saras
    C. India   D. Volan

97. For contribution in the field of trade, Padma Bhushan, 2007 was awarded to:
    A. LN. Mittal   B. S.B. Mittal
    C. Ratan Tata   D. Azim Premji

98. The HCF of $\dfrac{12}{10}, \dfrac{9}{8}$ and $\dfrac{84}{64}$ is:
    A. $\dfrac{1}{82}$ B. $\dfrac{3}{80}$
    C. $\dfrac{3}{320}$ D. $\dfrac{4}{82}$

99. The first Indian to get Nobel Prize is:
    A. Rabindra Nath Tagore
    B. C.V. Raman
    C. J.C. Bose
    D. Subhash Chandra Bose

100. Which latest satellite of INSAT series was launched in 2007?
    A. INSAT-2B   B. INSAT-2C
    C. INSAT-3D   D. INSAT-4B

101. If difference between the ages of X and Y is 12 years and the ratio of their ages is 3 : 7, then what is the age of Y?
A. 4 years
B. 7 years
C. 11 years
D. 21 years

102. $6.7 + 9 \{8- (2.6 + 1.5) + 12\}$ =?
A. 13.6
B. 31.6
C. 143.1
D. 149.8

103. The highest prize in literature of Indian government is:
A. Literature Prize
B. Lalit Kala Puraskar
C. Dada Saheb Phalke Puraskar
D. Jnanpith Puraskar

104. The area of a circle whose radius is 3.5 cm, is:
A. 12.5 cm^2
B. 22.5 cm^2
C. 28.5 cm^2
D. 38.5 cm^2

105. A sum of ₹ 6300 was lent at 5% rate of interest for 9 years. The simple interest will be:
A. ₹ 1840
B. ₹ 1942
C. ₹ 2742
D. ₹ 2835

106. In the following the Belghar wildlife sanctuary is known for:
A. Crocodile
B. Elephants
C. Tigers
D. None of these

107. International Gandhi Prize 2006 was given to:
A. Kofi Annan
B. Desmond Tutu
C. Yohi Sasakava
D. Sunderlal Bahuguna

108. The player of tournament of World Cup Cricket 2007 was:
A. Graeme Smith
B. Muttaih Muralitharan
C. Rahul Dravid
D. Glenn McGrath

109. If the compound interest on certain sum for 2 years at the rate of 10% p.a. is ₹ 630, the sum is:
A. ₹ 1000
B. ₹ 2000
C. ₹ 3000
D. ₹ 4000

110. The largest gland in human body to secrete bile is:
A. Gall bladder
B. Liver
C. Skin
D. Pancreas

111. The deepest lake of Asia is:
A. Rengali
B. Pulicut
C. Chilka
D. Baikal

112. Chalk : Lime : : Coal : ?
A. Carbon
B. Fire
C. Oven
D. Chimney

113. Odisha is a chief producer of:
A. Wheat
B. Cotton
C. Pulse
D. Jute

114. Which of the following is known for Bali journey?
A. Cuttak
B. Paradip
C. Gopalpur
D. Jajpur

115. In how many years will the simple interest on ₹ 6900 at the rate of 4% per annum be ₹ 2484?
A. 4 years
B. 7 years
C. 9 years
D. 12 years

116. In Forbes list, the richest man in the world is:
A. L.N. Mittal
B. Bill Gates
C. Queen Elizabeth
D. George Bush

117. To an astronomer sky appears:
A. White
B. Black
C. Light blue
D. Rich blue

118. The study of heredity is called:
A. Anatomy
B. Cytology
C. Psychology
D. Genetics

119. The last matches of Afro-Asian cricket championship were held in:
A. India
B. Pakistan
C. South Africa
D. Kenya

120. Who is the first Indian spaceman?
A. Homi Bhabha
B. Rakesh Sharma
C. Kalpana Chawla
D. Sunita Williams

121. Which city hosted the Arab league conference?
A. Dubai
B. Muscat
C. Riyadh
D. Doha

122. If STORMY is coded as QVMTKA, then WINTER will be coded as:
A. UGLRCO
B. UKLVCT
C. XKNVDT
D. XKLCVO

123. Barabat fort is situated at:
A. Cuttak
B. Khurda
C. Warangal
D. Ahmedabad

124. The Commonwealth Games–2010 was held in:
D. Colombo
B. Canberra
C. New Delhi
D. Dhaka

125. The dimensions of a rectangular hall are 5 m × 4 m × 3 m. A window occupies an area of 4 m^2. Without window the area of walls is:
A. 50 m^2
B. 54 m^2
C. 56 m^2
D. 60 m^2

126. The nature of carbon dioxide is:
A. Inflammable
B. Smellless
C. Yellowish
D. Sour

127. The largest store of bauxite has been found in the district of:
A. Nellore
B. Engule
C. Vishakhapattnam
D. Tulcher

128. X starts for his office and walks 500 m straight and turns left and walks 300 m. He again turns left and walks 500 m. He then turns right to walk 900 m. How far is he from his office?
A. 1000 m
B. 1100 m
C. 1200 m
D. 1300 m

129. Which of the following is a nonmetallic element?
A. Mercury
B. Manganese
C. Carbon
D. Gold

130. In respect of territorial area, the state of Andhra Pradesh is placed at:
A. Third
B. Fourth
C. Fifth
D. Sixth

131. The recently discovered earth like planet has been named–by the European scientists.
A. NW 58 IC
B. EU 58 IC
C. PL 58 IC
D. GL 58 IC

132. Karnam Malleswari is related to:
A. Weightlifting
B. Wrestling
C. Shotput
D. Long jump

133. 300 men can do a work in 16 days. To do $\dfrac{1}{4}$ of the work in 15 days, the number of men required is:
A. 80
B. 75
C. 60
D. 45

134. The south-west monsoon starts during:
A. May-June
B. June-July
C. July-August
D. August-September

135. The chairman of the Planning Commission in India is:
A. Dr. Manmohan Singh
B. Arjun Singh
C. P. Chidambaram
D. Pranab Mukherjee

136. Salarjung museum is located in:
A. Hyderabad
B. Delhi
C. Kolkata
D. Ahmedabad

137. The chief foodgrain crop of Andhra Pradesh is:
A. Ragi
B. Jowar
C. Wheat
D. Rice

138. If DEADLY is coded as GHDGOB, then MOTIVE will be coded as:
A. OQVKXG
B. NPUJWF
C. PRWLYH
D. QSXMZI

139. If A : B = 2 : 1 and B : C = 6 : 5, then A : B : C = ?
A. 2 : 6 : 5
B. 2 : 7 : 5
C. 4 : 10 : 7
D. 12 : 6 : 5

140. The state with lowest area is:
A. Lakshadwip
B. Puducherry
C. Goa
D. Delhi

141. 47 kmph is equivalent to:
A. 10.03 m/s
B. 11.04 m/s
C. 13.05 m/s
D. 14.06 m/s

142. Rocket is launched from:
A. Balasore
B. Sri Harikota
C. Trombay
D. Siachen

143. Who is the President of Afghanistan?
A. Pervez Musharraf
B. Hamid Karzai
C. M. Ahmedinejad
D. M. Abbaas

144. The first novelist of Odisha is:
A. Faqir Mohan Senapti
B. Gopinath Mohanty
C. Anant Patnaik
D. Manoj Das

145. A trader marks his goods at 20% higher than the cost price and then allows a discount of 10%. His gain per cent is:
A. 8%
B. 10%
C. 12%
D. 14%

146. The outermost layer of earth's atmoshphere is :
A. Troposphere
B. Lithosphere
C. Mesosphere
D. Ionosphere

147. X, Y and Z can complete a work in 7, 14 and 28 days respectively. They together can complete the work in:
A. 4 days
B. 8 days
C. 12 days
D. 16 days

148. A 140 m long train is moving at 70 kmph. It will cross a man running at 4 kmph in the same direction of train in:
A. 4.63 seconds
B. 5.63 seconds
C. 6.63 seconds
D. 7.63 seconds

149. 25 m is what per cent of 7.5 km?
A. 33%
B. 3.3%
C. 0.33%
D. 0.03%

150. A tap can fill a tank in 8 minutes and an other tap can empty the tank in 16 minutes. If both the taps are opened together, the tank will be filled in:
A. 8 minutes
B. 16 minutes
C. 20 minutes
D. 24 minutes

ANSWERS

1	2	3	4	5	6	7	8	9	10
A	A	A	A	C	C	C	B	C	B
11	12	13	14	15	16	17	18	19	20
D	A	B	D	D	C	D	C	A	D
21	22	23	24	25	26	27	28	29	30
C	A	B	B	A	D	B	A	C	C
31	32	33	34	35	36	37	38	39	40
D	C	C	B	B	B	B	C	B	D
41	42	43	44	45	46	47	48	49	50
A	C	D	C	C	C	A	B	B	C
51	52	53	54	55	56	57	58	59	60
A	B	B	D	B	D	A	D	D	A
61	62	63	64	65	66	67	68	69	70
A	C	D	C	C	B	D	C	A	C
71	72	73	74	75	76	77	78	79	80
A	D	D	C	B	B	C	C	D	B
81	82	83	84	85	86	87	88	89	90
C	C	B	D	B	C	A	D	B	B
91	92	93	94	95	96	97	98	99	100
D	D	A	B	D	B	B	B	A	D

101	102	103	104	105	106	107	108	109	110
D	D	D	D	D	A	C	D	C	B
111	112	113	114	115	116	117	118	119	120
C	A	C	A	C	B	B	D	A	B
121	122	123	124	125	126	127	128	129	130
C	B	A	C	A	B	B	C	C	B
131	132	133	134	135	136	137	138	139	140
D	A	A	B	A	A	D	C	D	A
141	142	143	144	145	146	147	148	149	150
C	A	B	A	A	D	A	D	C	B

EXPLANATORY ANSWERS

4. Suppose the principal is ₹ x.

As per the given condition,

$$\frac{x \times 13 \times 1}{100} - \frac{x \times 12.5 \times 1}{100} = 104$$

$$\Rightarrow \quad \frac{13x}{100} - \frac{12.5x}{100} = 104$$

$$\Rightarrow \quad \frac{0.5x}{100} = 104$$

$$\therefore \quad x = \frac{100 \times 104}{0.5}$$

$$= ₹\ 20800.$$

6. On dividing 2000 by 19, we get remainder = 5

$\therefore$ Required number = $19 - 5 = 14$.

9. Suppose three equal distances covered at different speeds x, y and z, then the average speed of the whole journey

$$= \frac{3xyz}{xy + yz + zx}$$

$\therefore$ Average speed

$$= \frac{3 \times 60 \times 30 \times 10}{30 \times 60 + 30 \times 10 + 10 \times 60}$$

$$= \frac{54000}{1800 + 300 + 600}$$

$$= \frac{54000}{2700} = 20 \text{ kmph.}$$

12. Compound Interest

$$= \text{Principal}\left[\left(1 + \frac{\text{Rate}}{100}\right)^{\text{Time}} - 1\right]$$

$$= 6000\left[\left(1 + \frac{12}{100}\right)^2 - 1\right]$$

$$= 6000\left[\left(\frac{28}{25}\right)^2 - 1\right]$$

$$= 6000\left(\frac{784 - 625}{625}\right)$$

$$= 6000 \times \frac{159}{625}$$

$$= ₹\ 1526.4$$

19. Weight of C = Total weight of (A + B + C) − Total weight of (A + B)

$$= 70 \times 3 - 90 \times 2$$

$$= 210 - 180 = 30 \text{ kg.}$$

24. $\because$ $\quad$ A : B = 5 : 7

$$A = 185$$

$\therefore$ $\quad$ $B = \dfrac{7}{5} \times 185 = 259.$

29. $\sqrt{24649} = 157.$

32. Required ratio = 50 ml : 2000 ml 1 : 40.

35. Observe the following pattern:

$$16 + 5 = 21$$
$$21 \div 3 = 7$$
$$13 + 5 = 18$$
$$18 \div 3 = 6$$
$$\therefore \quad 19 + 5 = \boxed{24}$$
$$24 \div 3 = \boxed{8}.$$

36. If there is a change of $x\%$ in the sides of two dimensional figures, then change in area

$$= \left(2x + \frac{x^2}{100}\right)\%$$

Given, $x = -5\%$

$$\therefore \quad \text{Required change} = \left(2 \times (-5) + \frac{(-5)^2}{100}\right)\%$$

$$= -10 + 0.25 = -9.75\%$$

Negative sign shows the decrease in area.

42.

$$? = 1 \div \frac{3}{7} \text{of} \frac{49}{10} + \frac{1}{7} - \frac{2}{7}$$

$$= 1 \div \left(\frac{3}{7} \times \frac{49}{10}\right) \frac{1}{7} - \frac{2}{7}$$

$$= 1 \div \frac{21}{10} - \frac{1}{7} - \frac{2}{7} = \frac{10}{21} - \frac{1}{7} - \frac{2}{7}$$

$$= \frac{10 - 3}{21} = \frac{7}{21} = \frac{1}{3}.$$

44. Population after 2 years

$$= 70000\left(1 + \frac{10}{100}\right)\left(1 + \frac{20}{100}\right)$$

$$= 70000 \times \frac{11}{10} \times \frac{6}{5} = 92400.$$

52. Suppose the number of one rupee, 50 paise and 5 paise coins are $3x$, $7x$ and $5x$ respectively.

From the question,

$$3x + \frac{5x}{2} + \frac{7x}{20} = 11.70$$

$$\Rightarrow \frac{60x + 50x + 7x}{20} = 11.70$$

$$\Rightarrow \quad 117x = 11.70 \times 20$$

$$\therefore \quad x = \frac{11.70 \times 20}{117} = 2$$

So, number of 50 paise coins = $5 \times 2 = 10$.

62. CP of the article

$$= \frac{100}{(100 - 19)} \times 3550$$

$$= \frac{100}{81} \times 3550 = ₹\ 4382.7$$

$$\approx ₹\ 4383.$$

63. $\because \quad 411 - 8 = 403 = 31 \times 13$
$$752 - 8 = 744 = 31 \times 24$$
$$1031 - 8 = 1023 = 31 \times 33$$

The largest number = HCF of 403, 744 and $1023 = 31$.

67. LCM of $\dfrac{2}{3}, \dfrac{4}{9}, \dfrac{5}{6}$ and $\dfrac{7}{12}$

$$= \frac{\text{LCM of } 2, 4, 5, 7}{\text{HCF of } 3, 9, 6, 12} = \frac{140}{3}.$$

70. Suppose total distance = x km

From the question,

$$\frac{x}{2 \times 40} + \frac{x}{2 \times 30} = 4$$

$$\Rightarrow \quad \frac{x}{80} + \frac{x}{60} = 4$$

$$\Rightarrow \quad \frac{3x + 4x}{240} = 4$$

$$\Rightarrow \quad 7x = 4 \times 240$$

$$\therefore \quad x = \frac{4 \times 240}{7} = 137.14 \text{ km}.$$

74. Suppose the man by 72 mangoes.

$$\text{CP of 72 mangoes} = \frac{9}{8} \times 72 = ₹\ 81$$

$$\text{SP of 72 mangoes} = \frac{8}{9} \times 72 = ₹\ 64$$

$$\text{Loss} = 81 - 64 = ₹\ 17$$

$$\therefore \quad \text{Loss\%} = \frac{17}{81} \times 100 = 20.98.$$

77. The given series is based on the following pattern:

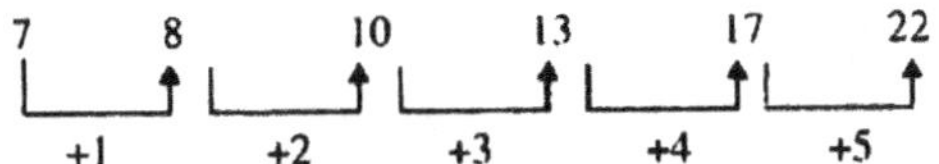

Hence, 22 will replace the question mark.

81. Required percentage

$$= \frac{3}{2} \times 100 = 150\%.$$

83. Distance covered in 15 minutes

$$= 120 \times \frac{15}{60} = 30 \text{ km.}$$

87. Total number of women in the group

$$= 1 + 1 + 3 \times (1 + 2) = 11.$$

88. Sum of runs scored in 3 matches

$$= 8 \times 52 - 50 \times 5$$
$$= 416 - 250 = 166$$

$$\therefore \text{ Required average} = \frac{166}{3} = 55.3.$$

91. Required time

$$= \frac{\text{Total distance (km)}}{\text{Speed (kmph)}} = \frac{200}{\frac{135}{3}} = \frac{200 \times 3}{135}$$

$$= 4.44 \text{ hours.}$$

94. Decimal equivalent of fractions:

$$\frac{7}{19} = 0.368 \qquad \frac{12}{16} = \frac{3}{4} = 0.75$$

$$\frac{11}{17} = 0.647 \qquad \frac{13}{18} = 0.72$$

$$\therefore \frac{12}{16} \text{ is the largest fraction.}$$

98. Required HCF

$$= \frac{\text{HCF of 12, 9 and 84}}{\text{LCM of 10, 8 and 64}} = \frac{3}{320}.$$

101. Suppose the present ages of X and Y are $3x$ and $7x$ years respectively.

From the question,

$$7x - 3x = 12$$
$$\Rightarrow \qquad 4x = 12$$

$$\Rightarrow \qquad x = \frac{12}{4} = 3$$

$$\therefore \qquad \text{Age of Y} = 7x = 7 \times 3 = 21 \text{ years.}$$

102. $? = 6.7 + 9 \{8 - (2.6 + 1.5) + 12\}$

$$= 6.7 + 9 \{8 - 4.1 + 12\}$$
$$= 6.7 + 9 \times 15.9$$
$$= 6.7 + 143.1 = 149.8.$$

104. Area of circle $= \pi r^2$

$$= \frac{22}{7} \times 3.5 \times 3.5 = 38.5 \text{ cm}^2.$$

105. Simple Interest

$$= \frac{6300 \times 5 \times 9}{100} = ₹ 2835.$$

109. Suppose principal $= x$,

then Compound Interest

$$= x \left[\left(1 + \frac{\text{Rate}}{100} \right)^{\text{Time}} - 1 \right]$$

$$\Rightarrow \qquad 630 = x \left[\left(1 + \frac{10}{100} \right)^2 - 1 \right]$$

$$\Rightarrow \qquad 630 = x \left[\left(\frac{121 - 100}{100} \right) \right]$$

$$\Rightarrow \qquad x = \frac{630 \times 100}{21} = ₹ 3000.$$

122.

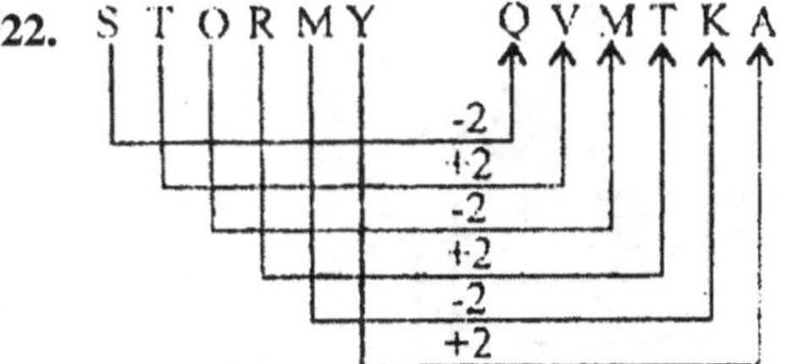

Similarly,

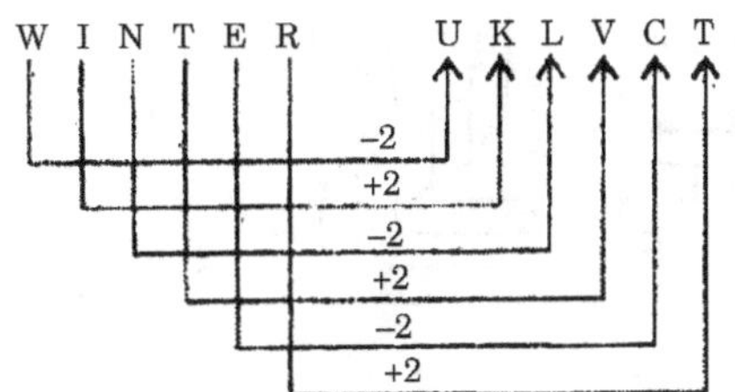

125. Area of the four walls excluding window

= 2(length + breadth) × height − area of window

= 2 (5 + 4) × 3 − 4

= 54 − 4 = 50 sq. m

128.

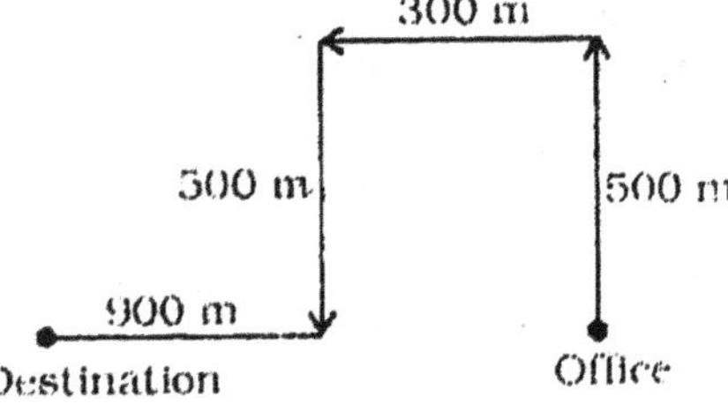

Required distance

= 900 + 300 = 1200 m.

133.

Work	Days	Men
W	16	300
$\dfrac{w}{4}$	15	x

$$\therefore \left.\begin{array}{c} w : \dfrac{w}{4} \\ 15 : 16 \end{array}\right\} :: 300 : x$$

$$\Rightarrow \quad w \times 15 \times x = \dfrac{w}{4} \times 16 \times 300$$

$$= W \times 4 \times 300$$

$$x = \dfrac{4 \times 300}{15} = 80.$$

138.

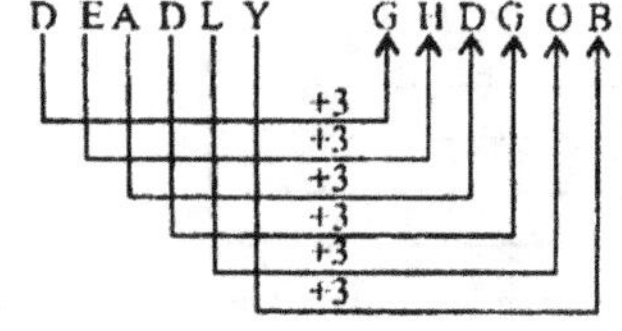

Similarly,

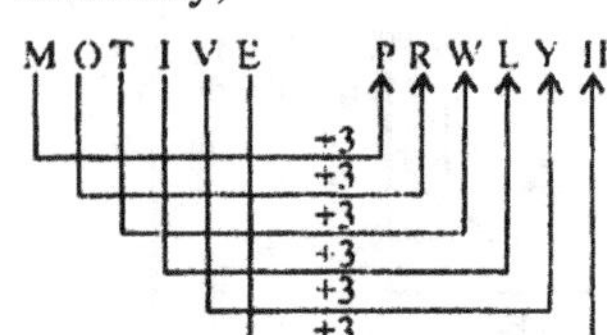

139. $\because$

$$A : B = 2 : 1$$
$$B : C = 6 : 5$$

$\therefore$
$$A : B : C = 2 \times 6 : 1 \times 6 : 1 \times 5$$
$$= 12 : 6 : 5.$$

141. $\because$

$$47 \text{ kmph} = \dfrac{47 \times 1000}{60 \times 60} \text{ m/sec}$$

$$= 13.05 \text{ m/sec.}$$

145. Suppose the CP of article = ₹ 100 and Marked price = ₹ 120

$\therefore$
$$SP = 120 \times \dfrac{90}{100} = ₹\, 108$$

$\Rightarrow$
$$\text{Profit \%} = \dfrac{8}{100} \times 100 = 8\%.$$

147. $\because$ X's 1 day's work = $\dfrac{1}{7}$

Y's 1 day's work = $\dfrac{1}{14}$

And, Z's 1 day's work = $\dfrac{1}{28}$

(X + Y + Z)'s 1 day's work

$$= \dfrac{1}{7} + \dfrac{1}{14} + \dfrac{1}{28} = \dfrac{4+2+1}{28} = \dfrac{7}{28} = \dfrac{1}{4}$$

$\therefore$ Hence, X, Y and Z together will do the work in 4 days.

148. Relative speed of the train

= (170 − 104) kmph = 66 kmph

$$= \dfrac{66 \times 5}{18} = \dfrac{55}{3} \text{ m/sec}$$

$\therefore$ Required time = $\dfrac{140}{55} \times 3 = 7.63$ seconds.

149. Required percentage

$$= \dfrac{25}{7500} \times 100 = 0.33\%.$$

150. Part of the tank filled by both the pipes in

1 minute = $\dfrac{1}{8} - \dfrac{1}{16} = \dfrac{1}{16}$

$\therefore$ Time taken to fill the tank = 16 minutes.

RAILWAY RECRUITMENT BOARD (RRB)
GROUP-'D' EXAM, 2006

1. Who among the following Gurus introduced the Gurmukhi Script for the spoken language of the Punjab?
   - A. Guru Nanak
   - B. Guru Angad
   - C. Guru Amardas
   - D. Guru Ramdas

2. Who was regarded as the greatest exponent of Guerilla tactics of Warfare?
   - A. Baji Rao-1
   - B. Balaji Vishwanath
   - C. Shivaji
   - D. Rajaram

3. Who founded the 'Servants' of India Society in 1905?
   - A. G.K. Ghokhale
   - B. Dadabhai Naoroji
   - C. Madan Mohan Malviya
   - D. Motilal Nehru

4. The famous 'Academy Awards' also known as 'Oscars' are related with:
   - A. Movies
   - B. Literature
   - C. Sports
   - D. All of these

5. The first sepoy who refused to use the greased cartridge and killed an Adjutant was:
   - A. Mangal Pandey
   - B. Shiv Ram
   - C. Hardev
   - D. Abdul Rahim

6. H5NI Virus causes:
   - A. AIDS
   - B. Blood Cancer
   - C. Bird Flu
   - D. Lung Cancer

7. The Tajmahal was designed by:
   - A. Ustad Mansur
   - B. Ustad Isa
   - C. Ustad Rohoni
   - D. Ustad Shamsher

8. The formation of Council of Ministers starts with the appointment of:
   - A. President
   - B. Speaker
   - C. Prime Minister
   - D. None of these

9. Nobody can become member of the Rajya Sabha until he/she attains the age of:
   - A. 30 years
   - B. 25 years
   - C. 21 years
   - D. 35 years

10. Who is the Chief Minister of Maharashtra at present?
    - A. Balasaheb Thackre
    - B. Gopinath Munde
    - C. Vilasrao Deshmukh
    - D. Narayan Rane

11. The normal tenure of a governor is:
    - A. 3 years
    - B. 5 years
    - C. Dependent on the tenure of Legislative Assembly
    - D. 6 years

12. Who has the right of Judicial Review in India?
    - A. President
    - B. High Court and Supreme Court
    - C. Prime Minister
    - D. Parliament

13. The minimum age required for contesting Panchayati Raj elections is:
    - A. 21 years
    - B. 18 years
    - C. 25 years
    - D. 30 years

14. What is the maximum age prescribed for the election to the post of President of India?
    - A. 58 years
    - B. 62 years
    - C. 60 years
    - D. No such limit

15. The Vice President holds his post:
    - A. as per the wishes of the President
    - B. for 4 years
    - C. for 5 years
    - D. for the period fixed by the Parliament

16. To an astronaut the outer space appears to be:
A. Blue
B. White
C. Black
D. Red

17. Due to which of the following phenomena. mirages are seen?
A. Interference of light
B. Total internal reflection of light
C. Scattering of light
D. Double refraction of light

18. The imaginary lines parallel to Equator are called:
A. Latitudes
B. Longitudes
C. Isobars
D. Isotherms

19. Where is the headquarters of the World Bank, which is also called "International Reconstruction and Development", situated?
A. New York
B. Paris
C. Zeneva
D. Washington

20. The scientific study of the earthquakes and related phenomena is known as:
A. Seismology
B. Geology
C. Both A and B
D. None of these

21. Conservation of energy means:
A. Energy can be created and destroyed
B. Energy can be created but cannot be destroyed
C. Energy can not be created but can be destroyed
D. Energy can neither be created nor be destroyed

22. The work done in lifting a weight of 20 kg upto a height one metre from the surface of the earth is:
A. Zero
B. 20 Joules
C. 200 Joules
D. None of these

23. Which of the following is not a part of human eye?
A. Femur
B. Iris
C. Pupil
D. Retina

24. Which of the following can be lifted by a hydrogen balloon?
A. One kg of water
B. One kg of copper
C. One kg pack of feathers
D. All are similar

25. The word "Mach" is used to measure:
A. Sound
B. Air
C. Ships
D. Aeroplanes

26. When velocity of a body is doubled its kinetic energy is:
A. doubled
B. halved
C. quadrupled
D. one-fourth

27. Which of the following has the equal atomic number and atomic weight?
A. Hydrogen
B. Helium
C. Oxygen
D. Nitrogen

28. The edible part of which of the following is a fruit?
A. Coconut
B. Groundnut
C. Pea
D. Wheat

29. The colour of milk of cow is yellow, due to the presence of:
A. Keratin
B. Riboflavin
C. Ribulose
D. None of these

30. There was industrial unrest in a city due to strike of employess of the Honda company. The city is:
A. New Delhi
B. Kolkata
C. Gurgaon
D. Meerut

31. The longest river in the world is:
A. Amazon
B. Nile
C. Mississippi
D. Brahmaputra

32. Who played the lead role in Hindi film "Iqbal"?
A. Nagesh Kookunur
B. Nasiruddin Shah
C. Shreyas Talpade
D. None of these

33. In which of the following fields the terms Bear and Bull are used?
A. Zoo
B. Agriculture
C. Share Market
D. Animal Husbandry

34. Who is the author of the book "Mein Kampf"?
A. Alexander the Great
B. Adolf Hitler
C. Sir Winston Churchill
D. Beneto Mussolini

35. Phulkan Commission is related with:
A. Reservation for Minorities
B. Tehlaka Defence Scandal
C. Improvement in civic services
D. Anti Sikh riots of 1984

36. Which state of India is the largest producer of rubber?
A. Karnataka   B. Kerala
C. Andhra Pradesh   D. Tamil Nadu

37. Why a stone is turned yellow or red?
A. Hydration   B. Oxidation
C. Carbonation   D. Ex-foliation

38. The ruling party at centre at present is:
A. the UPA   B. Congress
C. the NDA   D. BJP

39. Which of the following is the fastest train in India?
A. New Delhi-Bhopal Shatabdi
B. New Delhi-Mumbai Rajdhani
C. Mumbai-Ahmedabad Shatabdi
D. Toofan Express

40. There are .... States and .... Union Territories in India.
A. 25 and 6   B. 25 and 5
C. 28 and 7   D. 25 and 7

41. In which of the following stadia Sachin Tendulkar made his 35th century?
A. Chepauk
B. Green Park
C. Eden Gardens
D. Firoz Shah Kotla

42. Who among the following resigned from Council of Ministers due to Volcker controversy?
A. Natwar Singh   B. Digvijay Singh
C. Arjun Singh   D. None of these

43. Triple vaccine protects children from:
A. Whooping Cough, Tetanus and Tuberculosis
B. Whooping Cough, Tetanus and Diphtheria
C. Whooping Cough, Tuberculosis and Diphtheria
D. Tetanus, Tuberculosis and Diphtheria

44. Which of the following films won the Best Feature Film award at 52nd National Film Award announced in July, 2005?
A. Black
B. Mangal Pandey
C. Page-3
D. Hum Tum

45. What is the distance between two rails in Broad gauge line system?
A. 1.676 metres   B. 1.576 metres
C. 1.845 metres   D. 1.453 metres

46. Cow milk is a rich source of:
A. Vitamin B   B. Vitamin A
C. Vitamin D   D. Vitamin K

47. Ramesh was born on 21st October. He is younger to Sohan by 9 days. Gandhi Jayanti falls on Sunday this year. The day on which Sohan will celebrate his birthday is:
A. Sunday   B. Tuesday
C. Wednesday   D. Thursday

48. A squirrel starts climbing up a tree at the speed of 6 metres a minute but after each 6 metres it slips down 4 metres. It will be able to reach a top 120 metres height in:
A. 20 minutes   B. 60 minutes

C. 115 minutes   D. $1\frac{1}{2}$ hours

49. 'Central Rice Research Institute of India is located in:
A. Kolkata   B. Cuttack
C. Bangalore   D. Mysore

50. A clock buzzes 1 time at 1 O'clock, 2 times at 2 O'clock, 3 times at 3 O'clock and so on. What will be the total number of buzzes in a day?
A. 150   B. 156
C. 100   D. None of these

51. A man bought 5 shirts at ₹ 450 each, 4 trousers at ₹ 750 each and 12 pairs of shoes at ₹ 750 each. What is the average expenditure per article?
A. ₹ 900   B. ₹ 678.50
C. ₹ 800   D. ₹ 1000

52. In a class of 25 students 12 have taken Mathematics, 8 have taken Mathematics but not Biology. The number of students who have taken both Mathematics and Biology is:
A. 4
B. 8
C. 24
D. 36

53. Among 4 friends, Hari is twice the age of Gautam. Gopi is one and a half times elder than Gautam. Bala is 6 years elder than Gautam, but 6 years younger to Hari. Who is the eldest?
A. Bala
B. Gautam
C. Hari
D. Gopi

54. Ram and Shyam together can finish a job in 8 days. Ram can do the same job on his own in 12 days. How long will Shyam take to do the job by himself?
A. 16 days
B. 20 days
C. 24 days
D. 30 days

55. A ball hitting the ground bounces 10 metres above the ground. On each successive bounce its height decreases by 40%. Its height after 2 bounces will be:
A. 4 metres
B. 6 metres
C. 8 metres
D. 7 metres

56. If INDIA is written as 95491, then DELHI will be written as:
A. 45389
B. 45489
C. 45498
D. 45398

57. A lucky boy has been getting HEADS every time in 3 tosses of a coin. What is the probability that he will get HEADS again in the fourth tossing of the coin?
A. $\dfrac{1}{16}$
B. $\dfrac{1}{8}$
C. $\dfrac{1}{4}$
D. $\dfrac{1}{2}$

58. In 1 minute $\dfrac{3}{7}$ of a bucket is filled. The rest of the bucket can be filled in:
A. $\dfrac{7}{3}$ minutes
B. 2 minutes
C. $\dfrac{4}{3}$ minutes
D. None of these

59. If the day after tomorrow is Sunday, what was it day before yesterday?
A. Wednesday
B. Thursday
C. Friday
D. Saturday

60. Select the odd one out:
A. Delhi
B. Mumbai
C. Chennai
D. London

61. India won by what margin in recently played one-day international cricket series against Pakistan?
A. 4–1
B. 3–2
C. 5–0
D. Series draw

62. Which of the following is an important source of revenue of the states in India?
A. Sales Tax
B. Excise duty
C. Land revenue
D. Commercial Tax

63. How many countries are members of the United Nations Organisation?
A. 187
B. 154
C. 192
D. 199

64. 'Bibi ka Makbara' is situated in India at:
A. Hyderabad
B. Fatehpur Sikri
C. Aurangabad
D. Bijapur

65. Which of the following is the smallest country in the world in terms of area?
A. Tavalu
B. Vatican City
C. Monaco
D. The Maldives

66. Who were the first rulers to issue gold coins in India?
A. Mauryas
B. Indo-Greeks
C. Guptas
D. Kushans

67. Which of the following years is referred to as Great Divide in Indian demography?
A. 1901
B. 1921
C. 1945
D. 1959

68. In which of the following sectors maximum workforce is engaged in India?
A. Primary sector
B. Secondary sector
C. Tertiary sector
D. None of these

69. Which of the following is not an all India service?
A. Indian Polices Service
B. Indian Administrative Service
C. Indian Foreign Service
D. Indian Economic Service

70. Who is regarded as the 'Father of Modern Olympics'?
A. Robert Dover
B. Pierre De Coubertin
C. Theodosius-1
D. None of these

71. 'Hemlet' Cup is associated with which of the following games?
A. Volleyball
B. Badminton
C. Tennis
D. Handball

72. The colour of an opaque object is the colour which it:
A. absorbs
B. refracts
C. reflects
D. scatters

73. On which of the following principles does optical fibre work?
A. Total internal reflection
B. Refraction
C. Scattering
D. Interference

74. When was atom bomb dropped on Hiroshima?
A. August 6, 1945
B. August 8, 1942
C. August 9, 1945
D. August 6, 1944

75. Blue Revolution is related to
A. agriculture
B. iron and steel industry
C. irrigation
D. fishing

76. Which of the following Vedas was the earliest composition?
A. Rigveda
B. Samaveda
C. Yajurveda
D. Atharvaveda

77. Which was NOT one of the "Three Jewels" of Buddhism?
A. Buddha
B. Ahimsa
C. Dhamma
D. Sangha

78. At which of the following places did Mahavira, the Jaina Tirthankara, die?
A. Kusinagara
B. Vaishali
C. Rajagriha
D. Pavapuri

79. Which of the following is NOT among the "three Ratnas" or Gems of Jainism?
A. Full Knowledge
B. Action
C. Liberation
D. Belief in God

80. Prime Minister of India Dr. Manmohan Singh is a Member of Rajya Sabha. Which state is he elected from?
A. Assam
B. Punjab
C. Uttar Pradesh
D. Haryana

81. Hari Sena was the Poet–laureate of:
A. Ashoka
B. Samudragupta
C. Chandragupta
D. Harshwardhana

82. Who wrote the song "Vande Mataram"?
A. Bankim Chandra Chattopadhyay
B. Sharatchandra Chatterjee
C. Rabindranath Tagore
D. Mahatma Gandhi

83. Who shot dead General Dyer to take revenge of the Jallianwalla Bagh Tragedy?
A. Udham Singh
B. Madanlal Dhingra
C. Veer Savarkar
D. Khudiram Bose

84. The main feature of the Montague - Chelmsford Reforms (1919) was to provide
A. Provincial autonomy
B. Veto Power of Governor
C. Separate Communal Electorate
D. Dyarchy

85. Which of the following is not a feature of the Constitution of India?
A. Federal Government
B. Parliamentary Government
C. Presidential form of Judiciary
D. Independence of Judiciary

86. The Constitution of India provides:
A. Single citizenship
B. Double citizenship
C. Multinations citizenship
D. None of these

87. Which of the following is not a Fundamental Right?
A. Right against exploitation
B. Equality of opportunity
C. Right to freedom of religion
D. Right to strike

88. Who was the first to give the idea of Pakistan?
A. M.A. Jinnah
B. Shaukat Ali
C. Sir Sayyed Ahmed Khan
D. Mohammad Iqbal

89. At which of the following places Subhash Chandra Bose had established his "Azad Hind Fauz" and "Azad Hind Government"?
A. Burma   B. Japan
C. Malaya   D. Singapore

90. Akbar did not construct:
A. Purana Quila   B. Agra Fort
C. Allahabad Fort   D. Lahore Fort

91. Which of the following diseases is/are caused by a mutant gene?
A. Haemophilia
B. Sickle Cell Anaemia
C. Thalassimea
D. All of the above

92. The stories of which of the following are depicted in Ajanta painting?
A. Ramayana   B. Mahabharata
C. Jataka   D. Panchtantra

93. Kepler's law is associated with:
A. Law of Gravitation
B. Motion of planets
C. Law of Conservation of Energy
D. None of these

94. Two plane mirrors are kept parallel to each other. If an object is kept in between these two, how many images of this object would be formed?
A. Two   B. Infinite
C. Ten   D. Four

95. How far into the sea do the territorial waters of India extend?
A. 12 nautical miles   B. 6 nautical miles
C. 10 nautical miles   D. 8 nautical miles

96. All of the following diseases are caused by virus, except:
A. Jaundice   B. Influenza
C. Typhoid   D. Mumps

97. Leather shoes are often covered with patches of greenish fluffy mass during the rainy season, if unattended for sometime. This is due to the growth of:
A. Blue-green algae   B. Bacterium
C. Algae   D. Fungus

98. The gland that contains the thermostat of the body is:
A. pineal   B. pituitary
C. thyroid   D. hypothalamus

99. The transport of organic substances in plants it through:
A. Fibres   B. Phloem
C. Xylem   D. Wood

100. Malaria can be cured from a drug extracted from:
A. Belladona tree   B. Cinchona tree
C. Oak tree   D. Amaltas tree

101. Which of the following is not a parastite?
A. Louse   B. Mosquito
C. Housefly   D. None of these

102. Hardness of water is caused by soluble salts of:
A. Sodium and Potassium
B. Potassium and Ammonium
C. Sodium and Calcium
D. Calcium and Magnesium

103. She is a Pakistani actress detained by the immigration officers at Delhi airport, who was invited by the film maker Mahesh Bhatt to attend an Indo-Pak Peace March at Nizamuddin Dargah. Who is she?
A. Noor Phatima   B. Abida Hussain
C. Soha Ali   D. Meera

104. The deficiency of Vitamin 'A' causes:
A. Hair to fall
B. Dysentery
C. Night Blindness
D. Weakness

105. Which of the following human diseases is/are controlled by Heredity?
   A. Haemophilia   B. Leukamia
   C. Anaemia   D. All of these

106. Which of the following is not a component of DNA molecule?
   A. Adenine   B. Cytosine
   C. Thiamine   D. Uracil

107. In which of the following nitrogen is found?
   A. Fat   B. Protein
   C. Carbohydrate   D. Oil

108. The term related to Internet, is:
   A. World Wide Web
   B. Web Site, Homepage
   C. Navigator and Java
   D. All of the above

109. What is the average rate per minute of the heart beat of an adult?
   A. 60   B. 72
   C. 84   D. 96

110. The term of the Rajya Sabha is:
   A. 6 years   B. 2 years
   C. Permanent   D. 7 years

111. Abhijit Sawant earned fame in a television programme. Which of the following was that programme?
   A. Fame Gurkul
   B. Sa Re Ga Ma
   C. Indian Idol
   D. None of these

112. Which one of the pairs is not matched correctly?
   A. Vishwanathan Anand   -   Chess
   B. Kutirileeshwarn   -   Swimming
   C. M Vijayan   -   Tennis
   D. Kapil Dev   -   Cricket

113. "Swaraj is my birthright and I shall have it". Who gave this slogan?
   A. Subhash Chandra Bose
   B. M.K. Gandhi
   C. Bal Gangadhar Tilak
   D. J.L. Nehru

114. Which of the following Indian States shares boundaries with the maximum number of States?
   A. West Bengal   B. Madhya Pradesh
   C. Uttar Pradesh   D. Karnataka

115. The southernmost end of the Union of India lies in:
   A. Tamil Nadu
   B. Lakshadweep
   C. Andaman-Nicobar Islands
   D. Trivandrum

116. What effect do sand storms have on the temperature during summer?
   A. Temperature slightly increases
   B. Decrease in temperature
   C. Increase in temperature substantially
   D. Do not have any effect

117. Which place in India receives minimum rainfall?
   A. Leh   B. Jaisalmer
   C. Bikaner   D. Jodhpur

118. The maximum percentage of tribal population in India is of:
   A. Santhals   B. Bhils
   C. Mundas   D. Nagas

119. New Pension Scheme announced by the Central Government has been operative since:
   A. January 1, 2003   B. January 1, 2004
   C. April, 1, 2004   D. April 1, 2005

120. What is inflation?
   A. Increase in prices
   B. Rate of increase in prices
   C. Decrease in prices
   D. Stability in prices

121. Complete the series:
   9, 17, 29, 45, ...
   A. 60   B. 65
   C. 68   D. 70

122. Complete the series:
   3, 7, 15, 31, 63, ...
   A. 92   B. 115
   C. 127   D. 131

123. The average age of three boys is 15 years. If the ratio in their ages is 3 : 5 : 7, what is the age of the youngest boy?
A. 9 years
B. 15 years
C. 18 years
D. 21 years

124. A certain sum is invested on simple interest. If it trebles in 10 years, what is the rate of interest?
A. 18%
B. 20%
C. 22%
D. 25%

125. Pointing to a girl in the photograph, Amar said, "Her mother's brother is the only son of my mother's father". How is the girl's mother related to Amar?
A. Mother
B. Sister
C. Aunt or Mother
D. Grandmother

126. If today is Thursday, what will be the day after 363 days?
A. Sunday
B. Saturday
C. Thursday
D. None of these

127. In a certain code language, '145' means 'tall big boy' and '637' means 'beautiful little flower'. Which digit in that language means 'bright'?
A. 1
B. 3
C. 4
D. None of these

128. If + means ×; ÷ means –, × means ÷ and – means +, what will be the value of 4 + 11 ÷ 5 – 55 = ?
A. 94
B. –11
C. 79
D. –6

129. How many triangles does the given figure contain?

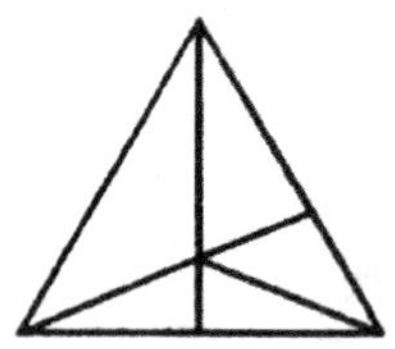

A. 12
B. 10
C. 6
D. 11

130. Amniocentesis is a technique related to:
A. use of ammonia
B. test of sex of embryo
C. eduction of children
D. simplification of domestic

131. Who among the following coined the term 'Gene' for factors controlling inheritance?
A. Gregory Mendel
B. Hugo de Vries
C. T. H. Morgan
D. W. Johanson

132. The main witness to Best Bakery incident Zahira Shekh was punished by the Supreme Court recently due to:
A. contempt of the Superme Court
B. absence on being summoned
C. involvement in conspiracy with the accused
D. charges against Teesta Setalvad

133. Mahmud of Gazni attacked India first in the year:
A. 1004
B. 1001
C. 1000
D. 999

134. The term "Pivot" is associated with which of the following games?
A. Golf
B. Swimming
C. Judo
D. Sumo Wrestling

135. Who was the first Muslim President of the Indian National Congress?
A. Hakim Ajmal Khan
B. Rafi Ahmad Kidwai
C. Abul Kalam Azad
D. Badruddin Taiyabji

136. Indian National Congress was founded in the year:
A. 1867
B. 1885
C. 1887
D. 1920

137. One of the pilgrimages of India was rocked by the bomb blast on March 7, 2006. Which of the following is that city?
A. Ayodhya
B. Ujjain
C. Varanasi
D. Mathura

138. No trace of .... has been found in the Indus Valley Civilization.
A. Sugarcane
B. Mustard
C. Sesame
D. Barley

139. 'ATM' (related with banking) is abbreviation for:
A. Automated Teller Machine
B. Any Time Money
C. All Time Money
D. None of these

140. Which country is the host of the World Cup Football, 2006?
A. Brazil   B. Germany
C. France   D. Argentina

141. Who was the first speaker of the Lok Sabha?
A. Hukum Singh
B. G.V. Mavalankar
C. G.S. Dhillon
D. Sarder Patel

142. The American astronaut of Indian origin who was killed in the accident during the return journey of Columbia spacecraft, was:
A. Kalpana Chawla   B. Rakesh Sharma
C. Deepak Thakur   D. None of these

143. Who is the auther of 'Devdas'?
A. K.M. Munshi
B. Sharat Chandra Chaterjee
C. Amrita Pritam
D. R.K. Narayana

144. Who was the President of India just before Dr. APJ Abdual Kalam?
A. Shankar Dayal Sharma
B. R. Venkataraman
C. K.R. Narayanan
D. R.K. Narayana

145. Which of the following wavelengths is the most effective in photosynthesis?
A. Blue
B. Green
C. White
D. All are equally effective

146. 10 men can finish construction of a wall in 8 days. How many men are needed to finish the work in half a day?
A. 80   B. 100
C. 120   D. 160

147. The, average height of the students in a class of X is 105 cm. If 20 more students with an average height of 120 cm join the class, what will the new average height be?
A. 105 cm   B. 110 cm
C. 112 cm   D. 115 cm

148. In a bag, there are coins of 50 paise, 25 paise and n rupee in the ratio of 5 : 6 : 2. If there are in all ₹ 42, how many 25 paise coins are there?
A. 60   B. 52
C. 34   D. 42

149. If $\sqrt{2^n} = 64$, the value one is:
A. 12   B. 6
C. 4   D. 2

150. The numbers 1, 3, 5, ... 25 are multiplied together. The number of zeros at the right end of the product is:
A. 1   B. 0
C. 2   D. 3

ANSWERS

1	2	3	4	5	6	7	8	9	10
B	C	A	A	A	C	B	C	A	C

11	12	13	14	15	16	17	18	19	20
B	B	A	D	C	C	B	A	D	A

21	22	23	24	25	26	27	28	29	30
D	C	A	C	D	C	A	A	B	C

31	32	33	34	35	36	37	38	39	40
B	C	C	B	B	B	B	A	A	C

41	42	43	44	45	46	47	48	49	50
D	A	B	C	A	A	C	C	B	B
51	**52**	**53**	**54**	**55**	**56**	**57**	**58**	**59**	**60**
B	A	C	C	B	A	D	C	B	D
61	**62**	**63**	**64**	**65**	**66**	**67**	**68**	**69**	**70**
A	A	C	C	B	D	B	A	D	B
71	**72**	**73**	**74**	**75**	**76**	**77**	**78**	**79**	**80**
C	C	A	A	D	A	B	D	C	A
81	**82**	**83**	**84**	**85**	**86**	**87**	**88**	**89**	**90**
B	A	A	D	C	A	D	D	D	A
91	**92**	**93**	**94**	**95**	**96**	**97**	**98**	**99**	**100**
D	C	B	B	A	C	D	D	B	B
101	**102**	**103**	**104**	**105**	**106**	**107**	**108**	**109**	**110**
C	D	D	C	A	D	B	D	B	C
111	**112**	**113**	**114**	**115**	**116**	**117**	**118**	**119**	**120**
C	C	C	C	C	B	A	A	B	B
121	**122**	**123**	**124**	**125**	**126**	**127**	**128**	**129**	**130**
B	C	A	B	C	D	D	A	A	B
131	**132**	**133**	**134**	**135**	**136**	**137**	**138**	**139**	**140**
D	C	C	A	D	B	C	A	A	B
141	**142**	**143**	**144**	**145**	**146**	**147**	**148**	**149**	**150**
B	A	B	C	B	D	D	D	A	B

EXPLANATORY ANSWERS

50. Total number of buzzes in a day

$= 2(1 + 2 + 3 + 4 + 5 + 6 + 7 + 8 + 9 + 10 + 11 + 12)$

$= 2 \times \dfrac{12 \times 13}{2}$

$= 2 \times 78 = 156.$

51. Cost of 5 shirts $= 5 \times ₹\,450 = ₹\,2250$

Cost of 4 trousers $= 4 \times ₹\,750 = ₹\,3000$

Cost of 12 pairs of shoes

$= 12 \times ₹\,750$

$= ₹\,9000$

Average expenditure

$= \dfrac{2250 + 3000 + 9000}{5 + 4 + 12}$

$= \dfrac{14,250}{21}$

$= ₹\,678.57$

$\cong ₹\,678.50.$

52. Required number of students

$= 12 - 8 = 4.$

53. Let the age of Gautam be x years

Age of Hari $= 2x$ years

Age of Bala $= (x + 6)$ years

$= (2x - 6)$ years

$\therefore \quad x = 12$ years

Age of Hari $= 2 \times 12$

$= 24$ years

Age of Gautam $= 12$ years

Age of Gopi $= \dfrac{3}{2}x$

$$= \dfrac{3}{2} \times 12 = 18 \text{ years}$$

Age of Bala $= 12 + 6 = 18$ years

Hence, Hari is eldest.

54. (Ram + Shyam)'s one day's work $= \dfrac{1}{8}$

Ram's one day's work $= \dfrac{1}{12}$

Then, Shyam's one day's work

$$= \dfrac{1}{8} - \dfrac{1}{12} = \dfrac{1}{24}$$

Therefore, Shyam will do the work in 24 days.

55. Height after 2nd bounce

$$= 10 - \dfrac{10 \times 40}{100} = 10 - 4 = 6 \text{ metres.}$$

56. As,

I	N	D	I	A
	14 (1+4)			
9	5	4	9	1

Similarly,

D	E	L	H	I
		1 + 2		
4	5	3	8	9

58. Remaining part

$$= 1 - \dfrac{3}{7} = \dfrac{7-3}{7} = \dfrac{4}{7}$$

Bucket is filled in $\dfrac{7}{3}$ minutes

Then, $\dfrac{4}{3}$ th part of bucket will be filled in

$\dfrac{7}{3} \times \dfrac{4}{7} = \dfrac{4}{3}$ minutes.

59. Today is Sunday

Yesterday was Friday

Hence, Day before Yesterday = Thursday.

60. Except London, all three are Indian cities.

121. 5, 9, 17, 29, 45, [65] with differences +4, +8, +12, +16, +20

122. 3, 7, 15, 31, 63, [127] with differences +4, +8, +16, +32, +64

123. Here, $\dfrac{3x + 5x + 7x}{3} = 15$

$$\Rightarrow \qquad 15x = 45$$

$$\therefore \qquad x = 3$$

The age of the youngest boy

$$= 3x = 3 \times 3 = 9 \text{ years.}$$

124.

$$\text{Rate} = \dfrac{I \times 100}{P \times T}$$

$$= \dfrac{200 \times 100}{100 \times 10} = 20\%.$$

125. Girl's maternal uncle is the only son of Amar's mother's father. Hence, girl's mother is either mother or maternal aunt of Amar.

126. $\dfrac{363}{7} = 51$ and also Remainder 6

Hence, Thursday + 6 = Wednesday.

127. ① 2 ③ ⟶ Bright little boy

① 4 5 ⟶ tall big boy

6 ③ 7 ⟶ beautiful little flower

Hence, bright → 2.

128. $4 + 11 \div 5 - 55 = ?$

$$? = 4 \times 11 - 5 + 55$$

(putting original signs)

$\Rightarrow \qquad ? = 44 - 5 + 55 = 94.$

129.

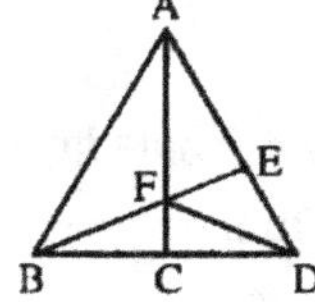

The triangles are:

Δ ABD, Δ ABC, Δ ACD, Δ ABF, Δ AFE, Δ FBD, Δ DEF, Δ FCD, Δ BFC, Δ BDE, Δ FDA, Δ ABE

Hence, total no. of triangles = 12.

146. In 8 days 10 men can finish the work.

So, in 1 day 10×8 men can finish the work.

Hence, in $\dfrac{1}{2}$ day $10 \times 8 \times 2$

= 160 men can finish the work.

147. $\text{New average} = \dfrac{10 \times 105 + 20 \times 120}{30}$

$$= \dfrac{1050 + 2400}{30}$$

$$= \dfrac{3450}{30}$$

$$= 115 \text{ cm.}$$

148. Let the number of coins of 50 paise, 25 paise and one rupee be $5x$, $6x$ and $2x$ respectively.

Then, $\dfrac{5}{2}x + \dfrac{6x}{4} + 2x = 42$

$\Rightarrow \qquad \dfrac{10x + 6x + 8x}{4} = 42$

$\Rightarrow \qquad 24x = 42 \times 4$

$\therefore \qquad x = \dfrac{42 \times 4}{24} = 7$

Hence, Number of 25 paise coins

$$= 6x = 6 \times 7 = 42.$$

149. $\sqrt{2^n} = 64$

$\Rightarrow \qquad 2^n = 64 \times 64$

$\Rightarrow \qquad 2^n = 2^6 \times 2^6$

$$= 2^{6+6}$$

$\therefore \qquad n = 6 + 6 = 12.$

150. The series consists of consecutive odd numbers. So, there will be no zero.

10 PRACTICE PAPERS

(501) Practice Paper—1

Railway Recruitment Board (RRB)
GROUP 'D'
Recruitment Exam

Directions (Qs. Nos. 1 to 4): *Select the missing number from the given responses.*

1.
   5   6   7   8
  10 18 21 40
   7   9 10 ?
  A. 20   B. 13
  C. 11   D. 15

2. 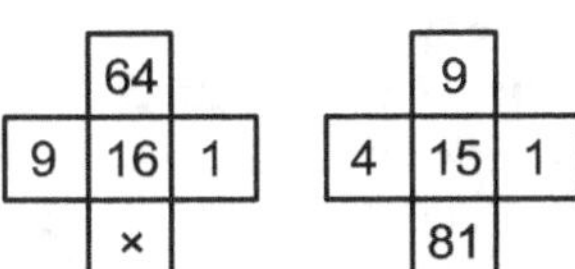
  A. 32   B. 4
  C. 2   D. 16

3. 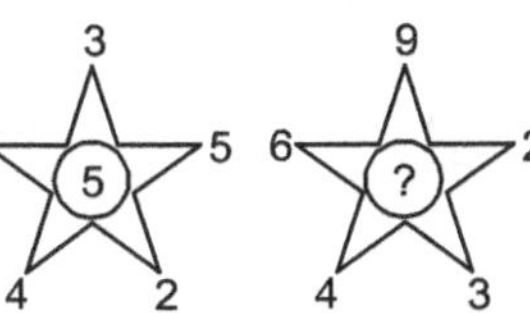
  A. 7   B. 10
  C. 11   D. 4

4. 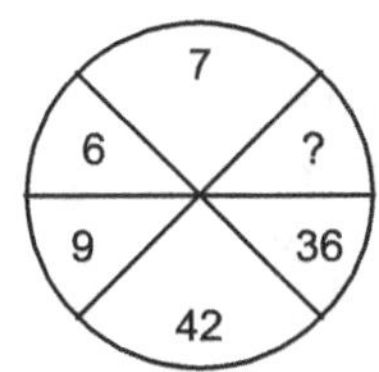
  A. 54   B. 34
  C. 78   D. 24

Directions (Qs. Nos. 5 to 13): *Select the related word/letters/number from the given alternatives.*

5. 414 : 636 :: 325 : ?
  A. 222   B. 547
  C. 636   D. 414

6. 32 : 28 :: 160 : ?
  A. 110   B. 80
  C. 140   D. 120

7. $\sqrt{AFI}$: 13 :: $\sqrt{DDA}$: ?
  A. 12   B. 21
  C. 24   D. 22

8. FE : HG :: ML : ?
  A. JI   B. QP
  C. PO   D. ON

9. Vacation : Holiday :: Vocation : ?
  A. Money   B. Career
  C. Degree   D. Pleasure

10. SNAKE : VQDNH :: CRADLE :: ?
  A. EVFGOF   B. FVDGPH
  C. FUDGOH   D. EUDGOH

11. Perch : Fresh water :: ? : Salt water
  A. Cod   B. Frog
  C. Crocodile   D. Snake

12. 196 : 256 :: ? : 400
  A. 324   B. 144
  C. 204   D. 452

13. Eyes : Tears :: ____ : ____
  A. Heart : Artery   B. Hunger : Bread
  C. Volcano : Lava   D. Sea : Water

14. If 'Stress' is coded as Rtress. Then 'Pulse' will be coded as:
  A. Qulse   B. Rulse
  C. Fulse   D. Oulse

Direction (Qs. No. 15): *Which conclusion is true with respect to the given statements.*

15. Statement:
  1. All squares are rectangles.
  2. All rectangles are polygons.

Conclusion
A. Square is a polygon.
B. Square is a rectangle and polygon.
C. Square is not a polygon.
D. Square is not a rectangle.

Directions (Qs. Nos. 16 & 17): *From the given alternative words, select the word which cannot be formed using the letters of the given word:*

16. Calculate
    A. Team   B. Tea
    C. Late   D. Cat

17. Correspondence
    A. Respond   B. Condense
    C. Respondent   D. Correspond

Directions (Qs. Nos. 18 to 20): *Which one set of letters when sequentially placed at the gaps in the given letter series shall complete it?*

18. oopqop _ qoo _ qo _ oqo _ pq
    A. poop   B. oppo
    C. opop   D. popo

19. _ _ babbba _ a _ _
    A. ababb   B. bbaba
    C. babbb   D. baaab

20. a _ baa _ baa _ ba
    A. bba   B. bab
    C. bbb   D. aab

21. Ali had ₹ 320. He spent 3/4 of it to buy a watch. Of the remainder, he used 1/8 of it to buy a pen. How much money is left?
    A. 120   B. 100
    C. 90   D. 70

Directions (Qs. Nos. 22 to 24): *A series is given, with one term missing. Choose the correct alternative from the given ones that will complete the series.*

22. 127, 131, 139, ?, 151, 157, 163, 167
    A. 141   B. 149
    C. 143   D. 147

23. 1, 1, 2, 3, 5, _?_, 13, 21
    A. 8   B. 7
    C. 6   D. 9

24. 361, _?_, 169, 121, 49, 25
    A. 324   B. 256
    C. 196   D. 289

25. Insert the arithmetical operations in the following numeric figure :
    $$4 \_ 3 \_ 4 = 48$$
    A. × ×   B. + −
    C. × +   D. + +

26. The sum of the perfect squares between 120 and 300 is:
    A. 1296   B. 1024
    C. 1204   D. 1400

27. A student goes to school at the rate of 2½ km/hr and reaches 6 minutes late. If he travels at the speed of 3 km/hr he is 10 minutes early. What is the distance to the school?
    A. 3¼ km   B. 3½ km
    C. 1 km   D. 4 km

28. A pipe can fill a tank in 24 hrs. Due to a leakage in the bottom, it is filled in 36 hrs. If the tank is half full, how much time will the leak take to empty the tank?
    A. 24 hrs.   B. 36 hrs.
    C. 72 hrs.   D. 48 hrs.

29. The ratio of two numbers is 3 : 4 and their L.C.M. is 120. The sum of numbers is:
    A. 70   B. 140
    C. 35   D. 105

30. If $\sqrt{33} = 5.745$, then the value of the following is approximately.
    $$\sqrt{\frac{3}{11}}$$
    A. 2.035   B. 0.5223
    C. 1   D. 6.32

31. Each side of a cube is decreased by 25%. Find the ratio of the volumes of the original cube and the resulting cube.
    A. 64 : 1
    B. 8 : 1
    C. 64 : 27
    D. 27 : 64

32. TF is a tower with F on the ground. The angle of elevation of T from A is such that $\tan x° = 2/5$ and AF = 200 m. The angle of elevation of T from a nearer point B is $y°$ with BF = 80 m. The value of $y°$ is:

A. 60° B. 45°
C. 75° D. 30°

Directions (Qs. Nos. 33 to 37): *The pie chart shows how the school funds is spent under different heads in a certain school. Using the pie chart answer the questions.*

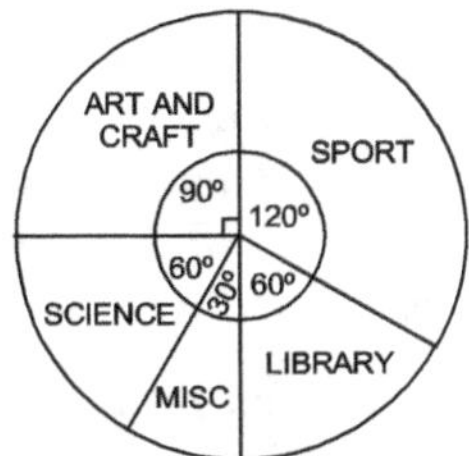

33. Which heads have the same amount of expenditure?
A. Misc and Library
B. Science and Misc
C. Sports and Science
D. Library and Science

34. Which head uses 25% of the funds?
A. Misc B. Sports
C. Art and Craft D. Library

35. Which head has the maximum expenditure?
A. Science B. Library
C. Sports D. Art and Craft

36. What percentage of the total expense is spent on library?
A. 24 B. 16.6
C. 20 D. 24.3

37. What is the ratio of expenditure on sports to that on art and craft?
A. 1 : 1 B. 2 : 1
C. 4 : 3 D. 1 : 4

38. Simon purchased a bicycle for ₹ 6810. He had paid a VAT of 13.5%. The list price of the bicycle was:
A. ₹ 6000 B. ₹ 6140
C. ₹ 5970.50 D. ₹ 6696.50

39. The base of a right prism is a trapezium whose lengths of two parallel sides are 10 cm and 6 cm and distance between them is 5 cm. If the height of the prism is 8 cm, its volume is:
A. 300 cm^3 B. 320 cm^3
C. 310 cm^3 D. 300.5 cm^3

40. The radius of a hemispherical bowl is 6 cm. The capacity of the bowl is: $\left(\text{Take } \pi = \dfrac{22}{7} \right)$
A. 495.51 cm^3 B. 345.53 cm^3
C. 452 cm^3 D. 452.57 cm^3

41. What is the position of the circumcentre of an obtuse-angled triangle?
A. It lies inside the triangle.
B. It is the mid point of the largest side.
C. It is the vertex opposite to the largest side.
D. It lies outside the triangle.

42. A man buys a TV priced at ₹ 16000. He pays ₹ 4000 at once and the rest after 15 months on which he is charged a simple interest at the rate of 12% per year. The total amount he pays for the TV is:
A. ₹ 18,200 B. ₹ 16,800
C. ₹ 17,800 D. ₹ 17,200

43. In a business A and C invested amounts in the ratio 2 : 1, whereas A and B invested amounts in the ratio 3 : 2. If their annual profit be ₹ 157300, then B's share in the profit is:
A. ₹ 24200 B. ₹ 48000
C. ₹ 36300 D. ₹ 48400

44. An epidemic broke out in a village in which 5% of the population died. Of the remaining, 20% fied out of panic. If the present population is 4655, then the population of the village originally was:
A. 5955 B. 6000
C. 5995 D. 6125

45. 50% of a number when added to 50 is equal to the number, The number is:
A. 75 B. 150
C. 50 D. 100

46. The difference between simple interest and the true discount on ₹ 2400 due 4 years hence at 5% per annum simple interest is:
A. ₹ 50
B. ₹ 80
C. ₹ 70
D. ₹ 30

47. The value of the following is:
$$\frac{(\tan 20°)^2}{(\operatorname{cosec} 70°)^2} + \frac{(\cot 20°)^2}{(\sec 70°)^2} + 2\tan 15°.\tan 45°.\tan 75°$$
A. 2
B. 3
C. 4
D. 1

48. If $\dfrac{x}{3} + \dfrac{3}{x} = 1$, then the value of x^3 is?
A. –27
B. 0
C. 27
D. 1

49. D and E are mid-points of sides AB and AC respectively of the $\triangle$ ABC. A line drawn from A meets BC at H and DE at K.
AK : KH = ??
A. 1 : 3
B. 1 : 2
C. 2 : 1
D. 1 : 1

50. If A, B, C are the angles of a $\triangle$ ABC, then following is equal to:
$$\sin\left(\frac{B+C}{2}\right)$$
A. $\sec \dfrac{B}{2}$
B. $\cos \dfrac{A}{2}$
C. $\sec \dfrac{A}{2}$
D. $\operatorname{cosec} \dfrac{A}{2}$

51. In which year was the first world environment day observed?
A. 1974
B. 1973
C. 1972
D. 1980

52. How many states are there in the Indian Union?
A. 30
B. 29
C. 27
D. 28

53. The battle of Plassey was fought between:
A. Mir Jafar and Robert Clive
B. Mir Khasim and Robert Clive
C. None of the options
D. Sirajudduala and Robert Clive

54. 'Red Data Book' provides an account of?
A. Endangered plants only
B. Extinct animals only
C. Endangered plants and animals
D. Fossil plants

55. The serious environmental degradation of Maldives is considered to be essentially due to:
A. High population density
B. Industrial pollution of water and air
C. Constant soil erosion
D. None of the options

56. Which of the following memories must be refreshed many times per second?
A. EPROM
B. ROM
C. Dynamic RAM
D. Static RAM

57. First human heart transplant was performed in:
A. 1972
B. 1955
C. 1959
D. 1967

58. Which of the following term is associated with Hockey?
A. Faceoff
B. Kickoff
C. Offside
D. Bodyline

59. The total utility from 9 units of commodity x is 20 and from 10 units is 15. Calculate the marginal utility from 10th unit.
A. 5
B. –5
C. –0.5
D. 0.5

60. The gas that causes suffocation and death when coal or coke is burnt in a closed room is:
A. Methane
B. Carbon di-oxide
C. Ethane
D. Carbon monoxide

61. Who was Akbar's famous revenue minister?
A. Humayun
B. Rana Pratap Singh
C. Todarmal
D. Tansen

62. When number of turns in a coil is trippled, without any change in the length of coil, its self inductance becomes?
A. one-third
B. nine times
C. six times
D. three times

63. The non-cooperation movement was called off due to?
A. Chauri Chaura Incident
B. Jallianwalla Bagh Tragedy
C. Poona pact
D. Gandhi-Irwin pact

64. Which was the first talkie film made in India?
A. Alam Ara
B. Mother India
C. Raja Harishchandra
D. Kisan Kanya

65. The directive principles incorporated in the Indian Constitution have been inspired by the constitution of:
A. Australia
B. Ireland
C. USA
D. Canada

66. When and where did the concept of Earth hour began?
A. In May, 2009 in Colombo, Sri Lanka
B. In June, 2007 in Christchurch, Newzealand
C. In April, 2008 in Tokyo, Japan
D. In March, 2007 in Sydney, Australia

67. Which factor is necessary for the development of democratic institutions?
A. Respect for individual rights
B. A one-party system
C. Strong military forces
D. An agricultural economy

68. The intensity ratio of waves is 25 : 9. What is the ratio of their amplitudes?
A. 5 : 3
B. 3 : 5
C. 25 : 9
D. 50 : 18

69. World's largest producer of coffee?
A. Brazil
B. Peru
C. Argentina
D. India

70. Soilless agriculture refers to:
A. Inter-cropping
B. Hygroponics
C. Sericulture
D. Hydroponics

71. Name the first Asian country to Orbit Mars.
A. Pakistan
B. China
C. India
D. Japan

72. Which of the following property of sound is affected by change in air temperature?
A. Amplitude
B. Intensity
C. Frequency
D. Wavelength

73. Barter transactions means:
A. Coins are exchanged for goods.
B. Goods are exchanged with gold.
C. Goods are exchanged with goods.
D. Money acts as a medium of exchange.

74. Who is the founder of the concept "Sarvodaya"?
A. Mahatma Gandhi
B. Vinobha Bhave
C. K.G. Mushroowala
D. None of these

75. The idea of parliamentary form of government is adapted from:
A. US
B. UK
C. Ireland
D. USSR

76. Who among the following was not a chief minister before he/she became the Prime Minister of India?
A. Morarji Desai
B. Charan Singh
C. Indira Gandhi
D. V.P. Singh

77. The instrument used to measure pressure:
A. Hygrometer
B. Thermometer
C. Aneroid Barometer
D. Anemometer

78. 'Cloud burst' means
A. Presence of scattered flakes of cloud in the sky.
B. Abnormally heavy downpour of rain, associated with a thunderstorm.
C. Sowing of seeds of a crop in cloudy weather.
D. Formation of artificial rain.

79. Which one of the following is odd?
A. POP
B. SNMP
C. IMAP
D. SMTP

80. What is the local name given to the parliament of Pakistan?
A. Majilis
B. Majlis-e-Shoora
C. Saeima-e-majilis
D. Jatia Parliament

81. National Renewal Fund (NRF) was instituted for the purpose of:
A. Restructuring and modernisation of industries.
B. Social security
C. Providing pension for retiring employees.
D. Rural reconstruction.

82. Who among the following rulers abolished Jaziya?
A. Akbar
B. Balban
C. Aurangzeb
D. Jahangir

83. Pick out the person associated with the coining of the term 'gene'.
A. Mendel
B. Waldeyer
C. Morgan
D. Johannsen

84. Who wrote the famous novel 'The Guide'?
A. R.K. Narayan
B. Chetan Bhagat
C. Satyajit Ray
D. Arundhati Roy

85. Which day is observed as World AIDS Day?
A. December 1st
B. December 20th
C. March 20th
D. March 1st

86. More than 50% of the world's coal deposits are held by:
A. USA, Russia and China
B. China, India and USA
C. India, Russia and USA
D. China, India and Russia

87. Who invented the Safety razor?
A. Steve Cher
B. Gillette
C. Lar Strauss
D. Steve Job

88. When was the last telegram sent in India?
A. July 14, 2013
B. July 30, 2013
C. August 1, 2013
D. June 14, 2013

89. If there is one million Mg^{2+} ions in $MgCl_2$, how many chloride ions are there?
A. Ten million
B. Half a million
C. One million
D. Two million

90. Which U.S. President announced the "New Deal" for economic recovery in the aftermath of the Great Depression?
A. Benjamin Franklin
B. Abraham Lincoln
C. J.F. Kennedy
D. Roosevelt

91. How many Nobel Prize awards are awarded each year?
A. 6
B. 8
C. 5
D. 10

92. The Industrial Development Bank of India was set up in:
A. July, 1964
B. July, 1966
C. July, 1962
D. July, 1968

93. Phycology is the study of:
A. Fungi
B. Lichens
C. Bacteria
D. Algae

94. The common name of sodium bicarbonate is:
A. Baking soda
B. Soda lime
C. Baking powder
D. Soda ash

95. A bullet of mass 'm' and velocity 'a' is fired in to a large block of wood of mass 'M'. The final velocity of the system is:
A. $\dfrac{m+M}{M}a$
B. $\dfrac{m}{m+M}a$
C. $\dfrac{m+M}{m}a$
D. $\dfrac{M}{m+M}a$

96. Which one of the following wood is used in making cricket bats?
A. Cedrus deodara
B. Linum usitatissimum
C. Morus alba
D. Salix purpurea

97. Which one of the following is not coal variety?
A. Lignite
B. Peat
C. Bituminous
D. Dolomite

98. Who was the first Indian to become member of British Parliament?
A. D.N. Wacha
B. D. Dadabhai Naoroji
C. Surendranath Banerjee
D. Firozshah Mehta

99. Dry ice is the solid form of:
A. Water
B. Carbon dioxide
C. Air
D. Nitrogen

100. What is 'Talcher' important for?
A. Atomic reactor
B. Cable industry
C. Hydro-electricity
D. Heavy water plant

ANSWERS

1	2	3	4	5	6	7	8	9	10
B	D	B	A	B	C	B	D	B	C

11	12	13	14	15	16	17	18	19	20
A	A	C	D	B	A	C	B	C	C

21	22	23	24	25	26	27	28	29	30
D	B	A	D	A	D	D	B	A	B

31	32	33	34	35	36	37	38	39	40
C	B	D	C	C	B	C	A	B	D

41	42	43	44	45	46	47	48	49	50
D	C	D	D	D	B	B	A	D	B

51	52	53	54	55	56	57	58	59	60
B	B	D	C	C	C	D	A	C	D

61	62	63	64	65	66	67	68	69	70
C	D	A	A	B	D	A	A	A	D

71	72	73	74	75	76	77	78	79	80
C	D	C	A	B	C	C	B	B	B

81	82	83	84	85	86	87	88	89	90
A	A	D	A	A	A	B	A	D	D

91	92	93	94	95	96	97	98	99	100
A	A	D	A	B	D	D	B	B	D

EXPLANATORY ANSWERS

1.

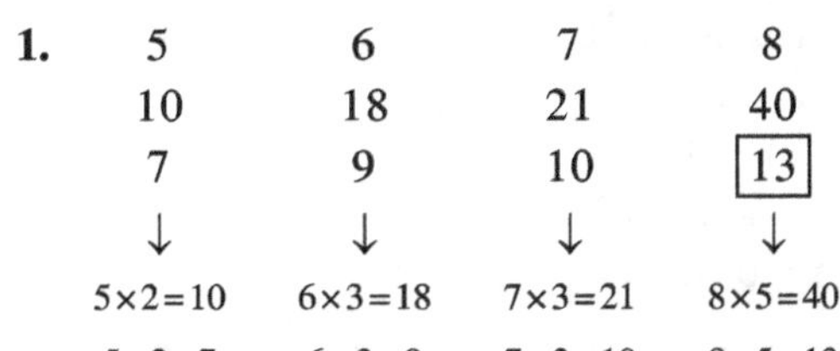

5	6	7	8
10	18	21	40
7	9	10	[13]
↓	↓	↓	↓

$5×2=10$ $6×3=18$ $7×3=21$ $8×5=40$

$5+2=7$ $6+3=9$ $7+3=10$ $8+5=13$

Hence, 13 will come at the place of question mark.

2.

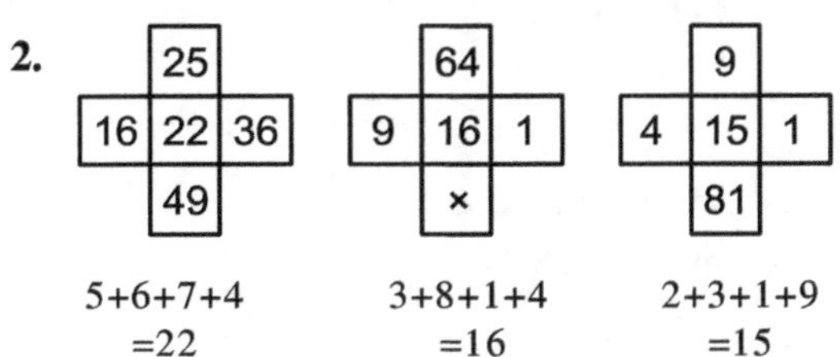

$5+6+7+4$
$=22$

$3+8+1+4$
$=16$

$2+3+1+9$
$=15$

Hence, 16 will come at the place of (×).

3.

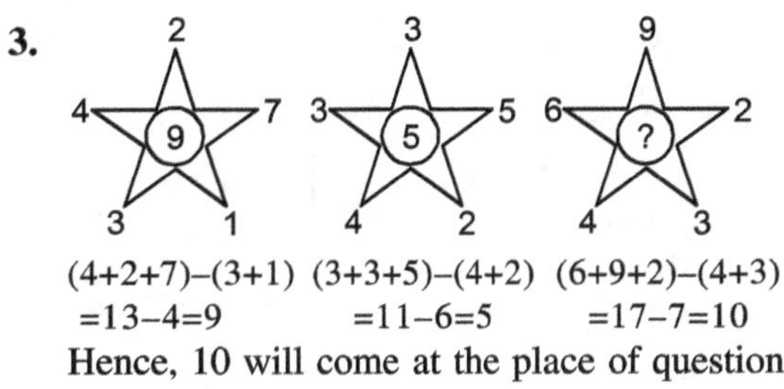

$(4+2+7)−(3+1)$ $(3+3+5)−(4+2)$ $(6+9+2)−(4+3)$
$=13−4=9$ $=11−6=5$ $=17−7=10$

Hence, 10 will come at the place of question mark.

4.

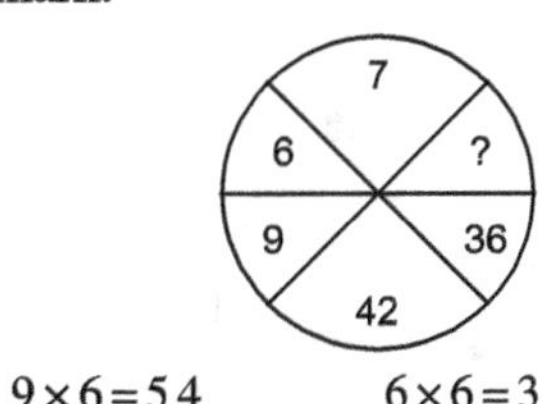

$9×6=54$ $6×6=36$ $7×6=42$

Hence, 54 will come at the place of the question mark.

5. $414 : 636 :: 325 : x$

$$414 + x = 636 + 325$$
$$x = 636 + 325 - 414$$
$$x = 547$$

Hence, 547 will come at the place of question mark.

6. $32 : 28 :: 160 : \boxed{x}$

$$32 \times x = 28 \times 160$$
$$x = \frac{28 \times 160}{32} = 28 \times 5 = 140$$

Hence, 140 will come at the place of question mark.

12. $196 : 256 :: x^2 : 400$

Taking square roots

$$14 : 16 :: x : 20$$
$$16 + x = 14 + 20$$
$$x = 14 + 20 - 16$$
$$x = 18$$
$$\therefore \quad x^2 = (18)^2 = 324$$

Hence, 324 will come at the place of question mark.

19. The series is bababb, bababb.

21. $320 - \dfrac{3}{4} \times 320$

$$= 320 - 240 = ₹\ 80$$

Now, $80 - \dfrac{1}{8} \times 80 = 80 - 10 = ₹\ 70$

Hence, the amount left $= ₹\ 70$

23. $1 \quad 1 \quad 2 \quad 3 \quad 5 \quad \boxed{8} \quad 13 \quad 21$

$$1 + 1 = 2$$
$$1 + 2 = 3$$
$$2 + 3 = 5$$
$$3 + 5 = 8$$
$$5 + 8 = 13$$
$$8 + 13 = 21$$

Hence, 8 will come at the place of question mark.

24. $361 \quad \boxed{289} \quad 169 \quad 121 \quad 49 \quad 25$

$$19^2 \quad 17^2 \quad 13^2 \quad 11^2 \quad 7^2 \quad 5^2$$

Hence, 289 will come at the place of question mark.

25. $4 \times 3 \times 4 = 48$

Hence, option (A) is correct.

26. Perfect squares between 120 and 300 are 121, 144, 169, 196, 225, 256, 289.

$$\therefore \quad \text{Sum} = 121 + 144 + 169 + 196$$
$$+ 225 + 256 + 289 = 1400$$

27. Let the distance $= x$ km.

$$\frac{x \times 2}{5} - \frac{6}{60} = \frac{x}{3} + \frac{10}{60}$$

$$\Rightarrow \quad \frac{2x}{5} - \frac{x}{3} = \frac{1}{6} + \frac{1}{10}$$

$$\Rightarrow \quad \frac{6x - 5x}{15} = \frac{5 + 3}{30} = \frac{8}{30} = \frac{4}{15}$$

$$\Rightarrow \quad \frac{x}{15} = \frac{4}{15} \qquad \Rightarrow x = 4$$

$\therefore$ Required distance $= 4$ km.

28. $\dfrac{1}{24} - \dfrac{1}{36} = \dfrac{3-2}{72} = \dfrac{1}{72}$

In 72 hrs. the leak can empty the full tank.

$\therefore$ Half full tank can empty the leak in 36 hrs.

29. Let the numbers are $3x$ and $4x$.

L.C.M. of $3x$ and $4x = 12x$

According to the question,

$$12x = 120$$
$$\Rightarrow \quad x = 10$$

$\therefore$ Numbers are 30 and 40

Sum of the numbers $= 30 + 40 = 70$

30. $\because \ \sqrt{33} = 5.745$

$$\therefore \quad \sqrt{\frac{3}{11}} = \frac{\sqrt{3 \times 11}}{\sqrt{11 \times 11}} = \frac{\sqrt{33}}{11}$$

$$= \frac{5.745}{11} = 0.5223 \ (\text{Approx.})$$

31. Let side of the cube $= x$

Volume of Cube $= x^3$

Now, $x - \dfrac{25}{100} x = \dfrac{75x}{100} = \dfrac{3x}{4}$

Volume of new cube $= \left(\dfrac{3x}{4}\right)^3 = \dfrac{27x^3}{64}$

Required ratio $= \dfrac{x^3 \times 64}{27x^3} = 64 : 27$

32.

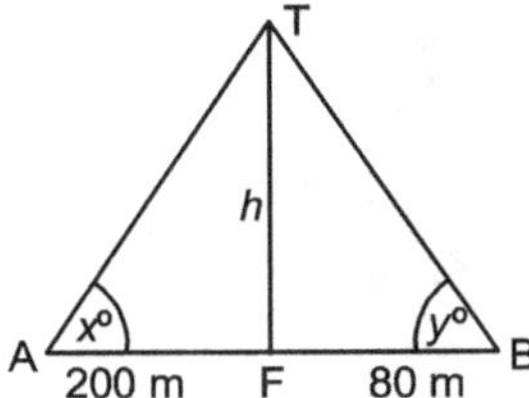

$\tan x^\circ = \dfrac{h}{200}$

$\Rightarrow \quad \dfrac{2}{5} = \dfrac{h}{200}$

$\Rightarrow \quad h = 80$ m

$\tan y^\circ = \dfrac{h}{80}$

$\Rightarrow \quad \tan y = \dfrac{80}{80} = 1$

$\Rightarrow \quad \tan y = \tan 45^\circ$

$\therefore \quad y = 45^\circ$

33. The same amount of expenditure
= Library and Science.

34. $\dfrac{90}{360} \times 100 = 25\%$

$\therefore$ 25% of the fund uses on Art and Craft.

35. $\dfrac{120}{360} \times 100 = \dfrac{100}{3}$

$= 33\dfrac{1}{3}\%$

On sports uses maximum expenditure.

36. Amount spent on Library

$= \dfrac{60}{360} \times 100$

$= \dfrac{100}{6} = 16.6\%$

37. Expenditure on Sports $= \dfrac{120}{360} \times 100 = \dfrac{100}{3}\%$

Expenditure on art and craft

$= \dfrac{90}{360} \times 100 = 25\%$

Required ratio $= \dfrac{100}{3} : 25$

$= \dfrac{100}{3} \times \dfrac{1}{25} = 4 : 3$

38. $100 + 13.5 = 113.5$

When C.P. ₹ 113.5, then list price = ₹ 100
When C.P. ₹ 6810, then list price

$= \dfrac{100}{113.5} \times 6810$

$= \dfrac{100 \times 10 \times 6810}{1135}$

$= \dfrac{100 \times 2 \times 6810}{227}$

$= 100 \times 2 \times 30 = ₹ 6000$

39. Required Volume $= \dfrac{1}{2} \times 5(10 + 6) \times 8$

$= 5 \times 16 \times 4 = 320$ cm^3

40. Volume of hemispherical bowl

$= \dfrac{2}{3} \pi r^3$

$= \dfrac{2}{3} \times \dfrac{22}{7} \times 6 \times 6 \times 6$

$= \dfrac{144 \times 22}{7} = \dfrac{3168}{7}$

$= 452.57$ cm^3

41. The circumcentre of an obtuse-angled triangle lies outside the triangle.

42. ₹ 16000 − 4000 = ₹ 12000

$\text{S.I.} = \dfrac{12000 \times 15 \times 12}{12 \times 100} = ₹ 1800$

Total amount paid for the T.V.

$= 12000 + 4000 + 1800 = ₹ 17800$

43. A : B = 3 : 2

$\Rightarrow$ B : A = 2 : 3 = 4 : 6

and A : C = 2 : 1 = 6 : 3

$\therefore$ B : A : C = 4 : 6 : 3

$\Rightarrow$ A : B : C = 6 : 4 : 3

$\therefore$ B's share = $157300 \times \dfrac{4}{13} = ₹\ 48400$

44. Let population of the village = 100

$$100 - \dfrac{5}{100} \times 100 = 95$$

$$95 - \dfrac{20}{100} \times 95 = 95 - 19 = 76$$

When present population is 76, then original population = 100

When present population is 4655, then original

population = $\dfrac{100}{76} \times 4655$

$$= \dfrac{465500}{76} = 6125$$

45. Let number = x

50% of x + 50 = x

$$\Rightarrow \dfrac{50}{100} \times x + 50 = x$$

$$\Rightarrow x - \dfrac{x}{2} = 50$$

$$\Rightarrow x = 100$$

Hence, number = 100

47. $\dfrac{\tan^2 20°}{\csc^2 70°} + \dfrac{\cot^2 20°}{\sec^2 70°} + 2\tan 15°.\tan 45°.\tan 75°$

$$= \dfrac{\tan^2 20°}{\sec^2 20°} + \dfrac{\cot^2 20°}{\csc^2 20°} + 2\tan 15° \cdot \cot 15° \times 1$$

$$[\because\ \tan 45° = 1]$$

$$= \dfrac{\sin^2 20}{\cos^2 20°} \times \cos^2 20° + \dfrac{\cos^2 20°}{\sin^2 20°} \times \sin^2 20° + 2$$

$$= (\sin^2 20° + \cos^2 20°) + 2$$

$$= 1 + 2 = 3$$

50. $\because$ A + B + C = 180°

$$\dfrac{A}{2} + \dfrac{B}{2} + \dfrac{C}{2} = \dfrac{180°}{2} = 90°$$

$$\dfrac{B}{2} + \dfrac{C}{2} = 90° - \dfrac{A}{2}$$

$$\sin\left(\dfrac{B+C}{2}\right) = \sin\left(90° - \dfrac{A}{2}\right) = \cos\dfrac{A}{2}$$

Railway Recruitment Board (RRB)
GROUP 'D'
Recruitment Exam

Directions (Qs. Nos. 1 to 9): *Select the related word/letters/number from the given alternatives.*

1. ABCXYZ : DEFUVW : : GHIRST : ___?___
   A. JKLOPQ   B. JOKPLN
   C. JNOPKL   D. MNOLKJ

2. ACE : BDF : : MOQ : ___?___
   A. MZU   B. MVT
   C. NPR   D. NZV

3. 8 : 23 : : 48 : ___?___
   A. 168   B. 112
   C. 90   D. 138

4. 5 : 28 : : 8 : ___?___ .
   A. 25   B. 67
   C. 40   D. 64

5. CAT : 3120 : : MAT : ___?___ .
   A. 13120   B. 12120
   C. 1312   D. 10120

6. Doctor : Hospital : : Teacher : ___?___ .
   A. School   B. Industry
   C. Field   D. Laboratory

7. 1st Prime Minister of India :
   Pt. Jawaharlal Nehru : :
   1st President of India : ___?___
   A. Dr. Zakir Hussain
   B. Dr. A.P.J. Abdul Kalam
   C. Dr. S. Radhakrishnan
   D. Dr. Rajendra Prasad

8. International Literacy Day : September 8 : :
   International Women's Day : ___?___ .
   A. April 22
   B. November 4
   C. March 8
   D. June 26

9. ZX : AC : : VT : ___?___ .
   A. AB   B. AE
   C. EG   D. DF

Directions (Qs. Nos. 10 to 17): *Find the word/letters/number from the given alternatives.*

10. A. 2, 3   B. 20, 21
    C. 9, 10   D. 24, 25

11. A. 56   B. 98
    C. 83   D. 64

12. A. Pond   B. River
    C. Ocean   D. Waterfall

13. A. Europe   B. Africa
    C. Asia   D. Canada

14. A. Flute   B. Piano
    C. Violin   D. Sitar

15. A. Litre   B. Yard
    C. Metre   D. Inch

16. A. QRS   B. XYZ
    C. STU   D. MLN

17. A. 3, 2, 4, 8   B. 4, 2, 3, 9
    C. 1, 2, 4, 7   D. 2, 3, 4, 9

18. Arrange the following in ascending order :
    1. Centimetre   2. Kilometre
    3. Decimetre   4. Metre
    A. 3, 1, 2, 4   B. 4, 2, 1, 3
    C. 1, 3, 4, 2   D. 2, 4, 3, 1

19. Which one of the given res-ponses would be
    a meaningful order of the following?
    1. House   2. Palace
    3. Bungalow   4. Hut
    A. 3, 2, 1, 4   B. 4, 1, 3, 2
    C. 1, 2, 3, 4   D. 2, 3, 1, 4

Directions (Qs. Nos. 20 and 21): *Which one set of letters when sequentially placed at the gaps in the given letter series shall complete it?*

20. a_ba_b_b_a_b
    A. bbabb
    B. abbab
    C. abaab
    D. aabba

21. m_m_am_a_
    A. amaa
    B. mama
    C. amam
    D. ammm

Directions (Qs. Nos. 22 to 27): *A series is given, with one term missing. Choose the correct alternative from the given ones that will complete the series.*

22. 1, 6, 13, 22, 33, __?__ .
    A. 46
    B. 44
    C. 47
    D. 43

23. ICE, JDF, KEG, LFH, __?__ .
    A. MGI
    B. HHI
    C. MIG
    D. MHG

24. EFGH, MNOP, QRST, __?__ .
    A. UVWX
    B. JIKH
    C. QRTS
    D. VLMN

25. BY, GT, LO, __?__ , VE
    A. QK
    B. QP
    C. PJ
    D. QJ

26. The difference between the circumference and diameter of a circle is 150 m. The radius of that circle is $\left(\text{Take } \pi = \dfrac{22}{7} \right)$
    A. 30 m
    B. 40 m
    C. 25 m
    D. 35 m

27. If the radius of a sphere be doubled, then the percentage of increase in volume is
    A. 600%
    B. 800%
    C. 500%
    D. 700%

28. A merchant offers 8% discount on all his goods and still makes a profit of 15%. If an item is marked ₹ 250, then its cost price is
    A. ₹ 230
    B. ₹ 187
    C. ₹ 180
    D. ₹ 200

29. If in a sale, the discount given on a saree is equal to one-fourth the marked price and the loss due to this discount is 15%, then the ratio of the cost price to the selling price is
    A. 10 : 17
    B. 20 : 17
    C. 3 : 4
    D. 4 : 3

30. Two numbers are in the ratio of 2 : 3. If their sum is 125, find the numbers.
    A. 20, 30
    B. 32, 78
    C. 50, 75
    D. 24, 36

31. A box contains 280 coins of one-rupee, 50-paise and 25-paise. The values of each kind of the coins are in the ratio of 8 : 4 : 3. Then the number of 50-paise coins is
    A. 80
    B. 90
    C. 70
    D. 60

32. The average age of P, Q and R is 5 years more than R's age. If the total ages of P and Q together is 39 years, then R's age is
    A. 16 years
    B. 14 years
    C. 12 years
    D. 24 years

33. If $5\sqrt{5} \times 5^3 \div 5^{-\frac{3}{2}} = 5^{a+2}$, then the value of a is:
    A. 4
    B. 5
    C. 6
    D. 8

34. The simplified value of $(0.2)^3 \times 200 \div 2000$ of $(0.2)^2$ is
    A. $\dfrac{1}{10}$
    B. 1
    C. $\dfrac{1}{100}$
    D. $\dfrac{1}{50}$

35. The odd one out from the sequence of numbers 19, 23, 29, 37, 43, 46, 47 is
    A. 37
    B. 19
    C. 23
    D. 46

36. The next number of the sequence $\dfrac{1}{2}, \dfrac{3}{4}, \dfrac{5}{8}, \dfrac{7}{16}, \dots$ is
    A. $\dfrac{9}{24}$
    B. $\dfrac{9}{32}$
    C. $\dfrac{10}{24}$
    D. $\dfrac{11}{32}$

37. The least number by which 20184 must be multiplied so as to make the product a perfect square is
A. 5   B. 6
C. 2   D. 3

38. One man or two women or three boys can do a piece of work in 88 days. One man, one woman and one boy will do it in
A. 48 days   B. 20 days
C. 44 days   D. 24 days

39. Two pipes A and B can separately fill a tank in 2 hours and 3 hours respectively. If both the pipes are opened simultaneously in the empty tank, then the tank will be filled in
A. 1 hour 15 minutes
B. 1 hour 20 minutes
C. 1 hour 12 minutes
D. 2 hours 30 minutes

40. The perimeter of a triangle is 54 m and its sides are in the ratio of 5 : 6 : 7. The area of the triangle is
A. $27\sqrt{2}$ m^2 B. 25 m^2
C. 18 m^2 D. $54\sqrt{6}$ m^2

41. The lengths of two parallel sides of a trapezium are 6 cm and 8 cm. If the height of the trapezium be 4 cm, then its area is
A. 30 sq. cm   B. 30 cm
C. 28 cm   D. 28 sq. cm

42. If the ratio of an external angle and an internal angle of a regular polygon is 1 : 17, then the number of sides of the regular polygon is
A. 36   B. 12
C. 20   D. 18

43. A bicycle wheel has a diameter (including the tyre) of 56 cm. The number of times the wheel will rotate to cover a distance of 2.2 km is
$$\left(\text{Assume } \pi = \frac{22}{7}\right)$$
A. 1875
B. 2500
C. 625
D. 1250

44. A tree of height 'h' metres is broken by a storm in such a way that its top touches the ground at a distance of 'x' metres from its root. Find the height at which the tree is broken. (Here $h > x$)
A. $\dfrac{h^2 + x^2}{4h}$ metres   B. $\dfrac{h^2 - x^2}{4h}$ metres
C. $\dfrac{h^2 + x^2}{2h}$ metres   D. $\dfrac{h^2 - x^2}{2h}$ metres

45. If $x^2 + ax + b$ is a perfect square, then which one of the following relations between a and b is true?
A. $b^2 = 4a$ B. $b^2 = a$
C. $a^2 = b$ D. $a^2 = 4b$

46. The average of two numbers is 8 and that of another three numbers is 3. The average of those five numbers is
A. 6   B. 5
C. 7   D. 5.5

47. A merchant loses 10% by selling an article. If the cost price of the article is ₹ 15, then the selling price of the article is
A. ₹ 12.30   B. ₹ 13.50
C. ₹ 13.20   D. ₹ 16.50

48. Yogita sold a plasma TV at 20% gain to Shyamla. Shyamla sold it to Deepa at 10% profit. If Deepa had to pay ₹ 33,000 for the plasma TV, find the cost price of the plasma TV for Yogita.
A. ₹ 35,000   B. ₹ 40,000
C. ₹ 30,000   D. ₹ 25,000

49. If 8% of x = 4% of y, then 20% of x is
A. 40% of y B. 80% of y
C. 10% of y D. 16% of y

50. At an election there were two candidates. A candidate got 38% vote and lost by 7200 number of votes. The total number of valid votes were
A. 16200
B. 30000
C. 13000
D. 13800

51. Universal adult franchise shows that India is a country which is
   A. Democratic   B. Sovereign
   C. Secular   D. Socialist

52. How many fundamental duties are there in our Indian Constitution?
   A. 12   B. 8
   C. 11   D. 9

53. In which year was Anti-Defection Bill passed by the Indian Parliament?
   A. 1990   B. 1995
   C. 1980   D. 1985

54. The World Trade Organisation (W.T.O.) came into effect in
   A. 1995   B. 1997
   C. 1990   D. 1993

55. Which Article of the Constitution enjoins the State to establish Village Panchayat?
   A. Article 44   B. Article 57
   C. Article 32   D. Article 40

56. The word 'Buddha' means
   A. An Enlightened one
   B. A Wanderer
   C. A Conqueror
   D. A Liberator

57. 1917 is known for
   A. End of the World War I
   B. The Russian Revolution
   C. Battle of Trafalgar
   D. Battle of Waterloo

58. What is meant by 'Capital Gain'?
   A. Appreciation in the money value of assets
   B. Additions to the capital invested in a business
   C. Part of profits added to the capital
   D. None of these

59. Which of the following listed is *not* a feature of organic farming?
   A. Use of synthetic fertilizers
   B. Very less energy consumption
   C. The non-use of chemical fertilizers and pesticides
   D. Soil is nurtured for future use by maintaining micro-organisms

60. Which of the schemes of the Government of India makes Indian cities free from slums?
   A. Rajiv Awas Yojana
   B. Antyodaya
   C. Indira Awas Yojana
   D. Central Rural Sanitation Programme

61. Indian economy is a
   A. Capitalistic economy
   B. Centralised economy
   C. Mixed economy
   D. Communistic economy

62. Who is called the 'Father of Economics'?
   A. Adam Smith   B. Alfred Marshall
   C. Max Muller   D. Karl Marx

63. The longest river in the world is
   A. Brahmaputra   B. Amazon
   C. Ganga   D. Nile

64. The main function of palisade parenchyma in leaf is
   A. Respiration
   B. Photosynthesis
   C. Transpiration
   D. Conduction

65. The harmful substances produced by the microbes are known as
   A. Hormones   B. Toxins
   C. Antibiotics   D. Pollutants

66. For immediate energy production in cells, one should take
   A. Vitamin C   B. Sucrose
   C. Glucose   D. Proteins

67. In human body, ligaments are made up of
   A. yellow fibres only
   B. yellow fibres and muscle fibres
   C. white fibres and some yellow elastic fibres
   D. white fibres only

68. Which one of the following types of malaria is pernicious malaria?
   A. Tertian   B. Malignant
   C. Vivax   D. Relapse

69. Who wrote the book 'Systema Naturae'?
   A. Darwin   B. Linnaeus
   C. Lamarck   D. Buffon

70. Who built the famous Vaikunta Perumal temple at Kanchipuram?
A. Nandi Varman II
B. Aparajita Varman
C. Narasimha Varman II
D. Parameshvara Varman II

71. U.N.O. was founded in the year
A. 1950 B. 1953
C. 1945 D. 1946

72. The first to invade India were the
A. Persians B. Arabs
C. Aryans D. Greeks

73. Niyamgiri hill is located in Kalahandi district of
A. Punjab B. Kerala
C. Odisha D. West Bengal

74. A cyclone occurs when
A. there is a low pressure in the centre and high pressure around
B. the pressure in the centre is equal to the pressure around
C. there is low pressure all around
D. there is a high pressure in the centre and low pressure around

75. The previous name of Zaire was
A. Congo B. Sierra Leone
C. Benin D. Liberia

76. The largest fresh water lake in India is
A. Wular Lake B. Nainital Lake
C. Dal Lake D. Bhimtal Lake

77. The Indian Supercomputer built by CRL, Pune which ranked fourth fastest in the world and most powerful in Asia is called
A. EKA
B. SAGA
C. Virgo
D. Param

78. A solution is
A. a solid dissolved in water
B. a mixture of two liquids
C. a homogeneous mixture of two or more substances
D. a solid dissolved in a liquid

79. The first organic compound synthesised in the laboratory was
A. Lactic acid
B. Glucose
C. Urea
D. Uric acid

80. The buffer action of blood is due to the presence of
A. Cl^- and HCO_3^- B. HCO_3^- and H_2CO_3
C. HCl and $NaCl$ D. Cl^- and CO_3^{2-}

81. Which one of the following contains maximum percentage of carbon?
A. Wrought iron B. High speed steel
C. Cast iron D. Stainless steel

82. Which of the following appeared to be with a significant potential for accumulation through food chains?
A. Lindane B. Carbaryl
C. DDT D. Parathion

83. A metal ball and a rubber ball, both having the same mass, strike a wall normally with the same velocity. The rubber ball rebounds and the metal ball does not rebound. It can be concluded that
A. Both suffer the same change in momentum
B. The initial momentum of the rubber ball is greater than that of the metal ball
C. The rubber ball suffers greater change in momentum
D. The metal ball suffers greater change in momentum

84. If the phase difference between two points is 120° for a wave with velocity of 360 m/s and frequency 500 Hz, then path difference between the two points is
A. 12 cm B. 24 cm
C. 1 cm D. 6 cm

85. If a body moves with a constant speed in a circle
A. no acceleration is produced in it
B. its velocity remains constant
C. no work is done on it
D. no force acts on it

86. The waves used in sonography are
A. Sound waves
B. Ultrasonic waves
C. Micro waves
D. Infrared waves

87. Fifth Generation Computers are
A. Data Interpreters
B. Data Controllers
C. Data Processors
D. Knowledge Processors

88. Name the oldest Indian civilization.
A. Mesopotamian civilization
B. Egyptian civilization
C. Indus Valley civilization
D. None of these

89. Who is the author of 'A Suitable Boy'?
A. Arundhati Roy
B. Khushwant Singh
C. Vikram Seth
D. None of these

90. Who was awarded the first Rajiv Gandhi National Sadbhavana Award?
A. Mother Teresa   B. Morarji Desai
C. J.R.D. Tata   D. None of these

91. International Literacy Day is observed on which one of the following days every year?
A. 28th March   B. 18th September
C. 8th September   D. 18th March

92. Who among the following Mughal rulers has been called the 'Prince of Builders'?
A. Shah Jahan   B. Babur
C. Akbar   D. Jahangir

93. Name the American film cartoonist who created Mickey Mouse and Donald Duck.
A. Steven Spielberg
B. Hanna Barbera
C. Warner Brothers
D. Walt Disney

94. An earthquake is also known as
A. Tremor   B. Temper
C. Teacher   D. None of these

95. Our atmosphere is divided into .... layers.
A. Four   B. Five
C. Two   D. Three

96. Lungs of a plant are
A. Flowers   B. Roots
C. Leaves   D. Stems

97. Who has authored the book titled 'Narendra Modi : A Political Biography'?
A. Jeffrey Dell   B. Kingsley Amis
C. Andy Marino   D. David Irving

98. Who invented the electric bulb?
A. Thomas Alva Edison
B. James Watt
C. Thomas More
D. None of these

99. Who invented aeroplane?
A. Hoffman   B. Wright Brothers
C. Edison   D. Stevenson

100. Who is called Rawalpindi Express?
A. Rahul Dravid
B. Imran Khan
C. Sachin Tendulkar
D. Shoaib Akhtar

ANSWERS

1	2	3	4	5	6	7	8	9	10
A	C	D	B	A	A	D	C	C	A

11	12	13	14	15	16	17	18	19	20
C	A	D	A	A	D	A	C	B	A

21	22	23	24	25	26	27	28	29	30
D	A	A	A	D	D	D	D	B	C

31	32	33	34	35	36	37	38	39	40
A	C	A	D	D	B	B	A	C	D

41	42	43	44	45	46	47	48	49	50
D	A	D	D	D	B	B	D	C	B
51	**52**	**53**	**54**	**55**	**56**	**57**	**58**	**59**	**60**
A	C	D	A	D	A	B	A	A	A
61	**62**	**63**	**64**	**65**	**66**	**67**	**68**	**69**	**70**
C	A	D	B	B	C	C	B	B	A
71	**72**	**73**	**74**	**75**	**76**	**77**	**78**	**79**	**80**
C	C	C	D	A	A	A	C	C	B
81	**82**	**83**	**84**	**85**	**86**	**87**	**88**	**89**	**90**
C	C	C	A	C	B	D	C	C	A
91	**92**	**93**	**94**	**95**	**96**	**97**	**98**	**99**	**100**
C	A	D	A	B	C	C	A	B	D

EXPLANATORY ANSWERS

1. ABC XYZ : DEF UVW :: GHI RST : JKL OPQ

2. ACE : BDF :: MOQ : NPR

3. 8 : 23 :: 48 : 138

8 × 138 = 1104

23 × 48 = 1104

4. 5 : 28 :: 8 : 67

$5^2 + 3$ $8^2 + 3$

5. C A T : 3 1 20 :: M A T : 13 1 20

3 1 20   13 1 20

10. 2, 3 both numbers are prime numbers.

11. 83 is prime number.

22. 1   6   13   22   33   46

+5   +7   +9   +11   +13

Hence, missing number of the series is 46.

26. According to the question,

$$C = 2\pi r \text{ and } d = 2r$$

$$C - d = 150$$

$$\Rightarrow \quad 2\pi r - 2r = 150$$

$$\Rightarrow \quad 2r(\pi - 1) = 150$$

$$\Rightarrow \quad r\left(\frac{22}{7} - 1\right) = \frac{150}{2} = 75$$

$$\Rightarrow \quad r = \frac{75 \times 7}{15} = 35\,\text{m}$$

Hence, radius of the circle = 35 m.

27. Volume of sphere $= \dfrac{4}{3}\pi r^3$

When radius increase two times then Volume of Sphere

$$= \frac{4}{3}\pi(2r)^3 = \frac{4}{3} \times 8\pi r^3$$

Increase in volume

$$= \frac{32\pi r^3}{3} - \frac{4}{3}\pi r^3$$

$$= \frac{28\pi r^3}{3}$$

% increase in volume

$$= \frac{\dfrac{28}{3}\pi r^3}{\dfrac{4}{3}\pi r^3} \times 100 = 700\%.$$

28.   M.P. = ₹ 250

$$\text{Discount} = \frac{8}{100} \times 250 = ₹\,20$$

$$\text{S.P.} = 250 - 20 = ₹\,230$$

$$100 + 15 = 115$$

When S.P. ₹ 115, then C.P. = ₹ 100

When S.P. ₹ 230, then C.P. = $\dfrac{100}{115} \times 230$

Hence, Cost price = ₹ 200.

29. Let marked price of saree = ₹ x

$$\text{Discount} = \frac{1}{4}x = \frac{x}{4}$$

$$\text{S.P.} = x - \frac{x}{4}$$

$$= \frac{3x}{4}$$

$$100 - 15 = 85$$

When S.P. ₹ 85, then C.P. = ₹ 100

When S.P. ₹ $\dfrac{3x}{4}$, then C.P.

$$= \frac{100}{85} \times \frac{3x}{4}$$

$$= \frac{15x}{17}$$

$$\therefore \quad \text{Required ratio} = \frac{\dfrac{15x}{17}}{\dfrac{3x}{4}}$$

$$= 20 : 17.$$

30. Let numbers are $2x$ and $3x$

According to the question,

$$2x + 3x = 125$$
$$\Rightarrow \qquad 5x = 125$$
$$\Rightarrow \qquad x = \frac{125}{5} = 25$$

Hence, numbers are 50 and 75.

32. Total age of P, Q and R = 3(R + 5)

$$\Rightarrow \quad P + Q + R = 3R + 15$$
$$\Rightarrow \quad 39 + R = 3R + 15$$
$$\Rightarrow \qquad 2R = 24$$
$$\Rightarrow \qquad R = 12 \text{ years.}$$

33. $5\sqrt{5} \times 5^3 \div 5^{-3/2} = 5^{a+2}$

$$\frac{(5)^{3/2} \times (5)^3}{(5)^{-3/2}} = 5^{a+2}$$

$$(5)^{3/2+3-(-3/2)} = 5^{a+2}$$

$$5^6 = 5^{a+2}$$

$$\Rightarrow \quad a + 2 = 6$$
$$a = 4$$

34. $(0.2)^3 \times 200 \div 2000 \,(0.2)^2$

$$= \frac{0.2}{10}$$

$$= \frac{2}{100} = \frac{1}{50}.$$

35. 19, 23, 29, 37, 43, 47 all are prime numbers but 46 is even number.

Hence required number is 46.

36. $\dfrac{1}{2}, \dfrac{3}{4}, \dfrac{5}{8}, \dfrac{7}{16}, \dots\dots$

The next number of the sequence is $\dfrac{9}{32}$.

37. $20184 = 2 \times 2 \times 2 \times 3 \times 29 \times 29$

$20184 \times 6 = 121104$ which is perfect square.

Hence, required least no. = 6.

38. 1 Man = 3 boys, 1 Woman = $\dfrac{3}{2}$ boys

$\therefore$ 1 man, 1 woman and 1 boy = $\dfrac{11}{2}$ boys

3 boys can do a work in 88 days

1 boy can do this work in 88 × 3 days

$\dfrac{11}{2}$ boys can do this work in $\dfrac{88 \times 3 \times 2}{11}$

= 48 days.

39. Tank filled by pipe A in 1 hour = $\dfrac{1}{2}$

Tank filled by pipe B in 1 hour = $\dfrac{1}{3}$

Tank filled by pipe (A + B) in hour

$$= \frac{1}{2} + \frac{1}{3} = \frac{3+2}{6} = \frac{5}{6}$$

Hence, tank will be filled by both the pipes together in $\frac{6}{5}$ hours = 1 hour 12 minutes.

40.

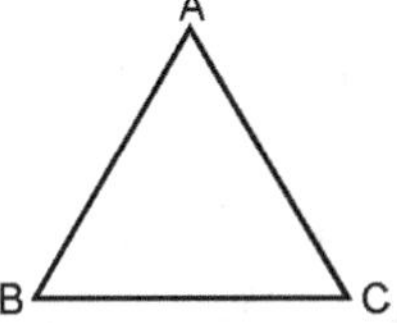

Let AB = $5x$ m, BC = $6x$ m and AC = $7x$ m

According to the question,

$5x + 6x + 7x = 54$

$\Rightarrow \quad 18x = 54$

$\Rightarrow \quad x = 3$

$\therefore$ AB = 15 m, BC = 18 m, AC = 21 m.

$$S = \frac{a+b+c}{2} = \frac{54}{2} = 27$$

$$\text{Area of } \Delta = \sqrt{s(s-a)(s-b)(s-c)}$$

$$= \sqrt{27(12)(9)(6)}$$

$$= \sqrt{9 \times 3 \times 3 \times 4 \times 9 \times 3 \times 2}$$

$$= 9 \times 3 \times 2 \times \sqrt{6} = 54\sqrt{6} \text{ m}^2.$$

41. Area of trapezium $= \frac{1}{2} \times h(b_1 + b_2)$

$$= \frac{1}{2} \times 4(6+8)$$

$$= 2 \times 14$$

$$= 28 \text{ cm}^2.$$

42. $\dfrac{\text{External angle}}{\text{Internal angle}} = \dfrac{1}{17}$

$$\Rightarrow \quad \frac{\dfrac{360}{n}}{180° - \dfrac{360°}{n}} = \frac{1}{17}$$

$$\Rightarrow \quad \frac{360}{180n - 360} = \frac{1}{17}$$

$$\Rightarrow \quad \frac{360}{180(n-2)} = \frac{1}{17}$$

$$\Rightarrow \quad n - 2 = 34$$

$$\Rightarrow \quad n = 36.$$

43. $C = \pi \times d$

$$= \frac{22}{7} \times 56 = 176 \text{ cm}$$

Distance = 2.2 km

$$\frac{22}{10} \times 1000 \times 100 \text{ cm} = 220000 \text{ cm}$$

$$\therefore \quad 176 \text{ cm} = 1 \text{ revolution}$$

$$\therefore \quad 220000 \text{ cm} = \frac{1}{176} \times 220000$$

$$= 1250$$

Hence required number of revolution = 1250.

44.

In Δ ACD, $\quad (h - y)^2 = y^2 + x^2$

$\Rightarrow \quad h^2 - 2hy + y^2 = y^2 + x^2$

$\Rightarrow \quad 2hy = h^2 - x^2$

$$\Rightarrow \quad y = \frac{h^2 - x^2}{2h}$$

Hence, the height at which the tree is broken

$$= \frac{h^2 - x^2}{2h} \text{ metres.}$$

46. Sum of two numbers = $8 \times 2 = 16$

and sum of three numbers = $3 \times 3 = 9$

Average of five numbers $= \dfrac{16+9}{5}$

$$= \frac{25}{5} = 5.$$

47. C.P. of the article = ₹ 15

$$100 - 10 = 90$$

When C.P. ₹ 100,

$$\text{then S.P.} = ₹\ 90$$

When C.P. ₹ 15,

$$\text{then S.P.} = \frac{90}{100} \times 15$$

$$= ₹\ \frac{135}{10}$$

$$= ₹\ 13.50.$$

48. Let C.P. of T.V. for Yogita = ₹ x

$$\text{S.P.} = x + \frac{20}{100} \times x = \frac{6x}{5}$$

$$\text{C.P. for Deepa} = \frac{6x}{5} + \frac{10}{100} \times \frac{6x}{5}$$

$$= \frac{120x + 12x}{100}$$

$$= \frac{132x}{100}$$

According to the question,

$$\frac{132x}{100} = 33000$$

$$\Rightarrow \quad x = \frac{33000 \times 100}{132} = 25000$$

Hence, cost price of the plasma TV for Yogita = ₹ 25000.

49. $\because \qquad 8\%$ of $x = 4\%$ of y

$$\therefore \qquad 20\% \text{ of } x = 20 \times \frac{4}{8}\% \text{ of } y$$

Hence, 20% of $x = 10\%$ of y.

50. Let total number of valid votes = x

According to the question,

62% of $x - 38\%$ of $x = 7200$

$$\Rightarrow \qquad 24\% \text{ of } x = 7200$$

$$\Rightarrow \qquad \frac{24}{100} \times x = 7200$$

$$\Rightarrow \qquad x = \frac{7200 \times 100}{24} = 30000$$

Hence, total number of votes = 30000.

Railway Recruitment Board (RRB)
GROUP 'D'
Recruitment Exam

Directions (Qs. Nos. 1 to 7) : *Select the related letters/words/number pair from the given alternatives.*

1. 85 : 40 : : 77 : ?
   A. 48   B. 49
   C. 50   D. 14

2. KNQT : LORU : : ADGJ : ?
   A. FHLO   B. DGEF
   C. MPVW   D. BEHK

3. DRIVEN : NEVIRD : : BEGUM : ?
   A. BGMUE   B. EBGMU
   C. MUGEB   D. MEUBG

4. Smell : Flower : : Taste : ?
   A. Salt   B. Food
   C. Sweet   D. Water

5. Introvert : Extrovert : : ?
   A. Extreme : Interim B. Against : Favour
   C. Action : Law   D. Angle : Tangent

6. Smoke : Pollution : : War : ?
   A. Victory   B. Treaty
   C. Destruction   D. Peace

7. 12 : 30 : : 18 : ?
   A. 42   B. 44
   C. 45   D. 36

Directions (Qs. Nos. 8 to 11) : *Find the odd letters/words/number pair from the given alternatives.*

8. A. 29 – 45   B. 48 – 68
   C. 71 – 87   D. 5 – 21

9. A. ADEG   B. EHIK
   C. LNOQ   D. TWXZ

10. A. Up : Down   B. Across : Along
   C. Small : Large   D. Day : Night

11. A. Hill   B. Plateau
   C. Plane   D. Mountain

12. If TRANSFER is coded as RTNAFSRE, then how ELEPHANT be coded in that code language?
   A. LEPEHATN   B. LEPEAHTN
   C. LEEPAHTN   D. LEPEAHNT

13. Which one of the given responses would be a meaningful order of the following in ascending order?
   1. Sending   2. Encoding
   3. Receiving   4. Decoding
   A. 4, 2, 1, 3   B. 1, 2, 3, 4
   C. 2, 1, 3, 4   D. 2, 4, 3, 1

14. Arrange the following words as per order in the English dictionary:
   1. Important   2. Impart
   3. Improvise   4. Improve
   A. 2, 1, 4, 3   B. 3, 4, 1, 2
   C. 2, 1, 3, 4   D. 1, 2, 3, 4

15. Which one set of letters when sequentially placed at the gaps in the given letter series shall complete it?
        bc_bca_cab_ab_a_ca
   A. cabac   B. abccb
   C. cabca   D. abcab

16. In the following letter series, how many B C N occur in such a way, that C is in the middle and B and N are on any one side?
   BCMXNCXNBXNCBNCB
   YBCXNBCNABONMZCB
   A. 2   B. 5
   C. 3   D. 4

Directions (Qs. Nos. 17 to 19) : *A series is given, with one term missing. Choose the correct alternative from the given ones that will complete the series.*

17. 7, 8, 11, 16, 23, ?
  A. 32 B. 37
  C. 40 D. 31

18. 3, 9, 6, 36, 30, ?
  A. 800 B. 950
  C. 400 D. 900

19. DKY, JFW, HIU, JHS, ?
  A. LGQ B. KGR
  C. KFR D. LFQ

20. A man said to a woman, "The only son of your brother, is the brother of my wife." How is that woman related to the wife of that man?
  A. Sister B. Mother
  C. Grandmother D. Aunt

21. If B = 2, BAG = 10, then BOX = ?
  A. 39 B. 41
  C. 52 D. 36

22. If DISC is coded as 8749 and ACHE is coded as 3950, then HEAD is coded as
  A. 5308 B. 3508
  C. 3805 D. 5038

23. If January 1st is a Friday, what is the first day of the month of March, in a leap year?
  A. Wednesday B. Thursday
  C. Friday D. Tuesday

24. Barun is taller than Sanjay, Bipul is taller than Barun. Krishna is also not as tall as Bipul, but is taller than Barun. Who is the tallest?
  A. Bipul B. Krishna
  C. Sanjay D. Barun

25. Rajan is younger than his father by 20 years. 5 years ago his father was 3 times elder than him. Find the present age of his father.
  A. 30 years B. 35 years
  C. 36 years D. 25 years

26. Let $\sqrt[3]{a} = \sqrt[3]{26} + \sqrt[3]{7} + \sqrt[3]{63}$. Then
  A. $a = 729$ B. $a < 729$ but $a > 216$
  C. $a < 216$ D. $a > 729$

27. The number of prime factors in $6^{333} \times 7^{222} \times 8^{111}$ is
  A. 1211
  B. 1221
  C. 1222
  D. 1111

28. If $x [-2\{-4 (-a)\}] + 5 [-2\{-2(-a)\}] = 4a$, then $x =$
  A. –2 B. –3
  C. –4 D. –5

29. $\sqrt{\dfrac{4\frac{1}{7} - 2\frac{1}{4}}{3\frac{1}{2} + 1\frac{1}{7}} \div \cfrac{1}{2 + \cfrac{1}{2 + \cfrac{1}{5 - \frac{1}{5}}}}}$ is equal to
  A. 2 B. 1
  C. 4 D. 3

30. If 120 is 20% of a number, then 120% of that number will be
  A. 120
  B. 360
  C. 720
  D. 20

31. In a division sum, the divisor is 3 times the quotient and 6 times the remainder. If the remainder is 2, then the dividend is
  A. 28 B. 50
  C. 48 D. 36

32. $\dfrac{1}{7} + \left(999\dfrac{692}{693} \right) \times 99$ is equal to
  A. 99900 B. 1
  C. 99000 D. 99800

33. The value of $\dfrac{\sqrt{72} \times \sqrt{363} \times \sqrt{175}}{\sqrt{32} \times \sqrt{147} \times \sqrt{252}}$ is
  A. $\dfrac{55}{28}$ B. $\dfrac{55}{42}$
  C. $\dfrac{45}{56}$ D. $\dfrac{45}{28}$

34. Zinc and copper are in the ratio 5 : 3 in 400 gm of an alloy. How much of copper (in grams) should be added to make the ratio 5 : 4?
A. 200
B. 50
C. 66
D. 72

35. The average age of A and B is 20 years. If A is to be replaced by C, the average would be 19 years. The average age of C and A is 21 years. The ages of A, B and C in order (in years) are
A. 22, 20, 18
B. 18, 22, 20
C. 18, 20, 22
D. 22, 18, 20

36. A reduction of 10% in the price of a commodity enables a person to buy 25 kg more for ₹ 225. The original price of the commodity per kg was
A. ₹ 1.50
B. ₹ 2
C. ₹ 1
D. ₹ 2.50

37. One type of liquid contains 20% water and the second type of liquid contains 35% of water. A glass is filled with 10 parts of first liquid and 4 parts of second liquid. The water in the new mixture in the glass is
A. $24\dfrac{2}{7}\%$
B. 37%
C. 46%
D. $12\dfrac{1}{7}\%$

38. If $x : y = 3 : 4$ and $y : z = 3 : 4$, then $\dfrac{x+y+z}{3z}$ is equal to
A. $\dfrac{37}{48}$
B. $\dfrac{13}{27}$
C. $\dfrac{1}{2}$
D. $\dfrac{73}{84}$

39. Mohan sold his watch at 10% loss. If he had sold it for ₹ 45 more, he would have made 5% profit. The selling price (in ₹) of the watch was
A. 270
B. 300
C. 900
D. 110

40. A vendor loses the selling price of 4 oranges on selling 36 oranges. His loss percent is
A. $11\dfrac{1}{2}\%$
B. $12\dfrac{1}{2}\%$
C. 9%
D. 10%

41. Successive discounts of 30% and 20% is equivalent to a single discount of
A. 10%
B. 50%
C. 40%
D. 44%

42. At the beginning of a partnership business, the capital of B was $\dfrac{3}{2}$ times that of A. After 8 months B withdrew $\dfrac{1}{2}$ of his capital and after 10 months A withdrew $\dfrac{1}{4}$ th of his capital. At the end of the year, if the profit incurred is ₹ 53,000, find the amount received by A.
A. ₹ 23,000
B. ₹ 30,800
C. ₹ 32,000
D. ₹ 30,000

43. If x, y, z are three sums of money such that y is the simple interest on x and z is the simple interest on y for the same time and at the same rate of interest, then we have
A. $y^2 = zx$
B. $z^2 = xy$
C. $xyz = 1$
D. $x^2 = yz$

44. A and B can together finish a work in 30 days. They worked together for 20 days and then B left. After another 20 days, A finished the remaining work. The number of days in which B alone can finish the work is
A. 60
B. 50
C. 48
D. 54

45. If $\dfrac{xy}{x+y} = a$, $\dfrac{xz}{x+z} = b$ and $\dfrac{yz}{y+z} = c$, where a, b, c are all non-zero numbers, then x equals to
A. $\dfrac{abc}{ab+bc+ac}$
B. $\dfrac{2abc}{ab+bc-ac}$
C. $\dfrac{2abc}{ab+ac-bc}$
D. $\dfrac{2abc}{ac+bc-ab}$

46. If $6x - 5y = 13$, $7x + 2y = 23$, then $11x + 18y =$
A. 15
B. −15
C. 51
D. 33

47. If $x + y + z = 13$ and $x^2 + y^2 + z^2 = 69$, then the value of $xy + z (x + y)$ is equal to
A. 60
B. 70
C. 40
D. 50

48. Two trains, of same length, are running in parallel tracks in the same direction with speed 60 km/hour and 90 km/hour respectively. The latter completely crosses the former in 30 seconds. The length of each train (in metres) is
A. 115
B. 125
C. 150
D. 100

49. A boat goes 24 km upstream and 28 km downstream in 6 hours. It goes 30 km upstream and 2 km downstream in 6 hours and 30 minutes. The speed of the boat in still water is
A. 8 km/hr
B. 9 km/hr
C. 12 km/hr
D. 10 km/hr

50. ABCD is a trapezium in which AB ∥ DC and AB = 2 CD. The diagonals AC and BD meet at O. The ratio of areas of triangles AOB and COD is
A. 1 : 4
B. 1 : 2
C. $1 : \sqrt{2}$
D. 4 : 1

51. Who said "Man is a social animal?"
A. Plato
B. Aristotle
C. Rousseau
D. Laski

52. "Marginal Cost" equals
A. the change in total cost divided by the change in quantity
B. total cost minus total benefit for the last unit produced
C. total cost divided by total benefit for the last unit produced
D. total cost divided by quantity

53. Extreme forms of markets are
A. Perfect competition; Monopolistic competition
B. Perfect competition; Oligopoly
C. Oligopoly; Monopoly
D. Perfect competition; Monopoly

54. A supply function expresses the relationship between
A. price and consumption
B. price and output
C. price and selling cost
D. price and demand

55. Goods which are meant either for consumption or for investment are called
A. Intermediate goods
B. Final goods
C. Giffen goods
D. Inferior goods

56. Variation in Cash Reserve Ratio and Open Market Operations are instruments of
A. Monetary policy
B. Budgetary policy
C. Trade policy
D. Fiscal policy

57. Which of the following subjects does not figure in the Concurrent List of the Constitution?
A. Trade unions
B. Stock Exchanges and futures markets
C. Protection of wild animals and birds
D. Forests

58. The President of India has the discretional power to
A. declare Financial Emergency
B. impose President's Rule in a state
C. appoint the Prime Minister
D. appoint the Chief Election Commissioner

59. The script of the Indus Valley Civilization is
A. Tamil
B. Kharosthi
C. Undeciphered
D. Brahmi

60. Which one of the following literary pieces was written by Krishna Devaraya?
A. *Katha Saristhaga*
B. *Kaviraja Marga*
C. *Ushaparinayam*
D. *Amukta Malyada*

61. Name three important forms of Satyagraha.
A. Revolution, plebiscite and boycott
B. Non-cooperation, civil disobedience and boycott
C. Boycott, civil disobedience and rebellion
D. Non-cooperation, revolution and referendum

62. Which Article empowers the President to impose Financial Emergency?
A. Article 360
B. Article 356
C. Article 364
D. Article 352

63. Who among the following played a prominent role during the "Reign of Terror" in France?
A. Montesquieu
B. Voltaire
C. Marat
D. Robespierre

64. The highest waterfall of India is in the state of
A. Karnataka
B. Andhra Pradesh
C. Assam
D. Maharashtra

65. Soil which is prone to intensive leaching due to rain is called
A. Red
B. Laterite
C. Black
D. Alluvial

66. The formation of "Mushroom rock" in desert region is an example of
A. Erosion
B. Deflation
C. Attrition
D. Abrasion

67. The "Grand Canyon" is on the river
A. Mississippi
B. Colorado
C. Columbia
D. Ohio

68. When the East India Company was formed, the Mughal emperor in India was
A. Akbar
B. Jehangir
C. Humayun
D. Aurangzeb

69. Which one of the following events did not take place during the Viceroyalty of Lord Curzon?
A. Partition of Bengal
B. Establishment of the Department of Archaeology
C. Second Delhi Durbar
D. Formation of Indian National Congress

70. Which gland in the human body regulates the secretion of hormones from the pituitary gland?
A. Hypothalamus gland
B. Thymus gland
C. Thyroid gland
D. Adrenal gland

71. The old and worn-out red blood corpuscles are destroyed in
A. Spleen
B. Liver
C. Stomach
D. Bone marrow

72. Subtropical high pressure belts are otherwise called
A. Roaring forties
B. Furious fifties
C. Screeching sixties
D. Horse latitudes

73. Self pollination will lead to
A. outbreeding
B. inbreeding
C. rare breeding
D. overbreeding

74. Hydroponics is a method of culture of plants without using
A. soil
B. water
C. light
D. sand

75. The non-green heterotrophic plants of plant kingdom are
A. fungi
B. mosses
C. ferns
D. algae

76. Centigrade and Fahrenheit temperatures are the same at
A. $-40°$
B. $32°$
C. $40°$
D. $-273°$

77. The dimensional formula for universal gravitational constant is
A. $M^{-1}L^3T^{-2}$
B. $M^{-1}L^3T^2$
C. ML^2T^{-2}
D. M^{-2}

78. In any spreadsheet, the address of the first cell is
A. A1
B. 0A
C. 1A
D. A0

79. Match List I with List II and choose the correct response:

List I	*List II*
(*a*) Vitamin B_1	1. Pyridoxine
(*b*) Vitamin B_2	2. Cyanocobalamin
(*c*) Vitamin B_6	3. Thismine
(*d*) Vitamin B_{12}	4. Riboflavin

A. (*a*) - 4, (*b*) - 1, (*c*) - 2, (*d*) - 3
B. (*a*) - 1, (*b*) - 2, (*c*) - 3, (*d*) - 4
C. (*a*) - 2, (*b*) - 3, (*c*) - 4, (*d*) - 1
D. (*a*) - 3, (*b*) - 4, (*c*) - 1, (*d*) - 2

80. Ohm's law is valid in case of
A. insulator
B. semiconductor
C. conductor
D. superconductor

81. The Laser is a beam of radiations which are
A. Coherent and non-monochromatic
B. Non-coherent and monochromatic
C. Coherent and monochromatic
D. Non-coherent and non-monochromatic

82. In electro-refining, the pure metal deposited on
A. anode
B. vessel
C. electrolyte
D. cathode

83. Which one of the following is correct matched?
A. Primary consumer – Leopard
B. Secondary consumer – Grass
C. Decomposer – Bacteria
D. Producer – Deer

84. The deciduous trees will
A. depend on others for their food
B. shed their leaves every year
C. not lose their leaves
D. synthesise their own food

85. Identify the DBMS among the following;
A. MS-Excel
B. MS-Access
C. MS-PowerPoint
D. PL/SQL

86. The database in which records are organised in a tree-like structure is
A. Object-oriented database
B. Network database
C. Hierarchical database
D. Relational database

87. Natural rubber is a polymer of
A. Styrene
B. Vinyl acetate
C. Propene
D. Isoprene

88. The pH of lemon juice is expected to be
A. more than 7
B. equal to 7
C. nothing can be predicted
D. less than 7

89. An example of heterocyclic compound is
A. Anthracene
B. Naphthalene
C. Furan
D. Benzene

90. Which of the following folk/tribal dances associated with Uttar Pradesh?
A. Veedhi
B. Thora
C. Tamasha
D. Rauf

91. Name the branch of Zoology that deals with the scientific study of animal behaviour:
A. Ecology
B. Physiology
C. Ethology
D. Anatomy

92. Which one of the following organizations and its headquarters are wrongly matched?

Organizations	Headquarters
A. International Civil Aviation Organization	– London
B. Interpol	– Lyon
C. Universal Postal Union	– Berne
D. Food and Agriculture Organization	– Rome

93. Which one of the following films was *not* directed by Satyajit Ray?
A. *Salaam Bombay*
B. *Aparajita*
C. *Charulata*
D. *Pather Panchali*

94. The endangered species are listed in what colour data book?
A. Blue
B. Black
C. Red
D. Green

95. Which country won the maximum number of medals in the Asian Athletic Championships held in Pune recently?
A. China
B. Japan
C. Saudi Arabia
D. Bahrain

96. Which Union Territory in India has two districts but none of its districts has common boundary with its other districts?
A. Chandigarh
B. Puducherry
C. Dadra and Nagar Haveli
D. Andaman and Nicobar Islands

97. The Keibul Lamjao, the only floating National Park in the world is in
A. Meghalaya
B. Manipur
C. Mizoram
D. Assam

98. Which one of the following days is not observed in the month of October?
A. International Day of Non-violence
B. Indian Air-force Day
C. U.N. Day
D. World Environment Day

99. Who is the author of the book *"The State of the Nation"*?
A. Fali S. Nariman
B. Mark Tully
C. Vinod Mehta
D. Kuldip Nayar

100. Among the following Nobel laureates, who was not a recipient of the Nobel Prize for Peace?
A. Norman Ernest Borlaug
B. Sir Winston Churchill
C. Woodrow Wilson
D. Linus C. Pauling

ANSWERS

1	2	3	4	5	6	7	8	9	10
B	D	C	B	B	C	C	B	C	B
11	**12**	**13**	**14**	**15**	**16**	**17**	**18**	**19**	**20**
C	B	C	A	B	C	A	D	A	D
21	**22**	**23**	**24**	**25**	**26**	**27**	**28**	**29**	**30**
B	D	D	A	B	B	B	B	B	C
31	**32**	**33**	**34**	**35**	**36**	**37**	**38**	**39**	**40**
B	C	A	B	D	C	A	A	A	D
41	**42**	**43**	**44**	**45**	**46**	**47**	**48**	**49**	**50**
D	A	A	A	D	C	D	B	D	D
51	**52**	**53**	**54**	**55**	**56**	**57**	**58**	**59**	**60**
B	A	D	B	B	A	B	C	C	D
61	**62**	**63**	**64**	**65**	**66**	**67**	**68**	**69**	**70**
B	A	D	A	B	D	B	A	D	A
71	**72**	**73**	**74**	**75**	**76**	**77**	**78**	**79**	**80**
A	D	B	A	A	A	A	A	D	C
81	**82**	**83**	**84**	**85**	**86**	**87**	**88**	**89**	**90**
C	D	C	B	B	C	D	D	C	B
91	**92**	**93**	**94**	**95**	**96**	**97**	**98**	**99**	**100**
C	A	A	C	A	B	B	D	A	B

EXPLANATORY ANSWERS

1. 85 : 40 :: 77 : ?

$8 \times 5 = 40,$

$7 \times 7 = 49$

∴ 49 is the answer.

7. 12 : 30 :: 18 : x

$$\frac{12}{30} = \frac{18}{x}$$

$$\Rightarrow \quad x = \frac{30 \times 18}{12} = 45.$$

17. 7, 8, 11, 16, 23, 32

+1, +3, +5, +7, +9

18. 3, 9, 6, 36, 30, 900

3×3, 6×6, 30×30

22.

D	I	S	C	A	C	H	E
8	7	4	9	3	9	5	0

H E A D is coded as 5 0 3 8.

23.
$$\begin{aligned}
\text{January} &= 31 \text{ days} \\
\text{February} &= 29 \text{ days (leap year)} \\
\text{March} &= \underline{1} \\
\text{Total} &= \underline{61 \text{ days}}
\end{aligned}$$

[Jan. Friday = 1, 8, 17, 22, 29.
Feb. Monday = 1, 8, 15, 22, 29]

First January is Friday

$\therefore \quad 61 \div 7 = 8\dfrac{5}{7}$

$8 \times 7 = 56 + 1 \text{ days} = 57 \text{ days} = \text{Friday}$

After 4 days = Tuesday.

24.
- Bipul
- Krishna
- Barun
- Sanjay

Bipul is the tallest.

25. Let present age of father = x years

$\therefore \qquad$ Rajan's age = $(x - 20)$ years

5 years ago father's age = $(x - 5)$ years

5 years ago Rajan's age = $(x - 20 - 5)$

$\qquad\qquad = (x - 25)$ years

According to the question,

$$(x - 5) = 3(x - 25)$$
$$x - 5 = 3x - 75$$
$$\Rightarrow \qquad 2x = 70$$
$$\Rightarrow \qquad x = 35$$

$\therefore \qquad$ Father's age = 35 years.

29.
$$\sqrt{\dfrac{4\frac{1}{7} - 2\frac{1}{4}}{3\frac{1}{2} + 1\frac{1}{7}} \div \cfrac{1}{2 + \cfrac{1}{2 + \cfrac{1}{5 - \frac{1}{5}}}}}$$

$$= \sqrt{\dfrac{\frac{29}{7} - \frac{9}{4}}{\frac{7}{2} + \frac{8}{7}} \div \cfrac{1}{2 + \cfrac{1}{2 + \cfrac{1}{\frac{25 - 1}{5}}}}}$$

$$= \sqrt{\dfrac{\frac{29}{7} - \frac{9}{4}}{\frac{7}{2} + \frac{8}{7}} \div \cfrac{1}{2 + \cfrac{1}{2 + \cfrac{5}{24}}}}$$

$$= \sqrt{\dfrac{\frac{29}{7} - \frac{9}{4}}{\frac{7}{2} + \frac{8}{7}} \div \cfrac{1}{2 + \cfrac{24}{53}}}$$

$$= \sqrt{\dfrac{\frac{29}{7} - \frac{9}{4}}{\frac{7}{2} + \frac{8}{7}} \div \dfrac{53}{130}}$$

$$= \sqrt{\dfrac{\frac{116 - 63}{28}}{\frac{49 + 16}{14}} \div \dfrac{53}{130}}$$

$$= \sqrt{\dfrac{53}{28} \times \dfrac{14}{65} \times \dfrac{130}{53}}$$

$$= \sqrt{1} = 1.$$

30. 20% of x = 120

$$\Rightarrow \qquad \dfrac{20}{100} \times x = 120$$

$$\Rightarrow \qquad \dfrac{x}{5} = 120 \Rightarrow x = 600$$

$\therefore \qquad$ 120% of $x = \dfrac{120}{100} \times 600$

$$= 120 \times 6$$
$$= 720.$$

31. Divident = Quotient × divisor + remainder

$$= 3x \times x$$

Divisor = $6 \times 2 = 12$

Quotient = $\dfrac{12}{3} = 4$

$\therefore \qquad$ Dividend = $4 \times 12 + 2 = 50.$

32. $\dfrac{1}{7}+\dfrac{692999}{693}\times 99 = \dfrac{693000}{7} = 99000.$

33. $\dfrac{\sqrt{72}\times\sqrt{363}\times\sqrt{175}}{\sqrt{32}\times\sqrt{147}\times\sqrt{252}}$

$$= \dfrac{6\sqrt{2}\times 11\sqrt{3}\times 5\sqrt{7}}{4\sqrt{2}\times 7\sqrt{3}\times 6\sqrt{7}}$$

$$= \dfrac{55}{28}.$$

34. Amount of copper $= \dfrac{3}{8}\times 400 = 150$ g

$$\dfrac{250}{150+x} = \dfrac{5}{4}$$
$$750 + 5x = 1000$$
$$\Rightarrow \qquad 5x = 250 \Rightarrow x = 50 \text{ gram.}$$

35. Total age of A and B $= 2\times 20 = 40$ years
Total age of B + C $= 2\times 19 = 38$ years
Total age of C + A $= 2\times 21 = 42$ years
$$2A + 2B + 2C = 40 + 38 + 42$$
$$\Rightarrow \qquad 2(A + B + C) = 120$$

$$\therefore \qquad A + B + C = \dfrac{120}{2} = 60 \text{ years}$$

$\therefore$ Age of A $= 60 - 38 = 22$ years
Age of B $= 60 - 42 = 18$ years
Age of C $= 60 - 40 = 20$ years
$\therefore$ The ages of A, B and C in order 22, 18, 20 years.

36. 10% reduction in ₹ 225 $= \dfrac{10\times 225}{100} = ₹\dfrac{45}{2}$

Reduced price of 25 kg $= ₹\dfrac{45}{2}$

Reduced price of 1 kg $= \dfrac{45}{2\times 25} = ₹\dfrac{9}{10}$/kg

According to the rule,
Percentage reduction = 10%
Percentage increase in the reduced price in order to restore the original price of sugar

$$= \left(\dfrac{100\times 10}{100-10}\right)\% = \dfrac{100\times 10}{90} = 11\dfrac{1}{9}\%$$

Hence to restore the original price, the reduced price will have to be increased by $11\dfrac{1}{9}\%$.

$\therefore$ Original Price $= ₹\dfrac{9}{10}+11\dfrac{1}{9}\%$ of $₹\dfrac{9}{10}$

$$= ₹\dfrac{9}{10}+\dfrac{100}{9\times 100}\times\dfrac{9}{10}$$

$$= \dfrac{9}{10}+\dfrac{1}{10} = \dfrac{10}{10} = ₹1/\text{kg.}$$

37. The percentage of Water in the mixture

$$= \left(\dfrac{10\times 20 + 4\times 35}{10+4}\right)\%$$

$$= \left(\dfrac{200+140}{14}\right)\%$$

$$= \left(\dfrac{340}{14}\right)\% = \dfrac{170}{7}\%$$

$$= 24\dfrac{2}{7}\%.$$

38. $\dfrac{x}{y} = \dfrac{3}{4},\ \dfrac{y}{z} = \dfrac{3}{4}$

$$4x = 3y$$

$$\Rightarrow \qquad x = \dfrac{3y}{4},\ \dfrac{y}{z} = \dfrac{3}{4}$$

$$3z = 4y$$

$$z = \dfrac{4y}{3}$$

$$\dfrac{x+y+z}{3z} = \dfrac{\dfrac{3y}{4}+y+\dfrac{4y}{3}}{3\times\dfrac{4y}{3}}$$

$$= \dfrac{\dfrac{9y+12y+16y}{12}}{\dfrac{12y}{3}}$$

$$= \dfrac{37y}{12}\times\dfrac{3}{12y} = \dfrac{37}{48}.$$

39. Let C.P. of the watch = $₹x$

In the first case, SP = $₹x - 10\%$ of x

$$= x - \frac{x}{10} = \frac{9x}{10}$$

In the second case,

$$SP = ₹\frac{9x}{10} + 45$$

$$= \frac{9x + 450}{10}$$

Profit = 5%

$$\text{C.P. of the watch} = \frac{S.P. \times 100}{100 + \text{gain}}$$

$$= \frac{\left(\dfrac{9x + 450}{10}\right) \times 100}{105}$$

$$= \left(\frac{9x + 450}{10}\right) \times \frac{100}{105}$$

$$= \frac{18x + 900}{21}$$

$$\Rightarrow \quad x = \frac{18x + 900}{21}$$

$$\Rightarrow \quad 21x - 18x = 900$$

$$\Rightarrow \quad 3x = 900$$

$$\Rightarrow \quad x = 300$$

$$\therefore \quad S.P. = \frac{9 \times 300}{10}$$

$$= ₹\,270$$

Hence selling price of the watch = $₹\,270$.

40. Let the selling price of 36 oranges = $₹\,36$

Then selling price of 4 oranges = $₹\,4$

$\therefore$ Loss = $₹\,4$

$\therefore$ Cost Price = $36 + 4$

$$= ₹\,40$$

$$\text{Loss } \% = \frac{\text{Loss}}{\text{C.P.}} \times 100$$

$$= \frac{4}{40} \times 100 = 10\%.$$

41. Single discount $= \left(x + y - \dfrac{xy}{100}\right)\%$

$$= \left(30 + 20 - \frac{30 \times 20}{100}\right)\%$$

$$= (50 - 6)\% = 44\%.$$

42. Let Capital of A = $₹\,x$

and Capital of B $= ₹\dfrac{3}{2} \times x = ₹\dfrac{3x}{2}$

Amount of A invested

$$= 10 \times x + \left(x - \frac{1}{4}x\right) \times 2$$

$$= 10x + \frac{6x}{4} = \frac{46x}{4} \text{ for 1 month}$$

Amount of B invested

$$= 8 \times \frac{3x}{2} + \left(\frac{3x}{2} - \frac{3x}{4}\right) \times 4$$

$$= 12x + 3x = 15x \text{ for 1 month}$$

Ratio of their investment

$$\frac{46x}{4} : \frac{15x}{1} = \frac{46x}{4} \times \frac{1}{15x} = 23 : 30$$

Amount received by A $= \dfrac{23}{53} \times 53000$

$$= ₹\,23 \times 1000$$

$$= ₹\,23{,}000$$

43. $y = \dfrac{x \times r \times t}{100} = \dfrac{xrt}{100}$

$$\Rightarrow \quad \frac{rt}{100} = \frac{y}{x} \qquad \qquad ...(i)$$

$$z = \frac{y \times r \times t}{100} \Rightarrow \frac{rt}{100} = \frac{z}{y} \qquad ...(ii)$$

From (i) and (ii)

$$\frac{y}{x} = \frac{z}{y} \Rightarrow y^2 = zx.$$

44. $(A + B)$'s 1 day work $= \dfrac{1}{30}$

$(A + B)$'s 20 days work $= \dfrac{1}{30} \times 20 = \dfrac{2}{3}$

Remaining work $= 1 - \dfrac{2}{3} = \dfrac{1}{3}$

$\dfrac{1}{3}$ part A can do alone in 20 days

A alone can do this work in 60 days

A's 1 day work $= \dfrac{1}{60}$

B's 1 day work $= \dfrac{1}{30} - \dfrac{1}{60} = \dfrac{2-1}{60} = \dfrac{1}{60}$

Hence, B can do this work alone in 60 days.

46.
$$6x - 5y = 13 \qquad]\times 2 \qquad ...(i)$$
$$7x + 2y = 13 \qquad]\times 5 \qquad ...(ii)$$
$$12x - 10y = 26$$
$$35x + 10y = 115$$
$$47x = 141 \qquad \Rightarrow x = 3$$

Putting the value of x in (iii), then we get
$$7x + 2y = 23 \Rightarrow 2y = 23 - 21 = 2$$
$$\Rightarrow \qquad y = 1$$

Value of $11x + 18y = 11(3) + 18(1)$
$$= 33 + 18 = 51.$$

47.
$$x + y + z = 13 \text{ and}$$
$$x^2 + y^2 + z^2 = 69$$
$$\therefore \quad (x + y + z)^2 = x^2 + y^2 + z^2 + 2\,(xy + yz + zx)$$
$$(13)^2 = 69 + 2\,(xy + yz + zx)$$
$$\Rightarrow \quad 169 - 69 = 2\,(xy + yz + zx)$$
$$\Rightarrow \quad 100 = 2\,(xy + yz + zx)$$
$$\Rightarrow \quad xy + yz + zx = \dfrac{100}{2} = 50$$
$$\therefore xy + z\,(x + y) = 50.$$

48. Relative speed of the trains
$$= 90 - 60 = 30 \text{ km/hr}$$
$$= 30 \times \dfrac{5}{18} = \dfrac{25}{3} \text{ m/s}$$

Distance covered in 30 seconds at this speed
$$= 30 \times \dfrac{25}{3} = 250 \text{ m}$$

$\therefore$ Length of each train $= \dfrac{250}{2} = 125$ m.

49. Let speed of men in still water is u km/hr.
and speed of current is v km/hr.

Upstream speed $= (u - v)$ km/hr

Downstream speed $= (u + v)$ km/hr

From question,
$$\dfrac{24}{u - v} + \dfrac{28}{u + v} = 6 \qquad ...(i)$$

and
$$\dfrac{30}{u - v} + \dfrac{21}{u + v} = 6.5 \qquad ...(ii)$$

from (i) and (ii), we have
$$\dfrac{140}{u + v} - \dfrac{84}{u + v} = 30 - 26$$

$$\dfrac{56}{u + v} = 4 \quad \Rightarrow u + v = 14 \qquad ...(iii)$$

from (i) and (iii),
$$\dfrac{24}{u - v} + \dfrac{28}{14} = 6 \quad \Rightarrow u - v = 6 \qquad ...(iv)$$

Finally, from (iii) and (iv), we have

Speed of boat in still water $= 10$ km/hr.

50.

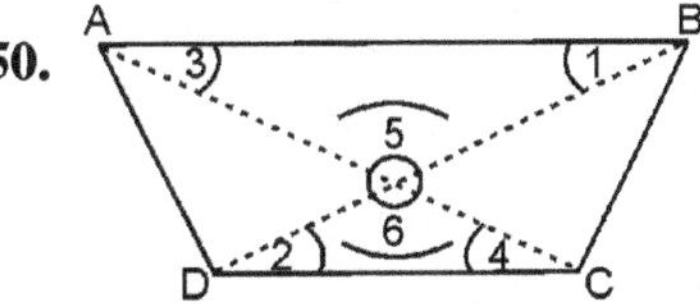

$\therefore$ ABCD is trapezium in which AB $\parallel$ CD and AB = 2CD

In $\triangle$ ABO and $\triangle$ DCO
$$\angle 1 = \angle 2 \text{ (alternate angle)}$$
$$\angle 3 = \angle 4 \text{ (alternate angle)}$$
$$\angle 5 = \angle 6 \text{ (V. opp. angle)}$$
$$\therefore \qquad \triangle AOB \sim \triangle COD \text{ (A.A.A.)}$$

$$\therefore \quad \dfrac{\text{area of } \triangle AOB}{\text{area of } \triangle COD} = \dfrac{(AB)^2}{(CD)^2}$$

$$= \dfrac{(2CD)^2}{CD^2} = 4 : 1.$$

Railway Recruitment Board (RRB)
GROUP 'D'
Recruitment Exam

Directions (Q. Nos. 1 to 6) : *Select the related letters/word/number from the given alternatives.*

1. Jewellery : Gold : : Furniture : ?
- A. Table
- B. Tree
- C. Wood
- D. Paint

2. Author : Novel : : Choreographer : ?
- A. Music
- B. Picture
- C. Make-up
- D. Dance

3. Rig : Ofd : : Met : ?
- A. Jbq
- B. Kcr
- C. Jcr
- D. Kbq

4. BDAC : FHEG : : NPMO : ?
- A. RQTS
- B. QTRS
- C. RTQS
- D. TRQS

5. 49 : 64 : : 144 : ?
- A. 186
- B. 121
- C. 256
- D. 169

6. SHOE : NCJZ : : REWA : ?
- A. WJBF
- B. CITY
- C. MZRV
- D. CAAR

Directions (Qs. Nos. 7 to 10) : *Select the one which is different from the other three responses.*

7.
- A. Tongue
- B. Teeth
- C. Nose
- D. Ear

8.
- A. Petrol – Car
- B. Electricity – Television
- C. Ink – Pen
- D. Dust – Vacuum cleaner

9.
- A. Light – Heavy
- B. Crime – Blame
- C. Short – Long
- D. Man – Woman

10.
- A. 343
- B. 512
- C. 729
- D. 144

Directions (Qs. Nos. 11 and 12) : *Which one of the given responses would be a meaningful order of the following?*

11.
1. Destination
2. Booking
3. Boarding
4. Travel
5. Planning
- A. 1, 2, 3, 4, 5
- B. 3, 4, 5, 1, 2
- C. 4, 3, 1, 2, 5
- D. 5, 2, 3, 4, 1

12.
1. Diagnosis
2. Doctor
3. Sick
4. Treatment
5. Recovery
- A. 1, 2, 3, 4, 5
- B. 3, 2, 1, 4, 5
- C. 2, 1, 3, 4, 5
- D. 4, 5, 1, 3, 2

13. Arrange the following words as per order in the dictionary:
1. Genuine
2. Genesis
3. Gender
4. Gentle
5. General
- A. 4, 5, 3, 2, 1
- B. 1, 5, 4, 3, 2
- C. 3, 5, 2, 4, 1
- D. 2, 5, 3, 1, 4

Directions (Qs. Nos. 14 to 17) : *A series is given, with one term/number/letters missing. Choose the correct alternative from the given ones that will complete the series.*

14. V, VIII, XI, XIV, ?, XX
- A. IX
- B. XXIII
- C. XV
- D. XVII

15. 3463, (2218) 1245

5324 (?) 3626
- A. 2312
- B. 1142
- C. 1698
- D. 1592

16. XGH, WIJ, VKL, UMN, _?_
   A. HOW   B. UJI
   C. TOP   D. SOP

17. SCD, TEF, UGH, _?_, WKL
   A. CMN   B. UJI
   C. VIJ   D. VJI

18. K is more beautiful than B. B is not beautiful as Y. J is not as beautiful as B or Y. Whose beauty is in the least degree?
   A. Y   B. K
   C. B   D. J

19. A person's present age is two-fifth of the age of his mother. After 8 years, he will one-half of the age of his mother. How old is the mother at present?
   A. 32 years   B. 36 years
   C. 40 years   D. 48 years

20. Raghu and Babu are twins. Babu's sister is Reema. Reema's husband is Rajan. Raghu's mother is Lakshmi. Lakshmi's husband is Rajesh. How is Rajesh related to Rajan?
   A. Uncle   B. Son-in-law
   C. Father-in-law   D. Cousin

21. If − stands for ÷, + stands for ×, ÷ stands for − and × stands for +, find out which one is correct.
   A. 49 + 7 − 3 × 5 ÷ 8 = 20
   B. 49 − 7 + 3 ÷ 5 × 8 = 24
   C. 49 × 7 + 3 ÷ 5 − 8 = 16
   D. 49 ÷ 7 × 3 + 5 − 8 = 26

Directions (Qs. Nos. 22 and 23) : *From the given alternatives select the word which **cannot** be formed using the letters of the given word.*

22. 'ANNIVERSARY'
   A. SAVE   B. VIEW
   C. YARN   D. VERY

23. 'REMEMBRANCE'
   A. REMEMBER   B. MEMBRANE
   C. NUMBER   D. EMBRACE

24. If MADRAS is written as DAMSAR, how can MUMBAI be written in that code?
   A. BAIUMM   B. MUMIAB
   C. IABMUM   D. MBIAUM

25. If DREAM is coded as 78026 and CHILD is coded as 53417, how can LEADER be coded?
   A. 102078   B. 102708
   C. 102087   D. 102780

26. The wrong number in the series

2, 9, 28, 65, 126, 216, 344 is :
   A. 9   B. 65
   C. 216   D. None of these

27. Eight consecutive numbers are given. If the average of the two numbers that appear in the middle is 4.5, then the sum of the eight given numbers is:
   A. 36   B. 48
   C. 54   D. 64

28. If $(1 \times 2 \times 3 \times 4 \times \ldots \times n) = \lfloor n$, then

$$\left(\lfloor 14 - \lfloor 13 - \lfloor 12\right) \text{ is equal to:}$$

   A. $14 \times 12 \times \left(\lfloor 12\right)$ B. $14 \times 12 \times \left(\lfloor 13\right)$

   C. $14 \times 13 \times \left(\lfloor 13\right)$ D. $13 \times 12 \times \left(\lfloor 12\right)$

29. A and B together can do a piece of work in 12 days, while B alone can finish it in 30 days. A alone can finish the work in:
   A. 15 days   B. 18 days
   C. 20 days   D. 25 days

30. A and B can do a job together in 12 days. A is 2 times as efficient as B. In how many days can B alone complete the work?
   A. 36   B. 12
   C. 18   D. 9

31. The marked price is 20% higher than cost price. A discount of 20% is given on the marked price. By this type of sale, there is:
   A. no loss no gain
   B. 4% gain
   C. 4% loss
   D. 2% loss

32. A chair listed at ₹ 350 is available at successive discounts of 25% and 10%. The selling price of the chair is:
   A. ₹ 240.25   B. ₹ 242.25
   C. ₹ 236.25   D. ₹ 230.25

33. A tradesman marks his goods at such a price that after allowing a discount of 15%, he makes a profit of 20%. What is the marked price of an article whose cost price is ₹ 170?
A. ₹ 220   B. ₹ 200
C. ₹ 240   D. ₹ 260

34. In two types of stainless steel, the ratio of chromium and steel are 2 : 11 and 5 : 21 respectively. In what proportion should the two types be mixed so that the ratio of chromium to steel in the mixed type become 7 : 32?
A. 1 : 2   B. 1 : 3
C. 2 : 3   D. 3 : 4

35. A sum of ₹ 7,000 is divided among A, B, C in such a way that the shares of A and B are in the ratio 2 : 3 and those B and C are in the ratio 4 : 5. The share of B is:
A. ₹ 1,600   B. ₹ 2,000
C. ₹ 2,400   D. ₹ 3,000

36. Tea worth ₹ 126 per kg and ₹ 135 per kg are mixed with a third variety in the ratio 1 : 1 : 2. If the mixture is worth ₹ 153 per kg, the price of the third variety per kg will be:
A. ₹ 169.5   B. ₹ 170.0
C. ₹ 175.5   D. ₹ 180.0

37. In the afternoon, a student read 100 pages at the rate of 60 pages per hour. In the evening, when she was tired, she read 100 more pages at the rate of 40 pages per hour. What was her average rate of reading, in pages per hour?
A. 48   B. 50
C. 60   D. 70

38. The mean weight of 34 students of a school is 42 kg. If the weight of the teacher be included, the mean rises by 400 grams. Find the weight of the teacher (in kg).
A. 66   B. 56
C. 55   D. 57

39. A cricketer has a mean score of 60 runs in 10 innings. Find out how many runs are to be scored in the eleventh innings to raise the mean score to 62?
A. 80   B. 81
C. 83   D. 82

40. A trader purchases a watch and a wall clock for ₹ 390. He sells them making a profit of 10% on the watch and 15% on the wall clock. He earns a profit of ₹ 51.50. The difference between the original prices of the wall clock and the watch is equal to:
A. ₹ 110
B. ₹ 100
C. ₹ 80
D. ₹ 120

41. A salesman expects a gain of 13% on his cost price. If in a month his sale was ₹ 7,91,000, what was his profit?
A. ₹ 91,000   B. ₹ 97,786
C. ₹ 85,659   D. ₹ 88,300

42. A merchant fixed the selling price of his articles at ₹ 700 after adding 40% profit to the cost price. As the sale was very low at this price level, he decided to fix the selling price at 10% profit. Find the new selling price.
A. ₹ 450   B. ₹ 490
C. ₹ 500   D. ₹ 550

43. A saves 20% of his monthly salary. If his monthly expenditure is ₹ 6,000, then his monthly savings is:
A. ₹ 1,200   B. ₹ 4,800
C. ₹ 1,500   D. ₹ 1,800

44. From 2008 to 2009, the sales of a book decreased by 80%. If the sales in 2010 were the same as in 2008, by what per cent did it increase from 2009 to 2010?
A. 80%   B. 100%
C. 120%   D. 400%

45. The speed of a bus is 72 km/hr. The distance covered by the bus in 5 seconds is:
A. 50 m   B. 74.5 m
C. 100 m   D. 60 m

46. Two men start together to walk a certain distance, one at 4 km/h and another at 3 km/h. The former arrives half an hour before the latter. Find the distance.
A. 6 km   B. 9 km
C. 8 km   D. 7 km

47. A person invests ₹ 12,000 as fixed deposit at a bank at the rate of 10% per annum simple interest. But due to some pressing needs he has to withdraw the entire money after 3 years, for which the bank allowed him a lower rate of interest. If he gets ₹ 3,320 less than what he would have got at the end of 5 years, the rate of interest allowed by the bank is:

A. $7\dfrac{8}{9}\%$ B. $8\dfrac{7}{9}\%$

C. $7\dfrac{5}{9}\%$ D. $7\dfrac{4}{9}\%$

48. The compound interest on ₹ 30,000 at 7% per annum for a certain time is ₹ 4,347. The time is:
A. 2 years   B. 2.5 years
C. 3 years   D. 4 years

49. A prism has as the base a right-angled triangle whose sides adjacent to the right angles are 10 cm and 12 cm long. The height of the prism is 20 cm. The density of the material of the prism is 6 gm/cubic cm. The weight of the prism is:
A. 3.4 kg   B. 4.8 kg
C. 6.4 kg   D. 7.2 kg

50. Three circles of radii 4 cm, 6 cm and 8 cm touch each other pairwise externally. The area of the triangle formed by the line-segments joining the centres of the three circles is:
A. $6\sqrt{6}$ sq. cm   B. $24\sqrt{6}$ sq. cm
C. $144\sqrt{13}$ sq. cm   D. $12\sqrt{105}$ sq. cm

51. The basic characteristic of a capitalistic economy is:
A. full employment
B. the private ownership of the means of production
C. absence of monopoly
D. large-scale production in primary industries

52. Which one of the following taxes is *not* a direct tax?
A. Gift tax   B. Wealth tax
C. Sales tax   D. Estate duty

53. UNDP prepares:
A. Index Number of Price Level
B. Physical Quality Index
C. Human Development Index
D. Standard of Living Index

54. Fiscal policy refers to
A. Sale and purchase of securities by RBI
B. Government taxes, expenditure and borrowings
C. Government borrowings from abroad
D. Sharing of its revenue by Central Government with States

55. Public opinion gets an authoritative expression in a democracy through:
A. Newspapers
B. Parliament
C. Pressure groups
D. Public meetings

56. Which one of the following is *not* a determining factor of a country's foreign policy?
A. National interests
B. Interdependence
C. Cultural conditions
D. Religious conditions

57. Who will act as the Chairman of Public Accounts Committee?
A. The Leader of the Opposition in Lok Sabha
B. The Leader of the House
C. The Speaker of the Lok Sabha
D. The Vice-President of India

58. Who was chosen unanimously as the President of India?
A. Dr. S. Radhakrishnan
B. Neelam Sanjiva Reddy
C. K.R. Narayanan
D. Dr. A.P.J. Abdul Kalam

59. The Constitution of India was passed by the Constituent Assembly on:
A. 17th October, 1949
B. 14th November, 1949
C. 26th November, 1949
D. 26th January, 1949

60. The power to decide an election petition is vested in the:
A. Parliament
B. Supreme Court
C. High Court
D. Election Commission

61. The 1857 Mutiny failed mainly because:
A. the British got French support
B. the British numbered more
C. of lack of planning and leadership
D. it was premature

62. *The Story of 'My Experiments with Truth'* is the autobiography of
A. Lala Lajpat Rai
B. Gopal Krishna Gokhale
C. Bal Gangadhar Tilak
D. Mahatma Gandhi

63. Who among the following made the Ganapati festival very popular in Maharashtra?
A. Gopal Krishna Gokhale
B. Annie Besant
C. Mahadev Ranade
D. Bal Gangadhar Tilak

64. The Mughal ruler who built the Buland Darwaza was:
A. Akbar   B. Babur
C. Humayun   D. Bahadur Shah

65. Diarchy in the provinces was introduced through the:
A. Indian Councils Act, 1861
B. Indian Councils Act, 1892
C. Government of India Act, 1919
D. Government of India Act, 1935

66. Which of the following is the world's largest desert?
A. Gobi
B. Sahara
C. The Great Australian Desert
D. Arabian Desert

67. The rate of erosion in a stream is lowest where:
A. breadth is greater
B. velocity is more
C. the river joins the sea
D. depth is greater

68. The name 'Sahyadri' is related to:
A. Western Ghats
B. Cyclone hazards
C. A rain-bearing wind
D. Himalayan Peak

69. Which of the following is *not* correctly matched?
A. Himachal Pradesh   — Shillong
B. Andhra Pradesh   — Hyderabad
C. Uttar Pradesh   — Lucknow
D. Arunachal Pradesh   — Itanagar

70. Tides in the sea have stored in them:
A. Hydraulic energy
B. Kinetic energy
C. Gravitational potential energy
D. A combination of all the three forms of energy

71. Delivery of developed foetus is scientifically called is:
A. Parturition   B. Oviposition
C. Abortion   D. Ovulation

72. Thyroxine hormone is secreted by:
A. Pituitary gland   B. Thyroid gland
C. Adrenal gland   D. Testes

73. The digestive juice which has no enzyme is:
A. Bile   B. Saliva
C. Intestinal juice   D. Gastric juice

74. An essential feature of seed germination is the presence of:
A. Minerals   B. Water
C. Light   D. Temperature

75. Plants that grow on stones and rocks are:
A. Halophytes   B. Aerophytes
C. Psammophytes   D. Lithophytes

76. Tactile hair is found in the body of:
A. Insects   B. Mammals
C. Reptiles   D. Birds

77. The source of energy in the Sun is:
A. nuclear fission
B. nuclear fusion
C. radioactivity
D. electrical energy

78. Which one of the following materials is used as controller in a nuclear reactor power generator?
A. Cadmium   B. Beryllium
C. Graphite   D. Heavy water

79. Banking of curves on road or railway track is done to provide:
A. centripetal force
B. centrifugal force
C. gravitational force
D. angular velocity

80. .... is a type of application software used for communication.
A. FTP   B. Word processing
C. Database   D. Image editing

81. A floppy disk is:
A. a semiconductor random-access memory
B. an EPROM
C. used as the primary memory in computer systems
D. made up of magnetic material

82. MDI stands for:
A. Multiple Document Interface
B. Multiple Design Interface
C. Multiple Design Interaction
D. Multiple Document Interaction

83. People die in an atmosphere of carbon dioxide because:
A. it is a poisonous gas
B. it destroys tissues
C. of want of oxygen
D. of suffocation

84. Which of the following acts as photosensitizer during photosynthesis?
A. Oxygen   B. Nitrogen
C. Chlorophyll   D. Chlorine

85. What happens when bleaching powder is left exposed to air?
A. It turns dark brown in colour
B. It turns yellow in colour
C. It gradually loses its oxygen
D. It gradually loses its chlorine

86. Arsenic pollution leads to:
A. White foot disease
B. Black foot disease
C. Dyslexia
D. Allergy

87. Which one of the following does *not* contribute to pollution?
A. Thermal Power Plant
B. Nuclear Power Plant
C. Hydroelectric Power Plant
D. Atomic Power Plant

88. Which of the following are the two major components of dry air (by volume)?
A. Nitrogen and Oxygen
B. Oxygen and Argon
C. Nitrogen and Ammonia
D. Oxygen and Carbon dioxide

89. Which one of the following is *not* an example of Lotic ecosystem?
A. Stream   B. Lagoon
C. Pond   D. Estuary

90. Permissible noise level at industrial area during daytime is:
A. 40 dB (A)   B. 75 dB (A)
C. 120 dB (A)   D. 140 dB (A)

91. Benazir Bhutto, the former Pakistan Prime Minister was assassinated in:
A. Hyderabad   B. Karachi
C. Rawalpindi   D. Islamabad

92. Which of the following is correctly matched?

Research Institutes	*Headquarters*
A. Leather Research Institute	— Lucknow
B. Rice Research Institute	— Cuttack
C. Silk Research Institute	— Bangalore
D. Sugar Research Institute	— Chennai

93. Who was affectionately known as the "Grand Old Man of India"?
A. Gopal Krishna Gokhale
B. Mahatma Gandhi
C. Bal Gangadhar Tilak
D. Dadabhai Naoroji

94. The colours of stars depend on their:
A. temperature
B. distance
C. radius
D. atmospheric pressure

95. Find the odd one out.

A.	IDBI	— Industrial Finance
B.	SIDBI	— Financial assistance to small industries
C.	FCI	— Financial assistance to commercial
D.	EXIM Bank	— Financing of export-import trade

96. Light from the Sun reaches us in nearly:
A. 8 min. B. 2 min.
C. 6 min. D. 4 min.

97. The State with largest gap in male and female literacy is:
A. Uttar Pradesh B. Madhya Pradesh
C. Rajasthan D. Kerala

98. "Better to reign in hell than serve in heaven." Who said these words?
A. William Shakespeare
B. Milton
C. William Wordsworth
D. Lord Tennyson

99. Comprehensive Test Ban Treaty (CTBT) is associated with the ban on which of the following?
A. Ban on certain organisations under UN laws
B. Ban on money laundering activities
C. Ban on nuclear tests for developing arsenals
D. Ban on terrorism

100. The Pulitzer Prize is associated with which of the following?
A. Environmental Protection
B. Civil Aviation
C. Journalism
D. Olympic Games

ANSWERS

1	2	3	4	5	6	7	8	9	10
C	D	A	C	D	C	B	D	B	D

11	12	13	14	15	16	17	18	19	20
D	B	C	D	C	C	C	D	C	C

21	22	23	24	25	26	27	28	29	30
B	B	C	B	B	C	A	A	C	A

31	32	33	34	35	36	37	38	39	40
C	C	C	A	C	C	A	B	D	A

41	42	43	44	45	46	47	48	49	50
A	D	C	D	C	A	D	A	D	B

51	52	53	54	55	56	57	58	59	60
B	C	C	B	B	D	A	B	C	D

61	62	63	64	65	66	67	68	69	70
C	D	D	A	C	B	A	A	A	D

71	72	73	74	75	76	77	78	79	80
A	B	A	B	D	A	B	A	A	A

81	82	83	84	85	86	87	88	89	90
D	A	C	C	D	B	C	A	C	B

91	92	93	94	95	96	97	98	99	100
C	B	D	A	C	A	C	B	C	C

EXPLANATORY ANSWERS

1. Jewellery are made from gold likewise Furniture are made from wood.

3. 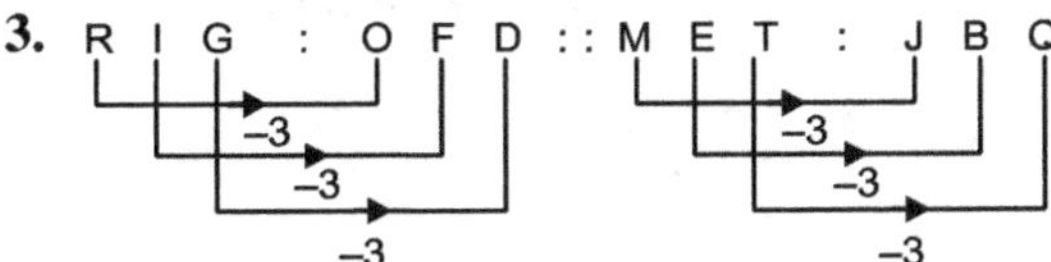

4. 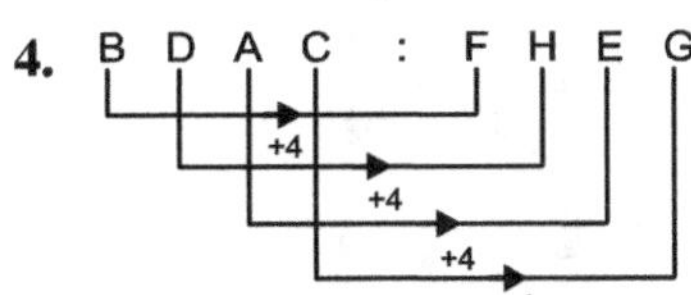

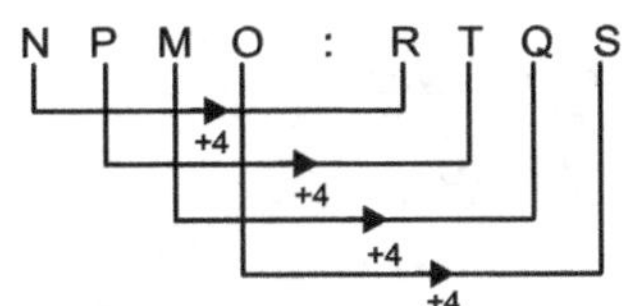

5. 49 : 64 :: 144 : ?

$(7)^2 : (8)^2 :: (12)^2 : (13)^2$

$(13)^2 = 169$

6. 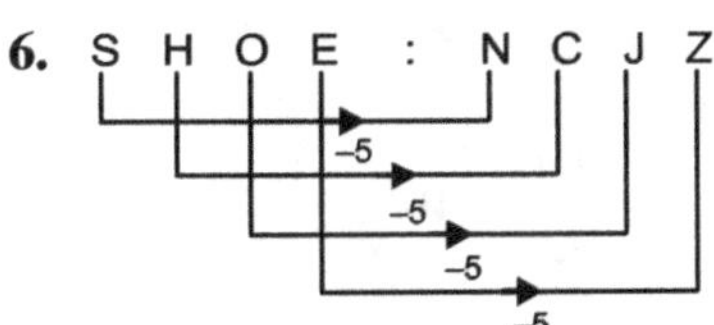

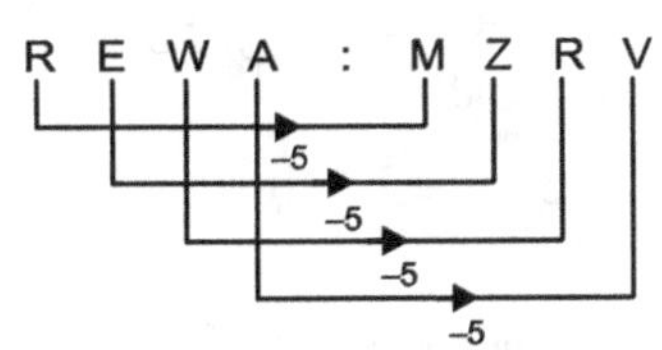

9. All given options except option B Crime–Blame are example of antonym.

10. All given options except option D 144 are cube of integer number, whereas '144' is a square of number 12.

11. When we plan for any journey, then we book tickets. On boarding the train or plane we start our travel. And our journey ended when we reached the destination.

12. One sick person go to the doctor, who diagnosis their problem and after proper treatment person recovered.

13. Gender, General, Genesis, Gentle, Genuine.

14. V, VIII XI, XIV, XVII XX

(5), (8), (11), (14), (17), (20)

15. 3463 (3463 − 1245 = 2218) 1245

5324 (5324 − 3626 = 1698) 3626

16. 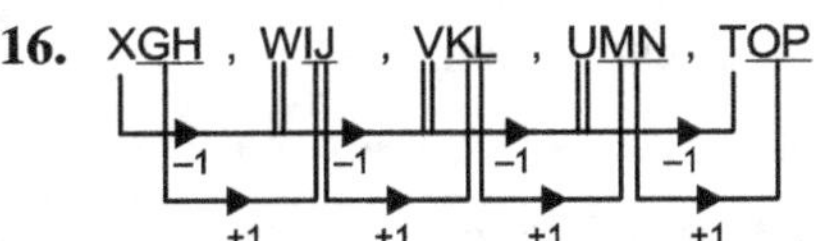

17. 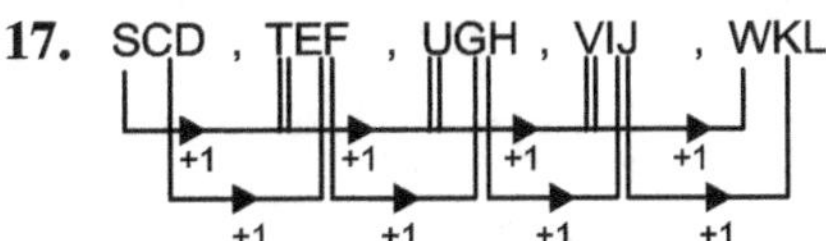

18. K > B > Y > J

19. Let present age of mother is x.

Then person's age is $= \dfrac{2}{5}x$

Age after 8 years,

$$\frac{2}{5}x + 8 = \frac{x}{2} + 4$$

$$\frac{x}{2} - \frac{2}{5}x = 8 - 4$$

$$\frac{(5-4)x}{10} = 4$$

$$x = 40 \text{ years}$$

24. 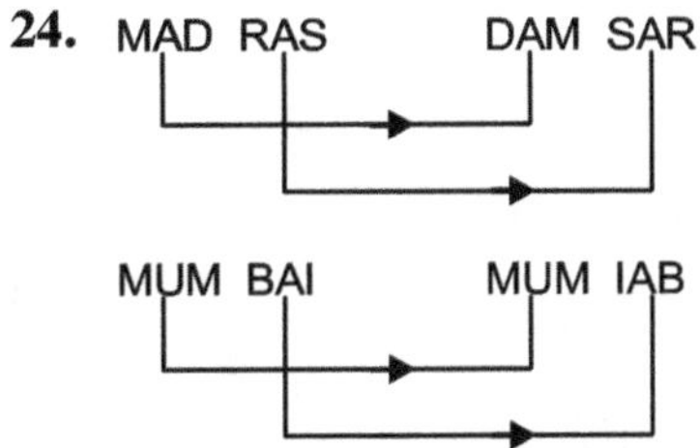

25.

$$\begin{array}{cccccccccc} \text{D} & \text{R} & \text{E} & \text{A} & \text{M} & \quad & \text{C} & \text{H} & \text{I} & \text{L} & \text{D} \\ \downarrow & \downarrow & \downarrow & \downarrow & \downarrow & & \downarrow & \downarrow & \downarrow & \downarrow & \downarrow \\ 7 & 8 & 0 & 2 & 6 & & 5 & 3 & 4 & 1 & 7 \end{array}$$

$$\begin{array}{cccccc} \text{L} & \text{E} & \text{A} & \text{D} & \text{E} & \text{R} \\ \downarrow & \downarrow & \downarrow & \downarrow & \downarrow & \downarrow \\ \boxed{1 \quad 0 \quad 2 \quad 7 \quad 0 \quad 8} \end{array}$$

26.

$$\begin{array}{ccccccc} 2 & 9 & 28 & 65 & 126 & \boxed{\dfrac{217}{216}} & 344 \\ \downarrow & \downarrow & \downarrow & \downarrow & \downarrow & \downarrow & \downarrow \\ 1^3+1 & 2^3+1 & 3^3+1 & 4^3+1 & 5^3+1 & 6^3+1 & 7^3+1 \end{array}$$

Hence, wrong number is 216

27. Let given consecutive numbers are

$x - 4, x - 3, x - 2, x - 1, x, x + 1, x + 2, x + 3$

Average of two middle terms

$$\frac{x-1+x}{2} = 4.5$$

$$\Rightarrow 2x - 1 = 2(4.5) = 9$$

$$\Rightarrow \quad 2x = 9 + 1 = 10$$

$$\Rightarrow \quad x = 5$$

Sequence is

$5 - 4, 5 - 3, 5 - 2, 5 - 1, 5, 5 + 1, 5 + 2, 5 + 3$

$1, 2, 3, 4, 5, 6, 7, 8$

Sum of given numbers

$= 1 + 2 + 3 + 4 + 5 + 6 + 7 + 8 = 36$

28. $\because (1 \times 2 \times 3 \times 4 \times \ldots \times n) = \lfloor n$

$$\therefore \left(\lfloor 14 - \lfloor 13 - \lfloor 12\right)$$

$$= \left(14 \times 13 \times \lfloor 12 - 13 \times \lfloor 12 - \lfloor 12\right)$$

$$= \lfloor 12 \left(14 \times 13 - 13 - 1\right)$$

$$= \lfloor 12 \left(14 \times 13 - 14\right)$$

$$= \lfloor 12 \times 14(13 - 1)$$

$$= 14 \times 12 \times \lfloor 12$$

29. $(A + B)$ can do a work in 12 days

$(A + B)$'s 1 day's work $= \dfrac{1}{12}$

B alone can do this work in 30 days

B's one day's work $= \dfrac{1}{30}$

A's one day's work $= \dfrac{1}{12} - \dfrac{1}{30}$

$$= \frac{5-2}{60} = \frac{3}{60} = \frac{1}{20}$$

Hence, A can do this work in 20 days.

31. Let cost price $= ₹ 100$

Marked price $= ₹ 100 + 20 = ₹ 120$

$$\text{Discount} = \frac{20}{100} \times 120 = ₹ 24$$

Selling price $= 120 - 24 = ₹ 96$

$$\text{Loss} = \text{CP} - \text{SP}$$

$$= 100 - 96 = ₹ 4$$

$$\text{Loss \%} = \frac{\text{loss}}{\text{CP}} \times 100$$

$$= \frac{4}{100} \times 100 = 4\%$$

32. List price of the chair $= ₹ 350$

$$\text{I discount} = \frac{25}{100} \times 350 = ₹ 87.5$$

$$350 - 87.5 = ₹ 262.5$$

$$\text{II discount} = \frac{10}{100} \times 262.5$$

$$= ₹ 26.25$$

Selling price $= 262.5 - 26.25$

$$= ₹ 236.25$$

33. Cost price = ₹ 170

$$\text{Profit} = \frac{20}{100} \times 170 = 34$$

$$\text{SP} = 170 + 34 = ₹\ 204$$

$$100 - 15 = 85$$

When SP is 85, then MP= ₹ 100

When SP is 204, then MP= $\dfrac{100}{85} \times 204$

$$= \frac{20}{17} \times 204$$

$$= 20 \times 12$$

$$\therefore \qquad \text{MP} = ₹\ 240$$

34.

Chromium	Steel
$\dfrac{2}{13}$	$\dfrac{11}{13}$
$\dfrac{5}{26}$	$\dfrac{21}{26}$

Let $x : y$ two types be mixed

$$\left(\frac{2}{13} \times \frac{x}{x+y} + \frac{5}{26} \times \frac{y}{x+y}\right):$$

$$\left(\frac{11}{13} \times \frac{x}{x+y} + \frac{21}{26} \times \frac{y}{x+y}\right)$$

$$\left(\frac{2x}{13(x+y)} + \frac{5y}{26(x+y)}\right):$$

$$\left(\frac{11x}{13(x+y)} + \frac{21y}{26(x+y)}\right)$$

$$\left(\frac{4x+5y}{26(x+y)}\right) : \left(\frac{22x+21y}{26(x+y)}\right)$$

According to the question,

$$\frac{4x+5y}{22x+21y} = \frac{7}{32}$$

$$\Rightarrow \quad 154x + 147y = 128x + 160y$$

$$\Rightarrow \quad 154x - 128x = 160y - 147y$$

$$\Rightarrow \qquad\qquad 26x = 13y$$

$$\Rightarrow \qquad \frac{x}{y} = \frac{13}{26} = \frac{1}{2}$$

Hence $x : y = 1 : 2$

35. A : B = 2 : 3 and B : C = 4 : 5

$$\text{A : B : C} = 8 : 12 : 15$$

$$\text{Share of B} = \frac{7000}{8+12+15} \times 12$$

$$= \frac{7000}{35} \times 12 = ₹\ 2400$$

36. Here, first two varieties of tea are mixed in equal ratio;

So, their average price = $\dfrac{126+135}{2} = ₹\ 130.50$

Let price of the third variety per kg be ₹ x; then mixture is formed by two varieties one at ₹ 130.50 per kg and other at ₹ x per kg in the same ratio 2 : 2 *i.e.*; 1 : 1

By the rule of alligation,

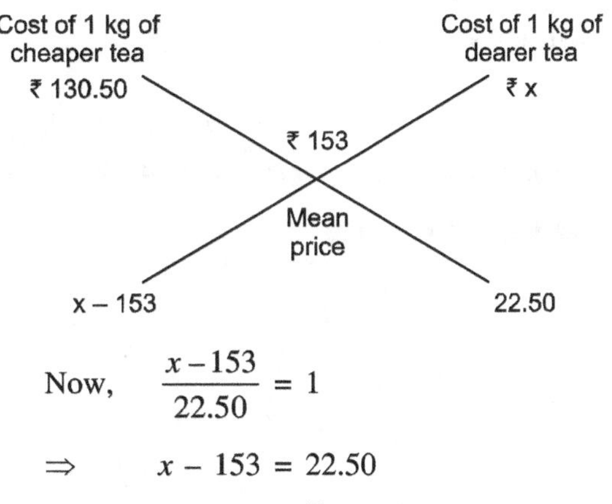

Now, $\quad \dfrac{x-153}{22.50} = 1$

$$\Rightarrow \qquad x - 153 = 22.50$$

$$\therefore \qquad\qquad x = ₹\ 175.50$$

37. 60 pages read in 1 hr

100 pages read in $\dfrac{1}{60} \times 100 = \dfrac{5}{3}$ hrs

Again 40 pages read in 1 hr

100 pages read in $\dfrac{1}{40} \times 100 = \dfrac{5}{2}$ hrs

Average rate $= \dfrac{200}{\dfrac{5}{3} + \dfrac{5}{2}} = \dfrac{200 \times 6}{25} = 48$ pages/hr.

38. Total weight of 34 students

$$= 34 \times 42 = 1428 \text{ kg}$$

Total weight with teacher

$$= 35 \times 42.4 = 1484 \text{ kg}$$

$\therefore$ Weight of the teacher

$$= 1484 - 1428 = 56 \text{ kg}$$

39. Total runs in 10 innings $= 60 \times 10 = 600$

Total runs in 11 innings $= 62 \times 11 = 682$

$\therefore$ Runs made in 11th innings $= 682 - 600 = 82$

41. Let CP $= ₹\,100$, profit $= 13\%$ of CP

SP $= 100 + 13 = ₹\,113$

When SP $= ₹\,113$, then CP $= ₹\,100$

When SP $= ₹\,791000$,

then CP $= \dfrac{100}{113} \times 791000$

$$\text{CP} = ₹\,100 \times 7000 = ₹\,700000$$

Profit $=$ SP $-$ CP $= 791000 - 700000 = ₹\,91000$

42. Let CP $= ₹\,x$ then

Profit $= \dfrac{40}{100} \times x = \dfrac{2x}{5}$

SP $=$ CP $+$ Profit $= x + \dfrac{2x}{5} = \dfrac{7x}{5}$

According to the question,

$$\dfrac{7x}{5} = 700$$

$$\Rightarrow \qquad x = 500$$

CP $= ₹\,500$

Profit $= 10\%$ of $500 = \dfrac{10}{100} \times 500 = ₹\,50$

Hence, new selling price $= 500 + 50 = ₹\,550$

43. When $₹\,80$ is expenditure, then salary is $₹\,100$

When $₹\,6000$ is expenditure, then salary

$$= ₹\dfrac{100}{80} \times 6000 = ₹\,7500$$

Saves $= 20\%$ of 7500

$$= \dfrac{20}{100} \times 7500 = ₹\,1500$$

Hence, monthly saving is $₹\,1500$.

45. $\qquad$ Speed $= 72$ km/hr

$$= 72 \times \dfrac{5}{18} \text{ m/s} = 20 \text{ m/s}$$

Distance covered in 5 seconds $= 20 \times 5$

$$= 100 \text{ m.}$$

46.

$$\xleftarrow{\hspace{2cm}} \ x \text{ km} \ \xrightarrow{\hspace{2cm}}$$

Time taken by first man $= \dfrac{\text{distance}}{\text{speed}} = \dfrac{x}{4}$ hrs.

Time taken by 2nd man $= \dfrac{\text{distance}}{\text{speed}} = \dfrac{x}{3}$ hrs.

According to the question,

$$\dfrac{x}{3} - \dfrac{x}{4} = \dfrac{1}{2}$$

$$\Rightarrow \quad \dfrac{4x - 3x}{12} = \dfrac{1}{2}$$

$$\Rightarrow \quad \dfrac{x}{12} = \dfrac{1}{2}$$

$$\Rightarrow \qquad x = 6$$

$\therefore$ Distance $= 6$ km

47.

$$p = ₹\,12000$$
$$r = 10\%$$
$$t = 5 \text{ years.}$$

$$\text{SI} = \frac{p \times r \times t}{100} = \frac{12000 \times 10 \times 5}{100} = ₹\,6000$$

Amount $= 12000 + 6000 = ₹\,18000$

But he got $18000 - 3320 = ₹\,14680$

$\text{SI} = 14680 - 12000 = ₹\,2680$

$$r = \frac{\text{SI} \times 100}{p \times t} = \frac{2680 \times 100}{12000 \times 3}$$

$$r = \frac{67}{9} = 7\frac{4}{9}\%$$

$\therefore$ The rate of interest allowed by the bank

$$= 7\frac{4}{9}\%$$

48.

$$p = ₹\,30000$$
$$r = 7\%$$
$$\text{CI} = ₹\,4347$$

$\therefore$
$$\text{A} = p + \text{CI}$$
$$= 30000 + 4347 = ₹\,34347$$

$$\text{A} = p\left(1 + \frac{r}{100}\right)^t$$

$$\Rightarrow \quad \frac{34347}{30000} = \left(1 + \frac{7}{100}\right)^t$$

$$\Rightarrow \quad \frac{11449}{10000} = \left(\frac{107}{100}\right)^t$$

$$\Rightarrow \quad \left(\frac{107}{100}\right)^2 = \left(\frac{107}{100}\right)^t$$

$$\Rightarrow \quad t = 2 \text{ years.}$$

49. Area of right triangle $= \dfrac{1}{2} \times b \times h$

$$= \frac{1}{2} \times 10 \times 12$$
$$= 60 \text{ cm}^2$$

Volume $= \text{Area} \times h = 60 \times 20 = 1200 \text{ cm}^3$

$$\text{D} = \frac{\text{M}}{\text{V}} \Rightarrow \text{M} = \text{D} \times \text{V}$$

$$= 6 \times 1200 = 7200 \text{ g}$$
$$= 7.2 \text{ kg}$$

50.

$$s = \frac{12 + 10 + 14}{2} = \frac{36}{2} = 18 \text{ cm}$$

Area of triangle

$$= \sqrt{s(s-a)(s-b)(s-c)}$$
$$= \sqrt{18 \times 6 \times 8 \times 4}$$
$$= \sqrt{6 \times 3 \times 6 \times 2 \times 2 \times 2 \times 2 \times 2}$$
$$= 24\sqrt{6} \text{ cm}^2.$$

Railway Recruitment Board (RRB)
GROUP 'D'
Recruitment Exam

Directions (Question Nos. 1 to 9): *Select the related word/letters/number from the given alternatives.*

1. Life : Death : Hope : ?
- A. Weep
- B. Pain
- C. Despair
- D. Sadness

2. Christian : Muslim : : ? : Quran
- A. Geeta
- B. Ramayan
- C. Angel
- D. Bible

3. Large : Enormous : : ?
- A. Cat : Tiger
- B. Warmth : Frost
- C. Plump : Fat
- D. Royal : Regale

4. BC : DI : : DE : ?
- A. PY
- B. FP
- C. EI
- D. RU

5. ACE : KIG : : MOQ : ?
- A. WUS
- B. WVU
- C. WVT
- D. WUT

6. DCEF : WXVU : : KJLM : ?
- A. QPRS
- B. STRQ
- C. PQNO
- D. NMKL

7. 3 : 27 : : 7 : ?
- A. 21
- B. 42
- C. 147
- D. 343

8. 9 : 28 : : 56 : ?
- A. 3
- B. 18
- C. 112
- D. 169

9. 12 : 35 : : 16 : ?
- A. 78
- B. 32
- C. 55
- D. 63

Directions (Question Nos. 10 to 18): *Select the one which is different from the other three responses.*

10.
- A. River
- B. Ocean
- C. Lake
- D. Rain

11.
- A. King
- B. Queen
- C. Royal
- D. Prince

12.
- A. Mango
- B. Apple
- C. Orange
- D. Guava

13.
- A. M
- B. N
- C. O
- D. P

14.
- A. GLOV
- B. CFKR
- C. ILQX
- D. ADIP

15.
- A. GOD
- B. RAT
- C. WAR
- D. PAPER

16.
- A. 363
- B. 484
- C. 1331
- D. 5462

17.
- A. 8 – 64
- B. 6 – 36
- C. 9 – 81
- D. 7 – 50

18.
- A. 121 – 196
- B. 144 – 225
- C. 36 – 83
- D. 16 – 49

19. Amongst the following words, which word appears second in order in the English dictionary?
- A. Complaint
- B. Complication
- C. Complement
- D. Compose

Directions (Question Nos. 20 and 21): *Which one of the given responses would be a meaningful order of the following words in ascending order?*

20.
1. Line
2. Angle
3. Square
4. Triangle
- A. 2, 1, 4, 3
- B. 3, 4, 1, 2
- C. 4, 2, 1, 3
- D. 1, 2, 4, 3

21.
1. Childhood
2. Adulthood
3. Infancy
4. Adolescence
5. Babyhood
- A. 4, 1, 3, 2, 5
- B. 3, 5, 1, 4, 2
- C. 2, 5, 1, 4, 3
- D. 5, 4, 2, 3, 1

22. Which one set of letters when sequentially placed at the gaps in the given letter series shall complete it?

L_NOO_ML_MNO_NML

A. MNLO   B. ONML
C. NLMO   D. LOMN

Directions (Question Nos. 23 to 25): *Choose the correct alternative from the given ones that will complete the series.*

23. AD, EH, IL, ?, QT
A. LM   B. MN
C. MP   D. OM

24. ABCD, IJKL, QRST, ?
A. YZAB   B. ABYZ
C. BAZY   D. YAZB

25. 2, 6, 14, 26, ?, 62
A. 52   B. 54
C. 44   D. 42

26. A number consists of two digits and the digit in the ten's place exceeds that in the unit's place by 5. If 5 times the sum of the digits be subtracted from the number, the digits of the number are reversed. Then the sum of digits of the number is
A. 11   B. 7
C. 9   D. 13

27. The greatest among the numbers

$\sqrt[4]{3}$, $\sqrt[5]{4}$, $\sqrt[10]{12}$, 1 is

A. 1   B. $\sqrt[5]{4}$

C. $\sqrt[4]{3}$ D. $\sqrt[10]{12}$

28. A fraction becomes $\dfrac{1}{6}$ when 4 is subtracted from its numerator and 1 is added to its denominator. If 2 and 1 are respectively added to its numerator and denominator, it becomes $\dfrac{1}{3}$. Then, the LCM of the numerator and denominator of the said fraction, must be
A. 14   B. 350
C. 5   D. 70

29. $(4^{61} + 4^{62} + 4^{63})$ is divisible by
A. 3   B. 11
C. 13   D. 17

30. The ratio of two numbers is 4 : 5 and their H.C.F. is 8. Then their L.C.M. is
A. 130   B. 140
C. 150   D. 160

31. Each interior angle of a regular polygon is 144°. The number of sides of the polygon is
A. 8   B. 9
C. 10   D. 11

32. There is a pyramid on a base which is a regular hexagon of side $2a$ cm. If every slant edge of this pyramid is of length $5a/2$ cm, then the volume of this pyramid is

A. $3a^3$ cm^3 B. $3\sqrt{2}\ a^3$ cm^3

C. $3\sqrt{3}\ a^3$ cm^3 D. $6a^3$ cm^3

33. Two solid right cones of equal heights and of radii r_1 and r_2 are melted and made to form a solid sphere of radius R. Then the height of the cone is

A. $\dfrac{4R^2}{r_1^2 + r_2^2}$ B. $\dfrac{4R}{r_1 + r_2}$

C. $\dfrac{4R^3}{r_1^2 + r_2^2}$ D. $\dfrac{R^2}{r_1^2 + r_2^2}$

34. The ratio of radii of two cones is 3 : 4 and the ratio of their heights is 4 : 3. Then the ratio of their volumes will be
A. 3 : 4   B. 4 : 3
C. 9 : 16   D. 16 : 9

35. The ratio of the areas of the circumcircle and the incircle of an equilateral triangle is
A. 2 : 1   B. 4 : 1
C. 8 : 1   D. 3 : 2

36. The area of the four walls of a room is 660 m^2 and its length is twice its breadth. If the height of the room is 11 m, then the area of its floor (in m^2) is
A. 120   B. 150
C. 200   D. 330

37. A cylindrical rod of iron whose height is eight times its radius is melted and cast into spherical balls each of half the radius of the cylinder. The number of such spherical balls is

A. 12   B. 16

C. 24   D. 48

38. A and B can do a piece of work in 10 days. B and C can do it in 12 days. A and C can do it in 15 days. How long will A take to do it alone?

A. 24 days   B. 20 days

C. 40 days   D. 30 days

39. A does half as much work as B in one-third of the time taken by B. If together they take 10 days to complete a work, then the time taken by B alone to do it would have been

A. 30 days   B. 25 days

C. 6 days   D. 12 days

40. A single discount equivalent to a discount series 20%, 20% and 10% is

A. 50%   B. 48.4%

C. 42.4%   D. 40.4%

41. If a shopkeeper marks the price of goods 50% more than their cost price and allows a discount of 40%, what is his gain or loss percent?

A. Gain of 10%   B. Loss of 10%

C. Gain of 20%   D. Loss of 20%

42. To get the ratio $p : q$ (for $p \neq q$), one has to add to each term of the ratio $x : y$, the number

A. $\dfrac{px + qy}{p - q}$ B. $\dfrac{qx - py}{p - q}$

C. $\dfrac{px - qy}{p - q}$ D. $\dfrac{py - qx}{p - q}$

43. Two containers have acid and water mixed respectively in the ratio 3 : 1 and 5 : 3. To get a new mixture with ratio of acid to water as 2 : 1, the two types have to be mixed in the ratio

A. 1 : 2   B. 2 : 1

C. 2 : 3   D. 3 : 2

44. a, b, c, d, e, f, g are consecutive even numbers, j, k, l, m, n are consecutive odd numbers. The average of all the numbers is

A. $3\left(\dfrac{a+n}{2}\right)$ B. $\left(\dfrac{l+d}{2}\right)$

C. $\dfrac{a+b+m+n}{4}$ D. $\dfrac{j+c+n+g}{4}$

45. The average of three numbers is 40. The first number is twice the second and the second one is thrice the third number. The difference between the largest and the smallest numbers is

A. 30   B. 36

C. 46   D. 60

46. By selling 12 oranges for ₹ 60, a man loses 25%. The number of oranges he has to sell for ₹ 100, so as to gain 25% is

A. 10   B. 11

C. 12   D. 15

47. The cost price of 400 lemons is equal to the selling price of 320 lemons. Then the profit percent is

A. 15%   B. 20%

C. 25%   D. 40%

48. A man spends 75% of his income. His income increased by 20% and he increased his expenditure by 15%. His savings will then be increased by

A. 33%   B. $33\dfrac{1}{3}\%$

C. 35%   D. 40%

49. 25 litres of salt solution contains 6% salt. How many litres of water must be added so as to get a resultant solution containing 5% salt?

A. 4 litres   B. 5 litres

C. 6 litres   D. 8 litres

50. The current of a stream runs at the rate of 4 km an hour. A boat goes 6 km and comes back to the starting point in 2 hours. The speed of the boat in still water is

A. 6 km/hour   B. 8 km/hour

C. 7.5 km/hour   D. 6.8 km/hour

51. Elasticity of demand measures the responsiveness of the quantity demanded of a good to a
A. change in the price of the good
B. change in the price of substitutes
C. change in the price of the complements
D. change in the price of joint products

52. Consumption function expresses the relationship between consumption and
A. savings   B. income
C. investment   D. price

53. 'Mixed economy' refers to
A. the co-existence of heavy, small scale and cottage industries
B. the promotion of agriculture as well as cottage industries
C. the co-existence of rich as well as poor
D. the co-existence of public as well as private sector

54. Which of the following is *not* a fixed cost?
A. Salaries of administrative staff
B. Rent of factory building
C. Property taxes
D. Electricity charges

55. Which of the following would *not* constitute an economic activity in Economics?
A. A teacher teaching students in his college
B. A teacher teaching students in a coaching institute
C. A teacher teaching his own daughter at home
D. A teacher teaching students under Sarva Shiksha Abhiyan Scheme

56. Zero hour is at the discretion of
A. Prime Minister
B. Speaker
C. Opposition leader
D. President

57. The Judges of High Court are administered oath of office by
A. The Chief Justice of High Court
B. The President of India
C. The Chief Justice of India
D. Governor of the State

58. Which slogan was given by the French Revolution to the world?
A. Liberty, Authority, Equaltiy
B. Liberty, Equality, Fraternity
C. Liberty, Law, Fraternity
D. Tradition, Authority, Law

59. The President of India can issue a proclamation of National Emergency only on the written recommendation of
A. The Prime Minister
B. The Cabinet consisting of only Cabinet Ministers of the Union
C. The Council of Ministers of the Union
D. Parliament

60. Parliament exercises control over public expenditure through
A. Advocate General
B. Comptroller and Auditor General
C. Commerce Minister
D. Finance Minister

61. Who was the court poet of Harsha Vardhana?
A. Bhani   B. Ravi Kirti
C. Bana   D. Vishnu Sharma

62. The 'Poorna Swaraj' resolution was adopted in the annual session of the Indian National Congress held at
A. Bomaby   B. Lahore
C. Calcutta   D. Madras

63. In which of the following countries were Buddha's idols disfigured and removed recently?
A. Pakistan   B. Turkey
C. Afghanistan   D. Iran

64. "Go back to Vedas." This call given by
A. Ramakrishna Paramahamsa
B. Vivekananda
C. Jyotiba Phule
D. Dayanand Sarswati

65. Which of the following pairs is *incorrect*?
A. Babar vs. Sangram Singh
B. Sher Shah vs. Humayun
C. Chengiz Khan vs. Alauddin Khilji
D. Akbar vs. Hemu

66. The natural gaps across the mountains which provide routes are called
A. Peaks   B. Dunes
C. Plateaus   D. Passes

67. Jhumming is shifting agriculture practised in
A. North-eastern India
B. South-western India
C. South-eastern India
D. Northern India

68. Frontal Rain is caused by
A. Convection currents
B. Winds from sea
C. Cyclonic activity
D. Condensation of water evaporated from mountains

69. The Palk Strait lies between
A. Bay of Bengal and Gulf of Manner
B. Andaman and Nicobar Islands
C. Rann of Kutch and Gulf of Khambhat
D. Lakshadweep and Maldives

70. Match the following :

	Rivers		Towns
(a)	Gomti	1.	Guwahati
(b)	Brahmaputra	2.	Rajahmundry
(c)	Godavari	3.	Tiruchirapalli
(d)	Kaveri	4.	Lucknow

	(a)	(b)	(c)	(d)
A.	3	4	2	1
B.	2	1	3	4
C.	4	1	2	3
D.	4	2	1	3

71. The example of hermaphrodite animal in which cross fertilisation occurs is
A. Hydra   B. Ascaris
C. Earthworm   D. Silkworm

72. Blubber is
A. a milky secretion of rubber plant
B. a layer of thick fat
C. a device to trap insects by some aquatic plants
D. fungal infection of rice plants

73. The coding segment of DNA is called
A. Codon   B. Muton
C. Intron   D. Exon

74. Fat soluble vitamins are
A. Tocopherol, Niacin, Cyanocobalamin
B. Calciferol, Carotene, Tocopherol
C. Ascorbic acid, Calciferol, Riboflavin
D. Thiamine, Carotene, Biotin

75. Silk is produced by
A. Egg of a silkworm
B. Pupa of silkworm
C. Larva of silkworm
D. Insect itself

76. Which of the following is an egg laying mammal?
A. Bat   B. Leafy ant-eater
C. Whale   D. Spiny ant-eater

77. A transformer works with
A. alternating current only
B. direct current only
C. both AC and DC
D. any signal

78. In the Earth, the weight of a body is maximum at the
A. North Pole   B. South Pole
C. Equator   D. Surface

79. The technique of collecting information about an object from a distance without making physical contact with it is
A. Remote sensing   B. Remote control
C. Remote accessing   D. Space shuttle

80. The head mirror used by E.N.T. doctors is
A. Concave   B. Convex
C. Plane   D. Plano-convex

81. A _______ is a high-speed network that connects local networks in a city or town.
A. LAN   B. MAN
C. WAN   D. TAN

82. PDA stands for
A. Personal Digital Assistant
B. Personal Development Agency
C. Personal Data Authority
D. Personal Data Array

83. Which of the following statements are correct about chloroform?
1. Liquid fuel
2. Anaesthetic in nature
3. Produces phosgene

4. Fire extinguisher
A. 1, 2 B. 1, 3
C. 2, 3 D. 4, 1

84. Which of the following is *not* a method of preparing oxygen?
A. Electrolysis of water
B. Fractional distillation of liquid air
C. Decomposition of potassium permanganate
D. Decomposition of manganese dioxide

85. Which one of the following is *not* a characteristic feature of alloys?
They are
A. Compounds
B. Mixtures
C. Solutions
D. Homogeneous systems

86. Permanent hardness of water may be removed by addition of
A. Alum
B. Sodium carbonate
C. Lime
D. Potassium Permanganate

87. Global warming is expected to result in
A. Increase in level of sea
B. Change in crop pattern
C. Change in coastline
D. Each of the above

88. Man can maintain an ecological balance in the biosphere by
A. deforestation
B. developing new breeds of cultivated plants and domesticated animals
C. using insecticides and pesticides
D. understanding the delicate balance in the relative number of organisms

89. Smog is a combination of
A. air and water vapour
B. water and smoke
C. fire and water
D. smoke and fog

90. Of the following, which one pollutes the air of a big city?
A. Copper B. Chromium
C. Lead D. Cadmium

91. Which State is famous for step-wells?
A. Maharashtra B. Gujarat
C. Odisha D. Manipur

92. First Indian Arctic Expendition was launched in the year
A. 2004 B. 2005
C. 2006 D. 2007

93. The river on which the reservoir for Indira Gandhi Canal has been built is
A. Sutlej B. Ravi
C. Luni D. Jhelum

94. Bihu is a festival that is observed in
A. West Bengal B. Maharashtra
C. Assam (Asom) D. Tamil Nadu

95. Bharat Ratna is designed like the leaf of
A. Banyan tree B. Peepal tree
C. Coconut tree D. Sandalwood tree

96. Radar is used to:
A. locate submerged submarines
B. receive signal from radio receivers
C. detect and locate distant objects
D. locate geostationary satellites

97. Optical fibre works on the principle of:
A. refraction
B. scattering
C. interference
D. total internal reflection

98. Which one of the following is in fact *not* a garden?
A. Hanging Gardens (Mumbai)
B. Eden Gardnes (Kolkata)
C. Vrindavan Gardnes (Mysore)
D. Khusro Gardnes (Lucknow)

99. The book "The Audacity of Hope" has been written by
A. Nayantara Sehgal B. Aravind Adiga
C. Vikram Seth D. Barack Obama

100. ISRO is the abbreviation for
A. Indian Scientific Research Organisation
B. Indian Space Research Organisation
C. International Space Research Organisation
D. International Scientific Research Organisation

ANSWERS

1	2	3	4	5	6	7	8	9	10
C	D	C	A	A	B	D	D	D	D

11	12	13	14	15	16	17	18	19	20
C	C	C	A	D	D	D	C	C	D

21	22	23	24	25	26	27	28	29	30
B	A	C	A	D	C	B	D	A	D

31	32	33	34	35	36	37	38	39	40
C	C	C	A	B	C	D	A	B	C

41	42	43	44	45	46	47	48	49	50
B	B	A	B	D	C	C	C	B	B

51	52	53	54	55	56	57	58	59	60
A	B	D	D	C	B	A	B	B	B

61	62	63	64	65	66	67	68	69	70
C	B	C	D	C	D	A	C	A	C

71	72	73	74	75	76	77	78	79	80
C	B	D	B	C	D	A	D	A	A

81	82	83	84	85	86	87	88	89	90
B	A	C	D	A	B	D	D	D	C

91	92	93	94	95	96	97	98	99	100
B	D	A	C	B	C	D	B	D	B

EXPLANATORY ANSWERS

4. 2 3   4 9   4 5   16 25
B C   D I   D E   P Y

5. A C E : K I G :: M O Q : W U S (+2 pattern)

6. D C E F : W X V U :: K J L M : S T R Q (+1 pattern)

9. $12 \times 3 - 1 = 35$

$16 \times 4 - 1 = 63.$

13. Rest there are consonent.

14. G L O V C F K R I L Q X A D I P (+5, +8, +3, +7 pattern; +3, +5, +5, +5)

15. Rest have only three letters.

16. Rest is divided by 11.

17. $8^2 = 64$, $6^2 = 36$, $9^2 = 81$, $\boxed{7^2 \neq 50}$

18. $11^2 - 14^2$, $12^2 - 15^2$, $4^2 - 7^2$.

23. A D E H I L M P Q T (+3 pattern; +1)

24. ABCD   IJKL   QRST   YZAB (+5 pattern)

25. 2   6   14   26   42   62 (+4, +8, +12, +16, +20)

27. $\sqrt[4]{3}$, $\sqrt[5]{4}$, $\sqrt[10]{12}$, 1

L.C.M of 4, 5 and 10 = 20

$$\sqrt[4]{3} = \sqrt[20]{3^5} = \sqrt[20]{243}$$

$$\sqrt[5]{4} = \sqrt[5\times4]{4^4} = \sqrt[20]{256}$$

$$\sqrt[10]{12} = \sqrt[10\times2]{12^2} = \sqrt[20]{144}$$

$$1 = 1 = 1$$

Clearly greatest number = 256

$\therefore$ $\sqrt[5]{4}$ is the greatest number.

28. Let fraction = $\dfrac{x}{y}$

According to the question,

$$\frac{x-4}{y+1} = \frac{1}{6}$$

$$6x - 24 = y + 1$$
$$6x - y = 25 \qquad ...(1)$$

and

$$\frac{x+2}{y+1} = \frac{1}{3}$$

$$3x + 6 = y + 1$$
$$3x - y = -5 \qquad ...(ii)$$

from (i) and (ii)

$$\begin{array}{r} 6x - y = 25 \\ 3x - y = -5 \\ -\quad+\quad\quad+ \\ \hline 3x = 30 \\ x = 10 \\ y = 35 \end{array}$$

$\therefore$ fraction = $\dfrac{x}{y} = \dfrac{10}{35}$

L.C.M of 10 and 35 = 70.

36. According to the question,
$$2(l + b)h = 660$$

$$(l + b)11 = \frac{660}{2} = 330$$

$$(l + b) = \frac{330}{11} = 30$$

$$2b + b = 30$$
$$b = 10$$
$$l = 20$$

Area = 20 × 10 = 200 m^2.

38. (A + B) one day's work = $\dfrac{1}{10}$ $\qquad$ ...(i)

(B + C) one day's work = $\dfrac{1}{12}$ $\qquad$ ...(ii)

(A + C) one day's work = $\dfrac{1}{15}$ $\qquad$ ...(iii)

equations (i) − (ii) gives

$$A + B - B - C = \frac{1}{10} - \frac{1}{12} = \frac{6-5}{60} = \frac{1}{60}$$

$$\therefore \qquad A - C = \frac{1}{60} \qquad ...(iv)$$

from equations (iii) and (iv)

$$A + C + A - C = \frac{1}{15} + \frac{1}{60}$$

$$2A = \frac{4+1}{60}$$

$$2A = \frac{5}{60}$$

$$A = \frac{5}{60 \times 2} = \frac{1}{24}$$

$\therefore$ A can do this work alone in 24 days.

45. Let numbers are a, b and c.
$$a + b + c = 3 \times 40 = 120$$
According to the question,
$$6c + 3c + c = 120$$
$$10c = 120$$
$$c = 12$$
$$\therefore \qquad a = 6 \times 12 = 72$$
$$b = 3 \times 12 = 36$$
$$c = 12 \times 1 = 12$$

Difference of greatest no. and smallest no. = 72 − 12 = 60.

47. According to the question,
$$400 - 320 = 80$$

$$\text{Profit \%} = \frac{80}{320} \times 100 = 25\%.$$

Railway Recruitment Board (RRB)
GROUP 'D'
Recruitment Exam

1. Select the number which does NOT belong to the given series:

   232, 343, 454, 564, 676
   - A. 676
   - B. 454
   - C. 343
   - D. 564

2. A bus left with some definite number of passengers. At the first stop, half the passengers left the bus and 35 boarded the bus. At the second stop $\frac{1}{5}$ th of the passengers left and 40 boarded the bus. Then, the bus moved with 80 passengers towards its destination without stopping anywhere. How many passengers were there originally?
   - A. 25
   - B. 30
   - C. 40
   - D. 50

3. If the day after tomorrow is Sunday, what day was tomorrow's day before yesterday?
   - A. Friday
   - B. Thursday
   - C. Monday
   - D. Tuesday

4. A man is 3 years older than his wife and four times as old as his son. If the son becomes 15 years old after 3 years, what is the present age of the wife?
   - A. 60 years
   - B. 51 years
   - C. 48 years
   - D. 45 years

5. X and Y are brothers. R is the father of Y. S is the brother of T and maternal uncle of X. What is T to R?
   - A. Mother
   - B. Wife
   - C. Sister
   - D. Brother

6. Suresh is 7 ranks ahead of Ashok in the class of 39 students. If Ashok's rank is 17th from the last, what is Suresh's rank from the start?
   - A. 16th
   - B. 23rd
   - C. 24th
   - D. 15th

7. A word/set of letters given in capital letters is followed by four answer words. Out of these only one **cannot** be formed by using the letters of the given word/set of letters. Find out that word:

   INDETERMINATE
   - A. DETERMINE
   - B. RETINUE
   - C. REMINDER
   - D. RETINA

8. A group of alphabets are given with each being assigned a numerical code. These have to be unscrambled into a meaningful word and the correct code so obtained may be indicated from the given responses:

R	A	H	K	S
1	2	3	4	5

   - A. 5 1 2 3 4
   - B. 5 4 2 1 3
   - C. 5 3 2 1 4
   - D. 5 3 1 2 4

9. A statement is given followed by two assumptions, (1), (2). You have to consider the statement to be true, even if it seems to be at variance from commonly known facts. You are to decide which of the given assumptions can definitely be drawn from the given statement. Indicate your answer.

   Statement: Theoretical education does not bring in economic advancement and it leads to a steady loss of confidence and money in the country.

Assumptions: (1) There is close relationship between development of confidence and economic development.

(2) Theoretical education makes priceless contribution for development of confidence

A. Only 1 is implicit
B. 2 is implicit
C. Both 1 and 2 are implicit
D. Both 1 and 2 are not implicit

10. Two statements are given followed by four conclusions, I, II, III and IV. You have to consider the statements to be true, even if they seem to be at variance from commonly known facts. You are to decide which of the given conclusions can definitely be drawn from the given statements. Indicate your answer.

Statement: (A) No cow is a chair.
(B) All chairs are tables

Conclusions: I. Some tables are chairs.
II. Some tables are cows.
III. Some chairs are cows.
IV. No table is a cow.

A. Either II or III follow
B. Either II or IV follow
C. Only I follows
D. All conclusions follow

11. If HONESTY is written as 5132468 and POVERTY as 7192068, how is HORSE written in a certain code?
A. 50124   B. 51042
C. 51024   D. 52014

12. In a certain code SISTER is written as RHRSDQ. How is UNCLE written in that code?
A. TMBKD   B. TBMKD
C. TVBOD   D. TMKBD

13. If 841 = 3, 633 = 5, 425 = 7, then 217 = ?
A. 6   B. 7
C. 8   D. 9

14. The following equations follow a common property. Find out the correct value to complete D:
A = 51 (714) 14; B = 61 (915) 15;
C = 71 (1136) 16; D = 81 (?) 17
A. (1377)   B. (1378)
C. (1356)   D. (1346)

15. After interchanging ÷ and =, 2 and 3 which one of the following statement becomes correct?
A. 15 = 2 ÷ 3   B. 5 ÷ 15 = 2
C. 2 = 15 ÷ 3   D. 3 = 2 ÷ 15

16. 25 * 2 * 6 = 4 * 11 * 0
Which set of symbols can replace * ?
A. ×, −, ×, +   B. +, −, ×, +
C. ×, +, ×, −   D. ×, +, +, ×

17. Find the missing number from the given responses:

5	6	12
4	3	4
2	3	?
18	27	96

A. 4   B. 5
C. 3   D. 6

18. Peter walked 8 kms. west and turned right and walked 3 kms. Then again he turned right and walked 12 kms. How far is he from the starting point?
A. 7   B. 8
C. 4   D. 5

19. Babu is Rahim's neighbour and his house is 200 metres away in the north west direction. Joseph is Rahim's neighbour and his house is located 200 metres away in the south west direction. Gopal is Joseph's neighbour and he stays 200 metres away in the south east direction. Roy is Gopal's neighbour and his house is located 200 metres away in the north east direction. Then where is the position of Roy's house in relation to Babu's?
A. South east   B. South west
C. North   D. North east

20. A group of friends are sitting in an arrangement one each at the corner of an octagon. All are facing the centre. Mahima is sitting diagonally opposite Rama, who is on Sushma's right. Ravi is next to Sushma and opposite Girdhar, who is on Chandra's left. Savitri is not on Mahima's right, but opposite Shalini. Who is on Shalini's right?
  A. Ravi
  B. Mahima
  C. Girdhar
  D. Rama

21. A cube has the following figures drawn on its five faces. The top surface is blank. The ellipse is between the cross and triangle. The square is on the right of the triangle. The ellipse and the square are opposite to each other. Which face is the circle on?
  A. On the top
  B. Opposite to ellipse
  C. Opposite to triangle
  D. At the bottom

Directions (Question Nos. 22 to 24): *Select the related word / letters / number / figure from the given alternatives.*

22. FOX : CUNNING : : RABBIT : ?
  A. Courageous B. Dangerous
  C. Timid   D. Ferocious

23. FLEXIBLE : RIGID : : CONFIDENCE : ?
  A. DIFFIDENCE
  B. INDIFFERENCE
  C. COWARDICE
  D. SCARE

24. AZCX : BYDW : : HQJO : ?
  A. GRFP   B. JPKM
  C. IPKN   D. GRJP

25. 40% of 1620 + 30% of 960 = ? % of 5200
  A. 12   B. 24
  C. 16   D. 18

26. How many perfect squares lie between 120 and 300?
  A. 5   B. 6
  C. 7   D. 8

27. $\left\{ \dfrac{(0.1)^2 - (0.01)^2}{0.0001} + 1 \right\}$ is equal to
  A. 1010   B. 110
  C. 101   D. 100

28. If there is a profit of 20% on the cost price of an article, the percentage of profit calculated on its selling price will be
  A. 24   B. $16\dfrac{2}{3}$
  C. $8\dfrac{1}{3}$ D. 20

29. If the cost price of 15 books is equal to the selling price of 20 books, the loss percent is
  A. 16   B. 20
  C. 24   D. 25

30. If an article is sold at 200% profit, then the ratio of its cost price to its selling price will be
  A. 1 : 2   B. 2 : 1
  C. 1 : 3   D. 3 : 1

31. If on a marked price, the difference of selling prices with a discount of 30% and two successive discounts of 20% and 10% is ₹ 72, then the marked price (in ₹) is
  A. 3,600   B. 3,000
  C. 2,500   D. 2,400

32. If an electricity bill is paid before due date, one gets a reduction of 4% on the amount of the bill. By paying the bill before due date a person got a reduction of ₹ 13. The amount of his electricity bill was
  A. ₹ 125   B. ₹ 225
  C. ₹ 325   D. ₹ 425

33. Successive discounts of 10%, 20% and 30% is equivalent to a single discount of
  A. 60%   B. 49.6%
  C. 40.5%   D. 36%

34. The price of an article was first increased by 10% and then again by 20%. If the last increased price be ₹ 33, the original price was
  A. ₹ 30   B. ₹ 27.50
  C. ₹ 26.50   D. ₹ 25

35. If each side of a square is increased by 10% its area will be increased by
A. 10%   B. 21%
C. 44%   D. 100%

36. The ratio of milk and water in mixtures of four containers are 5 : 3, 2 : 1, 3 : 2 and 7 : 4 respectively. In which container is the quantity of milk, relative to water, minimum?
A. First   B. Second
C. Third   D. Fourth

37. Two numbers are in the ratio 1 : 3. If their sum is 240, then their difference is
A. 120   B. 108
C. 100   D. 96

38. The ratio of income and expenditure of a person is 11 : 10. If he saves ₹ 9,000 per annum, his monthly income is
A. ₹ 8,000   B. ₹ 8,800
C. ₹ 8,500   D. ₹ 8,250

39. If $W_1 : W_2 = 2 : 3$, and $W_1 : W_3 = 1 : 2$, then $W_2 : W_3$ is
A. 3 : 4   B. 4 : 3
C. 2 : 3   D. 4 : 5

40. A copper wire of length 36 m and diameter 2 mm is melted to form a sphere. The radius of the sphere (in cm) is
A. 2.5   B. 3
C. 3.5   D. 4

41. The ratio of the radii of two wheels is 3 : 4. The ratio of their circumferences is
A. 4 : 3   B. 3 : 4
C. 2 : 3   D. 3 : 2

42. If the length of a rectangle is increased by 10% and its breadth is decreased by 10%, the change in its area will be
A. 1% increase   B. 1% decrease
C. 10% increase   D. No change

43. In how many years will sum of money double itself at $6\frac{1}{4}$ % simple interest per annum?
A. 24   B. 20
C. 16   D. 12

44. A sum of ₹ 12,000, deposited at compound interest becomes double after 5 years. How much will it be after 20 years?
A. ₹ 1,44,000   B. ₹ 1,20,000
C. ₹ 1,50,000   D. ₹ 1,92,000

45. In how many years will a sum of ₹ 800 at 10% per annum compound interest, compounded semi-annually becomes ₹ 926.10?
A. $1\frac{1}{2}$ B. $1\frac{2}{3}$
C. $2\frac{1}{3}$ D. $2\frac{1}{2}$

46. In a 100 m race, Kamal defeats Bimal by 5 seconds. If the speed of Kamal is 18 k.m./hr., then the speed of Bimal is
A. 15.4 k.m./hr.
B. 14.5 k.m./hr.
C. 14.4 k.m./hr.
D. 14 k.m./hr.

47. A train, 240 m long, crosses a man walking along the line in opposite direction at the rate of 3 km/h in 10 seconds. The speed of the train is
A. 63 km/h   B. 75 km/h
C. 83.4 km/h   D. 86.4 km/h

48. A boatman rows 1 km. in 5 minutes along the stream and 6 km. in 1 hour against the stream. The speed of the stream is
A. 3 km/hr.   B. 6 km/hr.
C. 10 km/hr.   D. 12 km/hr.

49. A can complete $\frac{1}{3}$ of a work in 5 days and B $\frac{2}{5}$ of the work in 10 days. In how many days both A and B together can complete the work ?
A. 10   B. $9\frac{3}{8}$
C. $8\frac{4}{5}$ D. $7\frac{1}{2}$

50. 7 men can complete a piece of work in 12 days. How many additional men will be required to complete double the work in 8 days ?
   A. 28   B. 21
   C. 14   D. 7

51. Tetra ethyl lead (TEL) is
   A. a catalyst in burning fossil fuel
   B. an antioxidant
   C. a reductant
   D. an antiknock compound

52. Curie point is the temperature at which
   A. Matter becomes radioactive.
   B. A metal loses magnetic properties.
   C. A metal loses conductivity.
   D. Transmutation of metal occurs.

53. The isotope used for the production of atomic energy is
   A. U-235   B. U-238
   C. U-234   D. U-236

54. The acceleration due to gravity at the equator
   A. is less than that at the poles
   B. is greater than that at the poles
   C. is equal to that at the poles
   D. does not depend on the earth's centripetal acceleration

55. Which of the following is not a nucleon ?
   A. Proton   B. Neutron
   C. Electron   D. Positron

56. The material used in the manufacture of lead pencil is
   A. Graphite   B. Lead
   C. Carbon   D. Mica

57. Angle of friction and angle of repose are
   A. equal to each other
   B. not equal to each other
   C. proportional to each other
   D. None of the above

58. Processor's speed of a computer is measured in
   A. BPS   B. MIPS
   C. Baud   D. Hertz

59. 'C' language is a
   A. Low level language
   B. High level language
   C. Machine level language
   D. Assembly level language

60. What happens to a person who receives the wrong type of blood ?
   A. All the arteries constrict.
   B. All the arteries dialates.
   C. The RBCs agglutinate.
   D. The spleen and lymphnodes deteriorate.

61. NIS stands for
   A. National Infectious diseases Seminar
   B. National Irrigation Schedule
   C. National Immunisation Schedule
   D. National Information Sector

62. If all bullets could not be removed from gun shot injury of a man, it may cause poisoning by
   A. Mercury   B. Lead
   C. Iron   D. Arsenic

63. Ringworm is a _____ disease.
   A. Bacterial   B. Protozoan
   C. Viral   D. Fungal

64. Pituitary gland is situated in
   A. the base of the heart
   B. the base of the brain
   C. the neck
   D. the abdomen

65. Who discovered cement?
   A. Agassit   B. Albertus Magnus
   C. Joseph Aspdin   D. Janseen

66. What is the reason for red colour of the soil in certain parts of India?
   A. Presence of magnesium
   B. Presence of phosphates
   C. Presence of ferric oxide
   D. Pressence of humus

67. Windows 7, the latest operating system from Microsoft Corporation has _______ Indian languages fonts.
   A. 14   B. 26
   C. 37   D. 49

68. TRIPS and TRIMS are the terms associated with
   A. IMF   B. WTQ
   C. IBRD   D. IDA

69. A Presidential Ordinance can remain in force
   A. For three months
   B. For six months
   C. For nine months
   D. Indefinitely

70. Which of the following when mixed with a metal forms amalgam?
   A. Aluminium
   B. Gold
   C. Silver
   D. Mercury

71. The first non-stop air-conditioned 'DURANTO' train was flagged off between
   A. Sealdah – New Delhi
   B. Mumbai – Howrah
   C. Bangalore – Howrah
   D. Chennai – New Delhi

72. Study of maps is called:
   A. Calligraphy
   B. Geography
   C. Geology
   D. Cartography

73. World AIDS day is held every year on:
   A. 1st of December
   B. 1st of January
   C. 14th of February
   D. 8th of March

74. Which one of the following states does not form part of Narmada River basin?
   A. Madhya Pradesh
   B. Rajasthan
   C. Gujarat
   D. Maharashtra

75. The first unmanned satellite built by ISRO was:
   A. Bhaskara-I
   B. Aryabhata
   C. Rohini
   D. Megha

76. The exchange of commodities between two countries is referred as
   A. Balance of trade
   B. Bilateral trade
   C. Volume of trade
   D. Multilateral trade

77. Soil erosion on hill slopes can be checked by
   A. Afforestation
   B. Terrace cultivation
   C. Strip cropping
   D. Contour ploughing

78. Who coined the word 'Geography'?
   A. Ptolemy   B. Eratosthenese
   C. Hecataus   D. Herodatus

79. Which of the following is called the "ecological hot spot of India"?
   A. Western Ghats
   B. Eastern Ghats
   C. Western Himalayas
   D. Eastern Himalayas

80. The art and science of map making is called
   A. Remote Sensing
   B. Cartography
   C. Photogrammetry
   D. Mapping

81. The age of the Earth can be determined by
   A. Geological Time Scale
   B. Radio-Metric Dating
   C. Gravity method
   D. Fossilization method

82. The monk who influenced Ashoka to embrace Buddhism was
   A. Vishnu Gupta
   B. Upa Gupta
   C. Brahma Gupta
   D. Brihadratha

83. The declaration that Democracy is a Government 'of the people, by the people; for the people' was made by
   A. George Washington
   B. Winston Churchill
   C. Abraham Lincoln
   D. Theodore Roosevelt

84. The Lodi dynasty was founded by
  A. Ibrahim Lodi   B. Sikandar Lodi
  C. Bahlol Lodi   D. Khizr Khan

85. Harshavardhana was defeated by
  A. Prabhakaravardhana
  B. Pulakesin II
  C. Narasimhavarma Pallava
  D. Sasanka

86. Who among the following was an illiterate?
  A. Jahangir   B. Shah Jahan
  C. Akbar   D. Aurangazeb

87. Which Governor General is associated with Doctrine of Lapse?
  A. Lord Ripon   B. Lord Dalhousie
  C. Lord Bentinck   D. Lord Curzon

88. India attained 'Dominion Status' on
  A. 15th January, 1947
  B. 15th August, 1947
  C. 15th August, 1950
  D. 15th October, 1947

89. Despotism is possible in a
  A. One party state
  B. Two party state
  C. Multi party state
  D. Two and multi party state

90. Marx belonged to
  A. Germany   B. Holland
  C. France   D. Britain

91. Which one of the following is the guardian of Fundamental Rights ?
  A. Legislature
  B. Executive
  C. Political parties
  D. Judiciary

92. Sarkaria Commission was concerned with
  A. Administrative Reforms
  B. Electoral Reforms
  C. Financial Reforms
  D. Centre-State relations

93. The Speaker of the Lok Sabha has to address his/her letter of resignation to
  A. Prime Minister of India
  B. President of India
  C. Deputy Speaker of Lok Sabha
  D. Minister of Parliamentary Affairs

94. A want becomes a demand only when it is backed by the
  A. Ability to purchase
  B. Necessity to buy
  C. Desire to buy
  D. Utility of the product

95. The terms "Micro Economics" and "Macro Economics" were coined by
  A. Alfred Marshall
  B. Ragner Nurkse
  C. Ragner Frisch
  D. J.M. Keynes

96. During periods of inflation, tax rates should
  A. increase
  B. decrease
  C. remain constant
  D. fluctuate

97. Which is the biggest tax paying sector in India?
  A. Agriculture sector
  B. Industrial sector
  C. Transport sector
  D. Banking sector

98. "Economics is what it ought to be" – This statement refers to
  A. Normative economics
  B. Positive economics
  C. Monetary economics
  D. Fiscal economics

99. The excess of price a person is to pay rather than forego the consumption of the commodity is called
  A. Price
  B. Profit
  C. Producers' surplus
  D. Consumers' surplus

100. Silver halides are used in photographic plates because they are
  A. oxidised in air
  B. soluble in hyposolution
  C. reduced by light
  D. totally colourless

ANSWERS

1	2	3	4	5	6	7	8	9	10
D	B	B	D	B	A	B	C	D	C

11	12	13	14	15	16	17	18	19	20
B	A	D	A	B	A	D	D	A	A

21	22	23	24	25	26	27	28	29	30
D	C	A	C	D	C	D	B	D	C

31	32	33	34	35	36	37	38	39	40
A	C	B	D	B	B	A	D	A	B

41	42	43	44	45	46	47	48	49	50
B	B	C	D	A	C	C	A	B	C

51	52	53	54	55	56	57	58	59	60
D	B	A	A	D	A	C	D	B	C

61	62	63	64	65	66	67	68	69	70
D	B	D	B	C	C	D	B	B	D

71	72	73	74	75	76	77	78	79	80
A	D	A	B	B	B	B	B	A	B

81	82	83	84	85	86	87	88	89	90
B	B	C	C	B	C	B	B	A	A

91	92	93	94	95	96	97	98	99	100
D	D	C	A	C	A	B	A	D	A

EXPLANATORY ANSWERS

2. Let there were x passengers originally.
The number of passengers after first stop

$$= \frac{x}{2} + 35$$

The number of passengers after second stop

$$= \left(\frac{x}{2} + 35\right)\frac{4}{5} + 40$$

From question,

$$\left(\frac{x}{2} + 35\right)\frac{4}{5} + 40 = 80$$

$$\Rightarrow \frac{x}{2} + 35 = \frac{40 \times 5}{4}$$

$$\Rightarrow \frac{x}{2} = 15$$

$$\therefore x = 30.$$

4. Present age of the son = 15 − 3 = 12 years
$\therefore$ Present age of the person = 12 × 4 = 48 years
$\therefore$ Present age of his wife = 48 − 3 = 45 years

5.

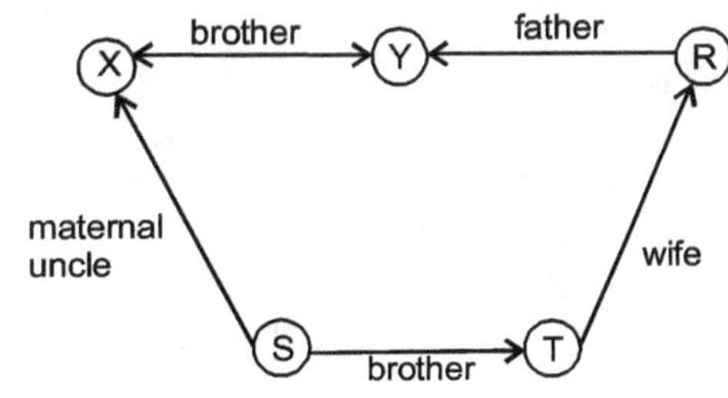

6.

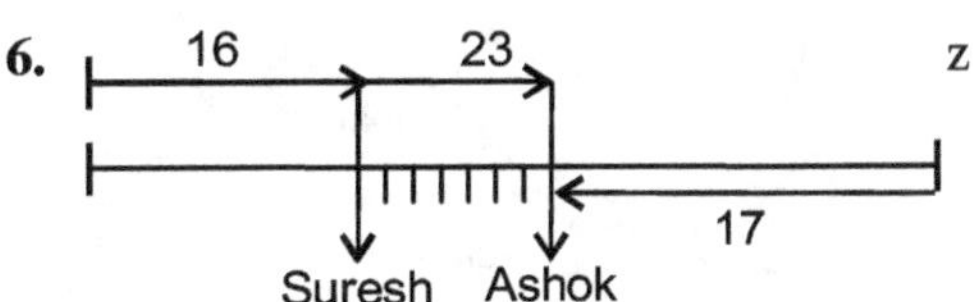

8. Meaningful word = SHARK

∴ code = 53214

10.

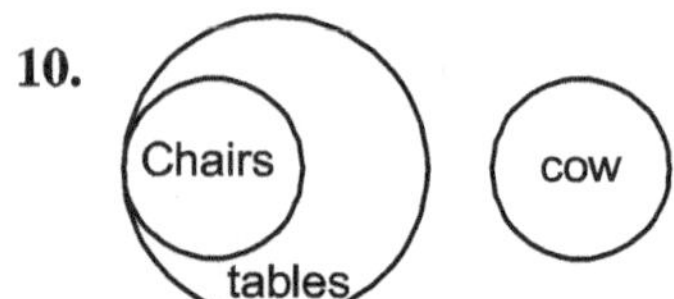

12.

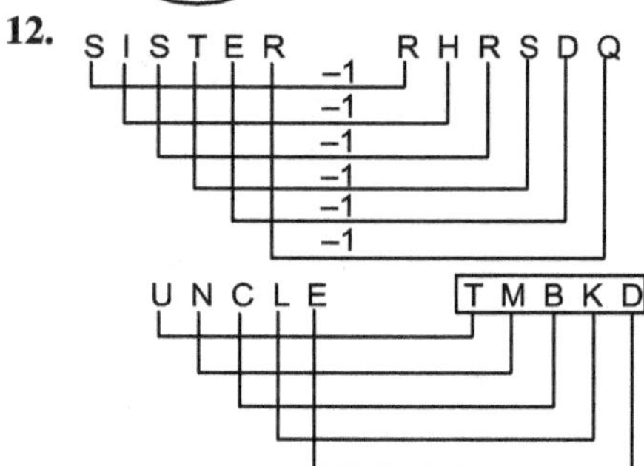

13.

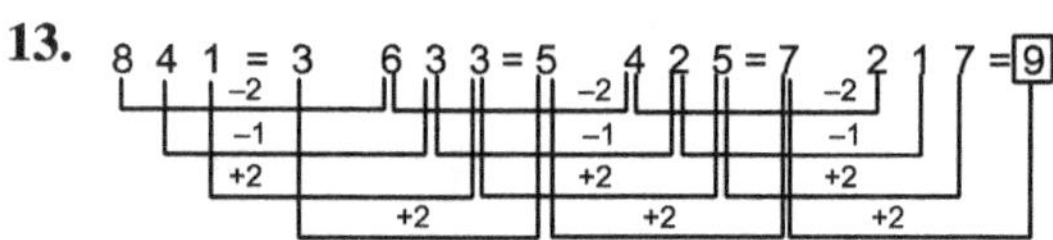

14. $51 \times 14 = 714$

$61 \times 15 = 915$

$71 \times 16 = 1136$

∴ $81 \times 17 = 1377.$

17. $5 + 4 \times 2 = 18$

$6 + 3 \times 3 = 27$

$12 + 4 \times 6 = 96$

19.

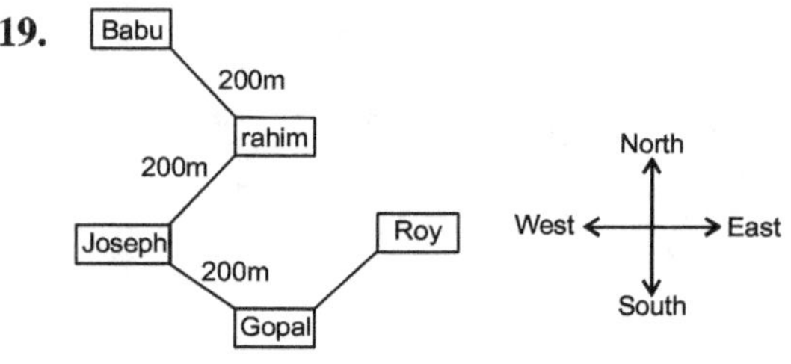

20.

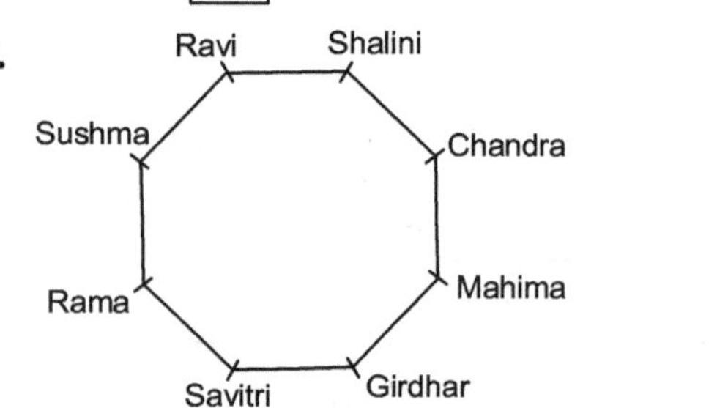

21.

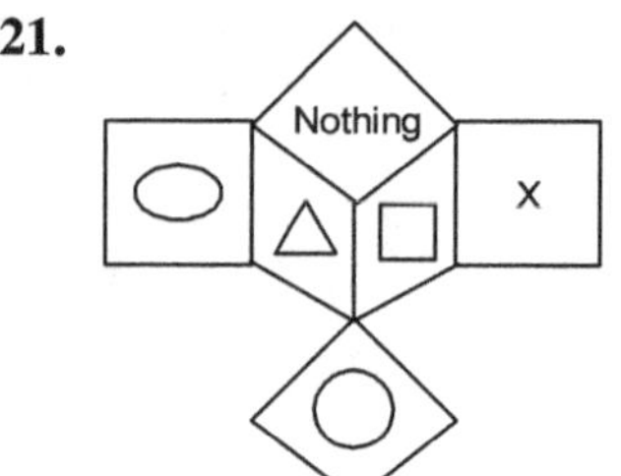

24.

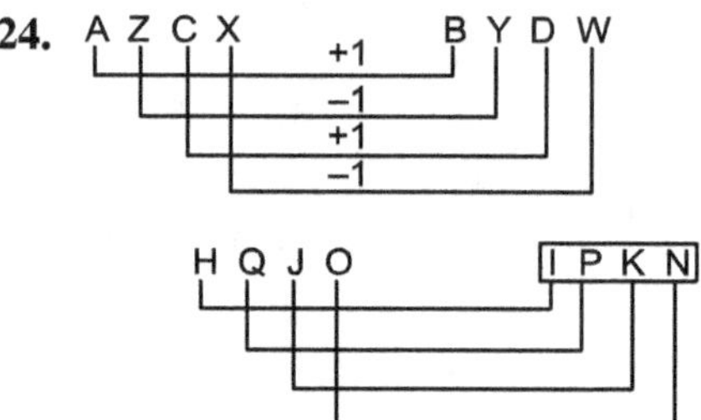

25. 40% of 1620 + 30% of 960 = x% of 5200

$$\frac{40}{100} \times 1620 + \frac{30}{100} \times 960 = \frac{x}{100} \times 5200$$

$$\Rightarrow \quad 648 + 288 = 52x$$

$$\Rightarrow \quad 936 = 52x$$

$$\Rightarrow \quad x = \frac{936}{52} = 18$$

Hence required number = 18

26. Clearly $11^2, 12^2, 13^2, 14^2, 15^2, 16^2$ and 17^2

total = 7

27. $\dfrac{(0.01 + 0.01)(0.1 - 0.01) + 0.0001}{0.0001}$

$$= \frac{0.0099 + 0.0001}{0.0001}$$

$$= \frac{0.01}{0.0001} = 100$$

30. Let   C.P. = ₹ x

then   S.P. = $x\left(1 + \dfrac{200}{100}\right)$

$$= 3x$$

∴   Ratio = $\dfrac{x}{3x} = 1 : 3.$

34. Let the price of an article = ₹ x

First increased by 10% = $x\left(1 + \dfrac{10}{100}\right) = \dfrac{11x}{10}$

Again Increased by 20%

$$= \frac{11x}{10}\left(1+\frac{20}{100}\right) = \frac{66x}{50}$$

Now according to question, $\dfrac{66x}{50} = 33$

$$\therefore \ x = \frac{33\times50}{66} = ₹\ 25.$$

35. Let side of square = x unit
then its area = x^2 sq. unit
Now side of the square increased by =

$$x\left(1+\frac{10}{100}\right)$$

$$= \frac{11x}{10}$$

$\therefore$ Area of new square = $\dfrac{121x^2}{100}$

Increase in area = $\dfrac{21x^2}{100}$

Increased % = $\dfrac{21x^2}{100\times x^2}\times100 = 21\%.$

37. Let the number are x and $3x$
$\therefore \ x + 3x = 240 \Rightarrow x = 60$
their difference = $180 - 60 = 120.$

40. Length of copper wire = 36 m = 3600 cm.

Diameter = 2mm $\therefore$ Radius = 1 mm = $\dfrac{1}{10}$ cm.

Now it is in the form of cylinder.

$\therefore$ Volume = $\pi r^2 h = \pi\dfrac{1}{100}\times3600 = 36\pi$

Now volume of sphere = $\dfrac{4}{3}\pi r^3$

$$36\pi = \frac{4}{3}\pi r^3$$

$\therefore \qquad\qquad r^3 = 27$
$\Rightarrow \qquad\qquad r = 3$ cm.

42. Let length of rectangle = l unit
breadth of rectangle = b unit
$\therefore$ Area = lb sq. unit.

Now from question length = $l\left(1+\dfrac{10}{100}\right)$

Also breadth = $b\left(1-\dfrac{10}{100}\right) = \dfrac{9l}{10}$

Area = $\dfrac{99lb}{100}$

Decrease in area = $lb\left(1-\dfrac{99}{100}\right) = \dfrac{lb}{100}$

$$= \frac{lb}{100\times lb}\times100$$

Required decrease % = 1%.

44. A = ₹ 24,000 P = ₹ 12,000, Let rate = $r\%$

$$\therefore \ 24000 = 12000\left(1+\frac{r}{100}\right)^5$$

$$2 = \left(1+\frac{r}{100}\right)^5$$

$$\therefore \ 2^4 = \left(1+\frac{r}{100}\right)^{20}$$

i.e., 16 times of principal
$\therefore$ Required amount = 16 × 12,000
$$= ₹\ 192,000.$$

Railway Recruitment Board (RRB)
GROUP 'D'
Recruitment Exam

Directions (Qs. No. 1-4): *Select the related word/ letters/number from the given alternatives.*

1. Rajiv Gandhi Airport : Hyderabad : : Indira Gandhi Airport : ?
   A. Mumbai B. Bangalore
   C. Delhi D. Kolkata

2. TEW : PAS : : IVX : ?
   A. ETR B. SQR
   C. ERT D. RNP

3. PEON : QGRR : : RUDE : ?
   A. MLNO B. SWGI
   C. TVSA D. STRR

4. 167 : 43 : : 245 : ?
   A. 75 B. 22
   C. 72 D. 91

Directions (Qs. No. 5-8): *Find out the odd word/ letters/number/number pair from the given alternatives.*

5. A. Hazy B. Cloudy
   C. Translucent D. Transparent

6. A. IDD B. AGG
   C. UTT D. REE

7. A. 286 B. 374
   C. 143 D. 279

8. A. 358 B. 853
   C. 538 D. 240

Directions (Qs. No. 9-12): *A series is given with one term missing. Choose the correct alternative from the given ones that will complete the series.*

9. Thousand, Ten thousand, Lakh, Ten lakh, ?
   A. Ones B. Hundred
   C. Ten crore D. Crore

10. ABC, BDF, DHL, ?
    A. RST B. HPX
    C. CDE D. EGF

11. IJ, PQ, XY, ?
    A. DE B. OP
    C. GH D. WV

12. 15, 32, 99, 400, ?
    A. 2001 B. 2004
    C. 2005 D. 1994

13. In the following question, two statements are given each followed by two conclusions I and II. You have to consider the statement to be true even if they seem to be at variance from commonly known facts. You have to decide which of the given conclusions, if any, follows from the given statements.

    Statements : I. All horses are bullocks.

    II. All bullocks are goats.

    Conclusions : I. All horses are goats.

    II. All goats are horses.

    A. Conclusion I follows
    B. Conclusion II follows
    C. Neither I nor II follows
    D. Both I and II follow

14. A racing event was organised in a jungle. The dog ran faster than the elephant but slower than the tiger. The deer was the fastest. The lion ran faster than the tiger. Who was the second to finish the race?
    A. Dog
    B. Deer
    C. Elephant
    D. Lion

15. Arrange the given words in the sequence in which they occur in the dictionary.
(*i*) Cover   (*ii*) Clandestine
(*iii*) Coward   (*iv*) Cajole
A. (*i*), (*iv*), (*iii*), (*ii*)   B. (*i*), (*ii*), (*iii*), (*iv*)
C. (*iv*), (*ii*), (*i*), (*iii*)   D. (*i*), (*iii*), (*iv*), (*ii*)

16. In a certain code language, 'NIGERIA' is written as '@#^\$?#*'. How is 'GINGER' written in that code language?
A. ^#\$@^?   B. ^#@^\$?
C. ^#@\$^?   D. #\$@\$^?

17. In the following question, select the missing number from the given series.

45	55	26
50	51	65
60	49	?

A. 19   B. 43
C. 64   D. 23

18. If "–" means "plus", "×" means "divide", "÷" means "multiply" and "+" means "minus", then
26 + 400 × 20 – 21 ÷ 12 = ?
A. 258   B. 219
C. 216   D. 230

19. Which set of letters when sequentially placed at the gaps in the given letter series shall complete it?
_BA_BBA_AB_B
A. ABAB   B. AAAB
C. BBAB   D. BBBA

20. A cat is chasing a mouse. The cat moves towards north for 25 m, takes a right turn and move 100 m, turns towards the south and moves 25 m further. Finally, it turns left and moves 55 m. What is the distance between the initial and the final position of the cat?
A. 185 m   B. 155 m
C. 190 m   D. 135 m

21. Hema was twice as old as Geeta 10 years ago. How old is Geeta today, if Hema will be 40 years old 10 years henceforth?
A. 15 years   B. 35 years
C. 25 years   D. 20 years

22. From the given alternatives, select the word which can be formed using the letters of the given word.
IMMEASURABLE
A. MEAT   B. BIBLE
C. BAILABLE   D. BLUE

23. If 2 × 16 = 8; 8 × 8 = 1; 6 × 12 = 12, then 12 × 144 = __?__.
A. 16   B. 24
C. 11   D. 12

24. Some equations are solved on the basis of a certain system. Using the same, solve the unsolved equation.
If 10 – 3 = 12, 12 – 4 = 13, 14 – 5 = 14, then 16 – 6 = __?__
A. 16   B. 18
C. 10   D. 15

25. The question given below is based upon the following set of codes:

Digit : 1 3 5 4 6 0 8 7 2
Code : A O Z L D T N H Q

Find the code for 21500.
A. SLOPH   B. QAZTT
C. SLPHO   D. SHLPO

26. The value of $\dfrac{\sqrt[6]{2}\left[(625)^{\frac{3}{5}} \times (1024)^{-\frac{6}{5}} \div (25)^{\frac{3}{5}}\right]^{\frac{1}{2}}}{\left(\sqrt[3]{128}\right)^{\frac{-5}{2}} \times (125)^{\frac{1}{5}}}$ is:
A. 10   B. 5
C. 2   D. 1

27. On simplification $\dfrac{4.669 \times 4.669 - 2.331 \times 2.331}{(4.669)^2 + (2.331)^2 + 4.669 \times 4.662}$ is equal to:
A. 0.331   B. 0.334
C. 1.669   D. 2.338

28. The value of 25 – 5 [2 + 3 {2 – 2 (5 – 3) + 5} – 10] ÷ 5 is:
A. 0   B. 1
C. 24   D. 25

29. If $1 + \cfrac{1}{\sqrt{5} + \cfrac{1}{\sqrt{5} + \cfrac{1}{\sqrt{5}}}} = a + b\sqrt{5}$, where a and b are rational numbers, then $(a - b)$ equals:

A. $\dfrac{29}{35}$ B. $\dfrac{6}{35}$

C. $\dfrac{19}{35}$ D. $\dfrac{41}{35}$

30. Let x be the least number which when divided by 5, 10, 12 and 15 leaves a remainder 2 in each case, but is divisible by 7. The sum of digits of x is:

A. 8   B. 9
C. 11   D. 13

31. H.C.F. of two numbers each of four digits is 103 and their L.C.M. is 187 times their H.C.F. The sum of the numbers is:

A. 4882   B. 4288
C. 2488   D. 2884

32. A person saves 40% of his income. His expenditure increases by 25% and his income also increases by 10%. Now his per cent saving are approximately:

A. 28   B. 30
C. 32   D. 35

33. The freight of machine amounts to 20% of its price. Had the price been 10% less than what it is, the total cost of machine would have been ₹ 4800 less. What is the price of the machine?

A. ₹ 40000   B. ₹ 42000
C. ₹ 45000   D. ₹ 48000

34. At an examination in which full marks were 1000, A got 10% less marks than B; B got 25% more than C and C got 20% less than D. If A got 720 marks, what percentage of full marks was obtained by D?

A. 70
B. 72
C. 75
D. 80

35. A dealer buys a table listed at ₹ 1200 and gets two successive discounts of 10% and 20%. He spends 10% of his cost price on transportation. At what price should he sell it to earn a profit of 20%?

A. ₹ 1045.44   B. ₹ 1140.48
C. ₹ 1150.56   D. ₹ 1164.52

36. The catalogue price of an article is ₹ 720. If it is sold at a discount of $16\dfrac{2}{3}\%$ of the catalogue price, the gain is 25%. If it is sold ₹ 160 below catalogue price, then what is the gain/loss per cent?

A. $16\dfrac{2}{3}\%$ gain   B. $16\dfrac{2}{3}\%$ loss

C. $6\dfrac{2}{3}\%$ gain   D. $6\dfrac{2}{3}\%$ loss

37. A vessel is full of a solution of alcohol and water in which their ratio is 4 : 3. If 14 litres of the solution are taken out and replaced by the same amount of water, then the ratio of alcohol and water in the resulting solution becomes 3 : 4. The capacity of the vessel, in litres, was:

A. 28   B. 35
C. 42   D. 56

38. A sum of ₹ 3535 is divided among A, B, C and D such that A : B = 1 : 2, B : C = 3 : 2 and C : D = 8 : 9. The difference in shares of B and D is:

A. ₹ 202   B. ₹ 303
C. ₹ 404   D. ₹ 505

39. A bag contains coins of one rupee, 50 paise and 25 paise. If these coins are in the ratio of 2 : 3 : 10 and the total amount of money in the bag is ₹ 288, then the number of 50 paise coin exceeds the number of one rupee coin by:

A. 48   B. 136
C. 184   D. 336

40. If $(x^2 - y^2) : (x^2 + y^2) = 3 : 5$, then $(x^2 + 2y^2) : (2x^2 - y^2)$ is equal to:

A. 4 : 3   B. 3 : 4
C. 7 : 6   D. 6 : 7

41. Two equal sums are lent out at the same time at 6% and 5% per annum simple interest respectively. The first is received 2 years earlier than the other and the amount in each case is ₹ 6400. Each sum is:

A. ₹ 3200   B. ₹ 4000
C. ₹ 4200   D. ₹ 4500

42. A certain sum amounts to ₹ 5832 in 2 years at 8% compound interest. The same sum will amount to ₹ x in 4 years at the same rate at simple interest. The value of x is:

A. ₹ 6200   B. ₹ 6400
C. ₹ 6600   D. ₹ 6800

43. A sum of ₹ 3903 is distributed between A and B such that A's share at 4% compound interest per annum in 7 years equals B's share at the same rate of compound interest in 9 years. The difference of shares of A and B is:

A. ₹ 153   B. ₹ 154
C. ₹ 253   D. ₹ 254

44. A batsman has a certain average runs for 16 innings. In the 17th innings he made a score of 85 runs thereby increasing his average by 3. What is his average after 17th innings?

A. 34   B. 35
C. 36   D. 37

45. The average age of 24 boys and x girls is 12 years 8 months. The average age of boys is 13 years and that of girls is 12 years. The difference of the number of boys and x is:

A. 7   B. 8
C. 9   D. 12

46. A person has to cover a distance of 240 km in 6 hours. If he covers one-third of the distance in two-third of the time, what must be his speed (in km/hour) to cover the remaining distance in the remaining time?

A. $33\frac{1}{3}$ B. $66\frac{2}{3}$
C. 40   D. 80

47. The difference between the time taken by two cars to travel a distance of 350 km is 2 hours 20 minutes. If the difference between their speeds is 5 km/hour, the speed (in km/h) of the car that takes less time to travel is:

A. 25   B. 30
C. 32   D. 40

48. Two motor-boats are approaching each other. One of them is moving downstream with a speed of u km/hour and the other upstream with a speed of w km/hour. In one hour, the total distance covered by them is s km. If the speed of each boat in still water is x km/hour, then:

A. $x = \dfrac{s}{2}$ B. $x = \dfrac{s}{3}$
C. $2x = 3s$ D. $3x = 2s$

49. A can do $\dfrac{1}{4}$ of a work in 5 days, while B can do $\dfrac{5}{6}$ of the same work in 25 days. They worked together for some time, then B left. If A completed the remaining work in 10 days, then B worked for:

A. 12 days   B. 10 days
C. 9 days   D. 6 days

50. A can do a piece of work in 9 days, B in $13\frac{1}{2}$ days and C in 18 days. They start working together, but A leaves 2 days and B 3 days before completion of work and C alone continues till the work is finished. In what time is the entire work completed?

A. 6 days   B. 8 days
C. 9 days   D. 10 days

51. Salts formed from strong acids and weak bases are:

A. Acidic   B. Basic
C. Neutral   D. Amphoteric

52. Aqueous solution of sodium chloride is called:

A. Brine   B. Aqua regia
C. Aerosol   D. Emulsion

53. The first shell or orbit in an atom is designated as:

A. K-shell   B. L-shell
C. M-shell   D. N-shell

54. Eka-Aluminium refers to:
A. Scandium   B. Gallium
C. Silicon   D. Germanium

55. The most electronegative atom in the modern periodic table is:
A. Fluorine   B. Chlorine
C. Bromine   D. Iodine

56. Carbon participates in bonding by:
A. Losing 4 electrons
B. Gaining 2 electrons
C. Gaining 4 electrons
D. Sharing 4 electrons

57. If in a solution, the OH^- concentration is greater than H^+ ion concentration, the solution will have pH:
A. less than 7   B. greater than 7
C. equal to 7   D. greater than 14

58. Electrical energy changes into chemical energy when current passes:
A. Electrolyte   B. Heater
C. Motor   D. Generator

59. The work done in taking a test charge 'q' around the complete circuit of the cell is called:
A. Potential difference   B. E.M.F
C. Volt   D. Ampere

60. The reciprocal of the resistance is ....
A. conductance   B. resistivity
C. capacitance   D. inductance

61. The temperature of an object is 60°C. Its value in Fahrenheit scale is:
A. 120°F   B. 130°F
C. 140°F   D. 110°F

62. The elements having same mass number but different atomic numbers are:
A. isobars   B. isomers
C. isotones   D. isotopes

63. Which is the longest part in the alimentary canal of human being?
A. Small intestine
B. Large intestine
C. Oesophagus
D. Stomach

64. How many pairs of legs are found in insects?
A. 02   B. 03
C. 04   D. 19

65. Identify the water-soluble vitamin from the following:
A. Vitamin A   B. Vitamin B_1
C. Vitamin D   D. Vitamin E

66. Which of the following activity is not responsible for greenhouse effect?
A. Use of solar car for transport
B. Use of wood as fuel
C. Emission from thermal power plant
D. Use of petrol vehicles for transport

67. Which cell organelle utilizes light energy during photosynthesis?
A. Mitochondria   B. Golgi body
C. Ribosome   D. Plastid

68. Identify the correctly matched pair from the following options:
A. Colon   –   Small Intestine
B. Bronchi   –   Lungs
C. Pons   –   Adrenal gland
D. Alveoli   –   Liver

69. Identify the micronutrients of crop plants from the following:
A. Magnesium   B. Manganese
C. Potassium   D. Sulphur

70. Number of Coliform is a measure for:
A. pH of water
B. chemical pollution in water
C. turbidity of water
D. microbial contamination of water

71. Which of the following substances is used to remove permanent hardness of water?
A. Gypsum   B. Plaster of paris
C. Washing soda   D. Benzene

72. Which of the following Metals will burn in air with dazzling brilliant light?
A. Copper   B. Iron
C. Magnesium   D. Zinc

73. The direction of induced current is obtained by:

A. Flemings right hand rule
B. Elock rule
C. Faraday's law
D. Fleming's left hand rule

74. The necessary condition for a conductor to obey Ohm's law:
A. voltage remains constant
B. current remains constant
C. temperature remains constant
D. nature of material

75. A particle having no charge and no mass is:
A. positron
B. neutron
C. electron
D. neutrino

76. Which of the following is the highest peak of Vindhya range in India?
A. Kalumar
B. Duphgarh
C. Lushai
D. Guru Shikhar

77. Which of the following River's source is Mahabaleshwar in Maharashtra?
A. Mahanadi
B. Krishna
C. Narmada
D. Godavari

78. Which of the following Dam is built in Kerala?
A. Tungbhadra
B. Cheruthoni
C. Koyna
D. Mettur

79. Which of the following belongs from Kharif crop in India?
A. Wheat
B. Barley
C. Cotton
D. Sesame

80. Which of the following Two-wheeler manufacturing units situated at Waluj, Aurangabad?
A. Bajaj
B. Hero
C. TVS
D. Honda

81. Who founded the Mughal empire in India?
A. Ibrahim Lodi
B. Babur
C. Nadir Shah
D. Shershah Suri

82. During First war of Independence, 1857, Kanpur region rose to oppose the British rule where Nana Saheb's Palace at ____ served as its headquarters.
A. Bithoor
B. Pokhraya
C. Fatehgarh
D. Bibighar

83. Gandhiji was imprisoned at ______ jail following 'Quit India' resolution in 1942.
A. Yervada
B. Aga Khan Palace
C. Transvaal
D. Bombay

84. Which of the following King did not belong to Mauryan dynasty?
A. Bindusar
B. Ashoka the great
C. Brihadratha
D. Harshvardhan

85. The capital of India was moved to Delhi from which city?
A. Bombay
B. Madras
C. Calcutta
D. Mysore

86. Which one among the following is not an Inert Gas?
A. Helium
B. Neon
C. Radon
D. Hydrogen

87. Vijayanagara's Empire ancient city of Hampi is situated in ______ state of southern India.
A. Tamil Nadu
B. Andhra Pradesh
C. Kerala
D. Karnataka

88. Which of the following Articles of Indian Constitution describes the abolition of untouchability?
A. Article 14
B. Article 15
C. Article 16
D. Article 17

89. Which of the following Indian state have the maximum representation in Lok Sabha?
A. Maharashtra
B. Uttar Pradesh
C. Tamil Nadu
D. Bihar

90. Which of the following is the study of spiders?
A. Arachnology
B. Anthropology
C. Apiology
D. Cynology

91. Which of the following folk dance belongs from Karnataka?
A. Balakat
B. Kolattam
C. Kargam
D. Padayani

92. Which of the following painting forms have been originated in Western Ghats of India?
A. Warli
B. Phad
C. Patachitra
D. Kalighat

93. "Losar" festival is celebrated in _______ State of India.
A. Assam
B. Manipur
C. Arunachal Pradesh
D. Meghalya

94. Which among the following is the largest memory size of a Computer?
A. Petabyte   B. Yottabyte
C. Terabyte   D. Gigabyte

95. What is the minimum age required to become the Prime Minister of India?
A. 21 years   B. 25 years
C. 30 years   D. 35 years

96. The source of river Narmada is
A. Amarkantak hills
B. Sahyadri hills
C. Maikal hills
D. Nilgiri hills

97. Who was the first Indian to travel in space?
A. Rakesh Sharma
B. Kalpana Chawla
C. Sunita Williams
D. Ravish Malhotra

98. Which among the following countries is not the member of ASEAN?
A. Singapore   B. Thailand
C. Indonesia   D. India

99. Which among the following place's Atomic Power station is newest one?
A. Kaiga   B. Tarapore
C. Kudankulam   D. Kakrapar

100. Dugong, a vulnerable marine mammal is found in the _______ Marine wildlife Sanctuary.
A. Malvan
B. Gihirmatha
C. Gulf of Mannar
D. Gulf of Kutch

ANSWERS

1	2	3	4	5	6	7	8	9	10
C	C	B	B	D	D	D	D	D	B
11	12	13	14	15	16	17	18	19	20
C	C	A	D	C	B	C	A	B	B
21	22	23	24	25	26	27	28	29	30
D	A	D	D	B	D	B	C	A	C
31	32	33	34	35	36	37	38	39	40
D	C	A	D	B	A	D	B	A	D
41	42	43	44	45	46	47	48	49	50
B	C	A	D	D	D	B	A	D	A
51	52	53	54	55	56	57	58	59	60
A	A	A	B	A	D	B	A	A	A
61	62	63	64	65	66	67	68	69	70
C	A	A	B	B	A	D	B	B	D
71	72	73	74	75	76	77	78	79	80
C	C	A	C	D	A	B	B	C	A
81	82	83	84	85	86	87	88	89	90
B	A	B	D	C	D	D	D	B	A
91	92	93	94	95	96	97	98	99	100
A	A	C	B	B	A	A	D	C	C

EXPLANATORY ANSWERS

1. Rajiv Gandhi Airport is situated in Hyderabad. and Indira Gandhi Airport is situated in Delhi.

2. Since,

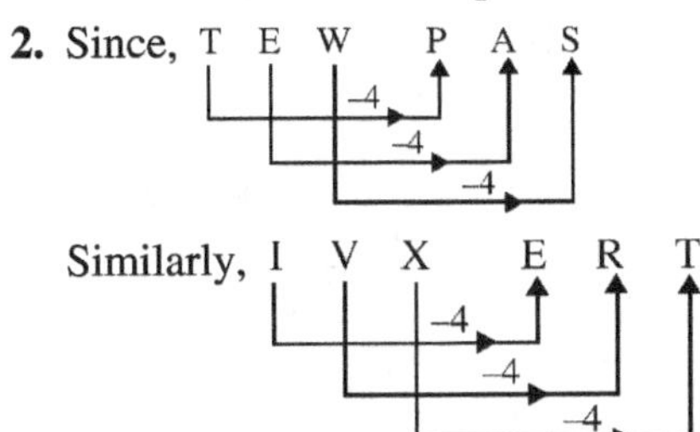

Similarly,

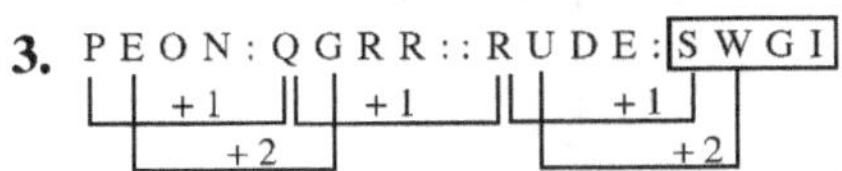

3. P E O N : Q G R R :: R U D E : S W G I

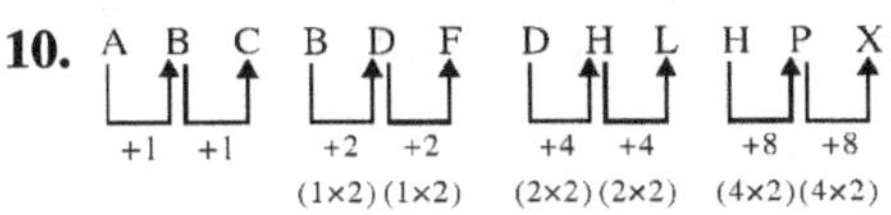

Hence, SWGI will come at the place of question mark.

4. 167 : 43 :: 245 : ?

$$7 \times 6 + 1 = 43$$

Similarly, $5 \times 4 + 2 = 22$

Hence, 22 will come at the place of question mark.

7. 286 $\Rightarrow$ 2 + 6 = 8

374 $\Rightarrow$ 3 + 4 = 7

143 $\Rightarrow$ 1 + 3 = 4

279 $\Rightarrow$ 2 + 9 = 11 $\neq$ 7

Hence, 279 is odd one out

8. 358 = 3 + 5 + 8 = 16

853 = 8 + 5 + 3 = 16

538 = 5 + 3 + 8 = 16

But 240 = 2 + 4 + 0 = 6.

9. Thousand, Ten thousand, Lakh, Ten Lakh ?

Hence, Crore will come at the place of question mark.

10.

A B C B D F D H L H P X

+1 +1 +2 +2 +4 +4 +8 +8

(1×2)(1×2) (2×2)(2×2) (4×2)(4×2)

12. 15 32 99 400 2005

×2+2 ×3+3 ×4+4 ×5+5

Hence, 2005 will come at the place of question mark.

13.

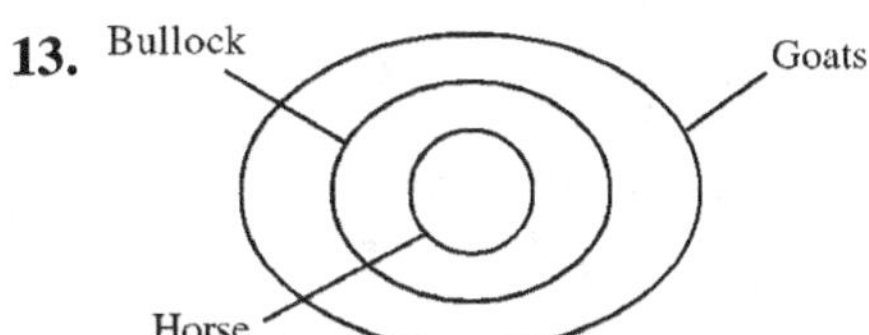

From Figure it is clear that all Horses are Goats.

14. Elephant $\rightarrow$ Dog $\rightarrow$ Tiger $\rightarrow$ Lion $\rightarrow$ Deer

$\because$ Deer was the fastest. The Lion ran faster than the Tiger.

Hence, Lion was the second to finish the race.

15. Cajole, Clandestine, Cover, Coward

Hence, Option (C) is correct.

16. Given:

N I G E R I A
↓ ↓ ↓ ↓ ↓ ↓ ↓
@ # ^ $? # *

Similarly, G I N G E R
↓ ↓ ↓ ↓ ↓ ↓
^ # @ ^ $?

Hence, Option (B) is correct.

17.

45	55	26
50	51	65
60	49	?

$45 + 50 + 60 = 155$

$55 + 51 + 49 = 155$

$26 + 65 + 64 = 155$

Hence, 64 will come at the place of question mark.

18. '−' means '+'; '×' means '÷'

'÷' means '×'; '+' means '−'

$26 - 400 \div 20 + 21 \times 12$

$= 26 - 20 + 252$

$= 278 - 20$

$= 258.$

19. ABAABBAAABBB

Hence, AAAB is correct option.

20.

$$AE = AD + DE$$
$$= 100 \text{ m} + 55 \text{ m}$$
$$= 155 \text{ m}$$

Hence, the distance between the initial and the final position of the cat = 155 m.

21. Let present age of Geeta is x years and Henna's age is y years.

10 years ago,

Geeta's age = $(x - 10)$ years

Hema's age = $(y - 10)$ years

$$2(x - 10) = y - 10$$
$$\Rightarrow \qquad 2x - y = 10 \qquad \qquad ...(i)$$

After 10 years,

Hema's age = 40 years

$$\Rightarrow \qquad y + 10 = 40$$
$$\Rightarrow \qquad y = 30$$

Putting the value of y in (i)

$$2x - 30 = 10$$
$$\Rightarrow \qquad 2x = 40$$
$$\Rightarrow \qquad x = 20$$

Hence, present age of Geeta = 20 years.

24. $10 - 3 = 12$

$(10 + 3) - (1 + 0) = 13 - 1 = 12$

$\qquad \qquad 12 - 4 = 13$

$(12 + 4) - (1 + 2) = 16 - 3 = 13$

$\qquad \qquad 14 - 5 = 14$

$(14 + 5) - (1 + 4) = 19 - 5 = 14$

$\therefore \qquad 16 - 6 = (16 + 6) - (1 + 6)$
$$= 22 - 7$$
$$= 15.$$

25.

1	3	5	4	6	0	8	7	2
↓	↓	↓	↓	↓	↓	↓	↓	↓
A	O	Z	L	D	T	N	H	Q

Hence, Code for

2	1	5	0	0	is
↓	↓	↓	↓	↓	
Q	A	Z	T	T	

26.

$$\frac{\sqrt[6]{2}\left[\left(5^4\right)^{\frac{3}{5}} \times \left(2^{10}\right)^{\frac{-6}{5}} \div \left(5^2\right)^{\frac{3}{5}}\right]^{\frac{1}{2}}}{\left(2^{\frac{7}{3}}\right)^{\frac{-5}{2}} \times \left(5^3\right)^{\frac{1}{5}}}$$

$$= \frac{\sqrt[6]{2}\left[5^{\frac{12}{5} - \frac{6}{5}} \times 2^{-12}\right]^{\frac{1}{2}}}{2^{\frac{-35}{6}} \times 5^{\frac{3}{5}}} = \frac{\sqrt[6]{2}\left[5^{\frac{6}{5} \times \frac{1}{2}} \times 2^{-6}\right]}{2^{\frac{-35}{6}} \times 5^{\frac{3}{5}}}$$

$$= \sqrt[6]{2}\left[5^{\frac{3}{5} - \frac{3}{5}} \times 2^{-6 + \frac{35}{6}}\right] = \sqrt[6]{2}\left[5^0 \times 2^{\frac{-1}{6}}\right]$$

$$= 2^{\frac{1}{6}} \times 2^{\frac{-1}{6}} \times 1 = 2^{\frac{1}{6} - \frac{1}{6}} \times 1$$

$$= 2^0 \times 1 = 1 \times 1 = 1.$$

27. Let $4.669 = a$ and $2.331 = b$

The given expression is

$$= \frac{a \times a - b \times b}{a^2 + b^2 + 2ab} = \frac{a^2 - b^2}{(a+b)^2}$$

$$= \frac{(a+b)(a-b)}{(a+b)(a+b)} = \frac{a-b}{a+b}$$

$$= \frac{4.669 - 2.331}{4.669 + 2.331} = \frac{2.338}{7} = 0.334.$$

28. $25 - 5[2 + 3\{2 - 2(5 - 3) + 5\} - 10] \div 5$

$= 25 - 5[2 + 3\{2 - 2 \times 2 + 5\} - 10] \div 5$

$= 25 - 5[2 + 3\{7 - 4\} - 10] \div 5$

$= 25 - 5[2 + 9 - 10] \div 5$

$= 25 - 5[1] \div 5$

$= 25 - 5 \div 5 = 25 - 1 = 24.$

29.

$$1 + \cfrac{1}{\sqrt{5} + \cfrac{1}{\frac{5+1}{\sqrt{5}}}} = 1 + \cfrac{1}{\sqrt{5} + \cfrac{\sqrt{5}}{6}} = 1 + \cfrac{1}{\frac{7\sqrt{5}}{6}}$$

$$= 1 + \frac{6}{7\sqrt{5}} \times \frac{\sqrt{5}}{\sqrt{5}} = 1 + \frac{6\sqrt{5}}{35}$$

$$1 + \frac{6\sqrt{5}}{35} = a + b\sqrt{5}$$

$$\Rightarrow \qquad a = 1 \text{ and } b = \frac{6}{35}$$

$$\therefore \qquad a - b = 1 - \frac{6}{35} = \frac{35-6}{35} = \frac{29}{35}.$$

30. L.C.M. of 5, 10, 12 and 15 = 60

Least no. = 60 + 2 = 62

But 62 is not divisible by 7

$$\therefore \qquad 60 \times 2 = 120 + 2 = 122$$

which is not divisible by 7

$$\therefore \qquad 60 \times 3 = 180 + 2 = 182$$

which is divisible by 7

Hence, required value of x = 182

Sum of the digits of x = 1 + 8 + 2 = 11.

31. $\because$ H.C.F. = 103

and L.C.M. = 103 × 187 = 19261

Let the numbers are $103x$ and $103y$

$$\text{L.C.M.} = 103xy$$

$$103xy = 19261$$

$$\Rightarrow \qquad xy = \frac{19261}{103} = 187$$

$$187 = 1 \times 187 \qquad (x = 1, y = 187)$$

or $\qquad 187 = 11$ and $y = 17$

$$(\because 11 \times 17 = 187)$$

when $x = 11$, then first no. = 103 × 11 = 1133

when $y = 17$, then 2nd no. = 103 × 17 = 1751

Sum of the numbers = 1133 + 1751 = 2884.

32. Let Man's income = ₹ 100

$$\text{Saving} = \frac{40}{100} \times 100 = ₹ 40$$

$$\text{Expenditure} = 100 - 40 = ₹ 60$$

$$\text{Now, his income} = 100 + \frac{10}{100} \times 100 = ₹ 110$$

$$\text{Expenditure} = 60 + \frac{25}{100} \times 60 = ₹ 75$$

$$\text{His saving} = 110 - 75 = ₹ 35$$

$$\text{Required \% saving} = \frac{35}{110} \times 100 = \frac{350}{11}$$

$$= 32\% \text{ (Approx.)}$$

33. Let the price of machine = ₹ x

$$\text{Freight} = \frac{20}{100} \times x = \frac{x}{5}$$

$$\text{C.P.} = x + \frac{x}{5} = \frac{6x}{5}$$

According to the question,

$$\frac{10}{100} \text{ of } \frac{6x}{5} = 4800$$

$$\Rightarrow \qquad 6x = 4800 \times 50$$

$$x = \frac{4800 \times 50}{6}$$

$$= 800 \times 50 = 40000$$

Hence, the price of machine = ₹ 40000.

34. Let D got 100 marks

$$\text{C got marks} = 100 - \frac{20}{100} \times 100 = 80$$

$$\text{Marks obtained by B} = 80 + \frac{25}{100} \times 80$$

$$= 80 + 20 = 100$$

$$\text{Marks obtained by A} = 100 - \frac{10}{100} \times 100$$

$$= 100 - 10 = 90$$

When A got 90 marks, then D got 100

When A got 720 marks, then D got

$$= \frac{100}{90} \times 720 = 800$$

$$\text{\% of D} = \frac{800}{1000} \times 100 = 80\%$$

Hence, marks obtained by D = 80%.

35.

$$\frac{10}{100} \times 1200 = ₹ 120$$

$$1200 - 120 = ₹ 1080$$

$$\text{Again, } \frac{20}{100} \times 1080 = ₹ 216$$

$$1080 - 216 = ₹ 864$$

$$\text{Transportation} = \frac{10}{100} \times 864 = ₹ 86.4$$

C.P. = 864 + 86.4 = 950.4

$$\text{Profit} = \frac{20}{100} \times 950.4$$

$$= 190.08$$

S.P. = 950.4 + 190.08

$$= ₹\ 1140.48.$$

36. $\qquad$ Discount = $16\dfrac{2}{3}\%$ of 720

$$= \frac{50}{3 \times 100} \times 720 = ₹\ 120$$

S.P. = 720 − 120 = ₹ 600

100 + 25 = 125

When S.P. ₹ 125, then C.P. = ₹ 100

When S.P. ₹ 600, then C.P. = $\dfrac{100}{125} \times 600$

C.P. = 4 × 120 = ₹ 480

Now S.P. = 720 − 160 = ₹ 560

Profit = 560 − 480 = ₹ 80

$$\text{Profit }\% = \frac{80}{480} \times 100$$

$$= \frac{50}{3} = 16\frac{2}{3}\%.$$

37. Let the vessel contains $4x\,l$ and $3x\,l$ of alcohol and water respectively

Amount of alcohol in 14 l solution

$$= \frac{4}{7} \times 14 = 8l$$

$$\text{Amount of water} = \frac{3}{7} \times 14 = 6l$$

According to the question,

$$\frac{4x - 8}{3x - 6 + 14} = \frac{3}{4}$$

$$\Rightarrow \qquad \frac{4x - 8}{3x + 8} = \frac{3}{4}$$

$$\Rightarrow \qquad 16x - 32 = 9x + 24$$

$$\Rightarrow \qquad 7x = 56 \Rightarrow x = 8$$

∴ Capacity of vessel = $7x = 7 \times 8 = 56\ l.$

38. $\qquad \dfrac{A}{B} = \dfrac{1}{2} \Rightarrow A = \dfrac{B}{2}$

$$\frac{B}{C} = \frac{3}{2} \Rightarrow C = \frac{2B}{3}$$

$$\frac{C}{D} = \frac{8}{9} \Rightarrow D = \frac{9C}{8} = \frac{9}{8} \times \frac{2B}{3} = \frac{3B}{4}$$

A + B + C + D = 3535

$$\Rightarrow \qquad \frac{B}{2} + B + \frac{2B}{3} + \frac{3B}{4} = 3535$$

$$\Rightarrow \qquad \frac{6B + 12B + 8B + 9B}{12} = 3535$$

$$\Rightarrow \qquad 35B = 12 \times 3535$$

$$\Rightarrow \qquad B = \frac{12 \times 3535}{35}$$

$$= 12 \times 101 = 1212$$

$$D = \frac{3B}{4} = \frac{3}{4} \times 1212$$

$$= 3 \times 303 = 909$$

B − D = 1212 − 909 = 303

Hence, the difference in shares of B and D

$$= 303.$$

39. Let the number of ₹ 1, 50 paise and 25 paise *coins* be $2x$, $3x$ and $10x$ respectively.

According to the question,

$$\frac{2x}{1} + \frac{3x}{2} + \frac{10x}{4} = 288$$

$$\Rightarrow \qquad \frac{8x + 6x + 10x}{4} = 288$$

$$\Rightarrow \qquad 24x = 4 \times 288$$

$$\Rightarrow \qquad x = \frac{4 \times 288}{24}$$

$$= 4 \times 12 = 48$$

Number of ₹ 1 coins = $2x = 2 \times 48 = 96$

Number of 50 paise coins

$$= 3x = 3 \times 48 = 144$$

Difference = 144 − 96 = 48.

40. $\because \quad \dfrac{x^2 - y^2}{x^2 + y^2} = \dfrac{3}{5}$

$\Rightarrow \quad 5x^2 - 5y^2 = 3x^2 + 3y^2$

$\Rightarrow \quad 2x^2 = 8y^2$

$\Rightarrow \quad x^2 = 4y^2$

Now, $\dfrac{x^2 + 2y^2}{2x^2 - y^2} = \dfrac{4y^2 + 2y^2}{8y^2 - y^2} = \dfrac{6y^2}{7y^2} = \dfrac{6}{7}$

Hence, $(x^2 + 2y^2) : (2x^2 - y^2) = 6 : 7$.

41. $\dfrac{P \times r_1 \times (t - 2)}{100} = \dfrac{P \times r_2 \times t}{100}$

$\Rightarrow \quad 6 \times (t - 2) = 5t$

$\Rightarrow \quad 6t - 12 = 5t$

$\Rightarrow \quad t = 12 \text{ years}$

$$\text{S.I.} = \dfrac{P \times 6 \times 10}{100} = \dfrac{3P}{5}$$

$$P + \text{S.I.} = 6400$$

$$P + \dfrac{3P}{5} = 6400$$

$\Rightarrow \quad 8P = 6400 \times 5$

$\Rightarrow \quad P = \dfrac{6400 \times 5}{8} = 4000$

Hence, each sum = ₹ 4000.

42. Let, $\qquad P = ₹\ 100$

$$A = 100 \left(1 + \dfrac{8}{100}\right)^2$$

$$= 100 \times \dfrac{27}{25} \times \dfrac{27}{25} = \dfrac{2916}{25}$$

When amount ₹ $\dfrac{2916}{25}$, then P = ₹ 100

When amount ₹ 5832, then P

$$= \dfrac{100 \times 25}{2916} \times 5832$$

$\therefore \qquad P = ₹\ 5000$

Now, $\qquad \text{S.I.} = \dfrac{5000 \times 8 \times 4}{100} = 1600$

$\therefore \qquad$ Amount = 5000 + 1600 = ₹ 6600.

43. Let A's share = ₹ x

and B's share = $3903 - x$

According to the question,

$$\dfrac{\left(1 + \dfrac{4}{100}\right)^9}{\left(1 + \dfrac{4}{100}\right)^7} = \dfrac{x}{3903 - x}$$

$\Rightarrow \qquad \left(1 + \dfrac{4}{100}\right)^2 = \dfrac{x}{3903 - x}$

$\Rightarrow \qquad \left(\dfrac{26}{25}\right)^2 = \dfrac{x}{3903 - x}$

$$\dfrac{676}{625} = \dfrac{x}{3903 - x}$$

$\Rightarrow 676 \times 3903 - 676x = 625x$

$\Rightarrow \qquad 1301x = 676 \times 3903$

$\Rightarrow \qquad x = \dfrac{676 \times 3903}{1301}$

$$= 676 \times 3 = 2028$$

A's Share = ₹ 2028

B's Share = $3903 - 2028 = ₹\ 1875$

The difference of shares of A and B

$$= 2028 - 1875 = ₹\ 153.$$

44. Let average for 16 innings be x

then, $\qquad \dfrac{16x + 85}{17} = x + 3$

$\Rightarrow \qquad 16x + 85 = 17x + 51$

$\Rightarrow \qquad 17x - 16x = 85 - 51 \Rightarrow x = 34$

Hence, average after 17 innings

$$= 34 + 3 = 37.$$

45. Total age of 24 boys and x girls

$$= (24 + x) \times 12\dfrac{8}{12} = (24 + x) \times \dfrac{38}{3}$$

Total age of 24 boys = 24×13

Total age of x girls = $12 \times x$

$$(24 + x) \times \dfrac{38}{3} = 24 \times 13 + 12x$$

$\Rightarrow \quad 24 \times 38 + 38x = 24 \times 13 \times 3 + 36x$

$\Rightarrow \qquad\qquad 2x = 24 \times 39 - 24 \times 38$

$\qquad\qquad\qquad = 24\,(39 - 38)$

$\Rightarrow \qquad\qquad 2x = 24 \times 1 = 24$

$\Rightarrow \qquad\qquad x = 12$

Required difference $= 24 - 12 = 12$.

46. 240 km travelled in 6 hours

$\dfrac{1}{3}$ of 240 km = 80 km and $\dfrac{2}{3}$ of 6 hours

$$= \dfrac{2}{3} \times 6 = 4 \text{ hours}$$

Remaining distance $= 240 - 80 = 160$ km

Remaining time $= 6 - 4 = 2$ hours

$$\text{Speed} = \dfrac{160}{2} = 80 \text{ km/hour.}$$

47. Let speed of slow car $= x$ km/hr

and speed of fast car $= (x + 5)$ km/hr

According to the question,

$$\dfrac{350}{x} - \dfrac{350}{x+5} = 2\dfrac{20}{60}$$

$\Rightarrow \qquad 350\left(\dfrac{x+5-x}{x(x+5)}\right) = \dfrac{7}{3}$

$\Rightarrow \qquad\qquad x^2 + 5x = 750$

$\Rightarrow \qquad\qquad x^2 + 5x - 750 = 0$

$\Rightarrow \quad x^2 + 30x - 25x - 750 = 0$

$\Rightarrow \quad x(x + 30) - 25(x + 30) = 0$

$\Rightarrow \qquad (x - 25)\,(x + 30) = 0$

$\Rightarrow \qquad\qquad x = 25 \text{ or } x = -30$

Hence, speed of slow car $= 25$ km/hr

Speed of fast car $= (25 + 5) = 30$ km/hr.

48. $\qquad$ Average speed $= \dfrac{\text{Total distance}}{\text{Total time}}$

$\Rightarrow \qquad\qquad x = \dfrac{S}{2}.$

49. A can do full work in 20 days

and B can do this work in 30 days

$\because$ A works alone for 10 days

$\therefore$ Work done by A in 10 days $= \dfrac{10}{20}$ work

$\therefore$ A + B do together $1 - \dfrac{10}{20} = \dfrac{10}{20}$ work

Now, A + B do 1 work in

$$\dfrac{20 \times 30}{20 + 30} = \dfrac{600}{50} = 12 \text{ days}$$

$\therefore$ A + B do $\dfrac{10}{20}$ work in $12 \times \dfrac{10}{20} = 6$ days

Hence, B worked for 6 days.

50. Let the work be finished in x days

According to the question,

$$\dfrac{x-2}{9} + \dfrac{2(x-3)}{27} + \dfrac{x}{18} = 1$$

$\Rightarrow \qquad \dfrac{x-2}{9} + \dfrac{2x-6}{27} + \dfrac{x}{18} = 1$

$\Rightarrow \qquad \dfrac{6(x-2)+2(2x-6)+3x}{54} = 1$

$\Rightarrow \quad 6x - 12 + 4x - 12 + 3x = 54$

$\Rightarrow \qquad\qquad 13x - 24 = 54$

$\Rightarrow \qquad\qquad 13x = 78$

$\Rightarrow \qquad\qquad x = 6$

Hence, the work be finished in 6 days.

Railway Recruitment Board (RRB)
GROUP 'D'
Recruitment Exam

1. Constant efforts to achieve something
   A. Perseverance
   B. Attempt
   C. Enthusiasm
   D. Vigour

2. The minimum voting age in India is:
   A. 16 years
   B. 18 years
   C. 21 years
   D. 24 years

3. If in a certain code CAT is written as DBU, then DOG will be written as:
   A. EOH
   B. DHP
   C. EPH
   D. HPE

4. Which of the following word does not figure in the Preamble of the Indian Constitution?
   A. Sovereign
   B. Democratic
   C. Socialist
   D. Welfare

5. If you write down all the numbers from 1 to 100, then how many times do you write 3?
   A. 11
   B. 18
   C. 20
   D. 21

6. The first Home Minister of Independent India was
   A. Jagjivan Ram
   B. Sardar Vallabhbhai Patel
   C. Maulana Abdul Kalam Azad
   D. Pandit Govind Ballabh Pant

7. The chemical name of table salt is :
   A. Potassium Chloride
   B. Calcium Chloride
   C. Sodium Chloride
   D. Magnesium Sulphate

8. What is the missing term in the following series: 11, 12, 17, 18, 23, 24, ____
   A. 27
   B. 29
   C. 30
   D. 35

9. River Nile flows in which country?
   A. Peru
   B. Egypt
   C. Canada
   D. Vietnam

10. Introducing Reeta, Monica said, "She is the only daughter of my father's only daughter." How is Monica related to Reeta?
    A. Aunt
    B. Niece
    C. Cousin
    D. Mother

11. Which game is Saina Nehwal associated with?
    A. Tennis
    B. Golf
    C. Boxing
    D. Badminton

12. Which British officer was responsible for the Jallianwala Bagh massacre?
    A. Maj Sleeman
    B. General Dyer
    C. Sir Arthur Wellesly
    D. Col Manson

13. If + means $\div$, $\div$ means –, – means ×, × means +, then $12 + 6 \div 3 - 2 \times 8 =$
    A. –2
    B. 2
    C. 8
    D. 4

14. Bhajan Sopori is associated with:
    A. Flute
    B. Shehnai
    C. Santoor
    D. Tabla

15. Who amongst the following was called as "Frontier Gandhi"?
    A. Lala Lajpat Rai
    B. Mohd. Ali Jinnah
    C. Khudiram Bose
    D. Khan Abdul Gaffar Khan

16. If $x^2 + x - 12 = 0$, values of x will be:
    A. –3, 4
    B. 3, –4
    C. –3, –4
    D. 3, 4

17. In which country is the famous Wimbledon Tennis Championship played?
A. England   B. France
C. Germany   D. USA

18. Dandi March is associated with:
A. Home Rule Movement
B. Non-cooperation Movement
C. Civil Disobedience Movement
D. Quit India Movement

19. 1st May is observed as:
A. UN Day
B. World AIDS Day
C. World Literacy Day
D. International Labour Day

20. What type of mirror is used by motorists to see road behind them?
A. Convex   B. Concave
C. Plain   D. Concavo-Convex

21. Which one of the following is a natural fibre?
A. Jute   B. Nylon
C. Acrylic   D. Polyester

22. Choose the correctly spelt word:
A. Exemple   B. Example
C. Exampel   D. Exampal

23. On a vertical pole, a monkey climbs 30 feet in one hour and then rests for a while during which he slips down 20 feet. He again starts climbing and slips back in the same manner. If he begins his ascent at 8 am, at what time will he first touch a flag on the pole at 120 feet from the ground?
A. 4 pm   B. 5 pm
C. 6 pm   D. 7 pm

24. At room temperature, the metal that remains liquid is:
A. Mercury   B. Platinum
C. Lead   D. Zinc

25. Which is known as carbolic acid?
A. Phenol   B. Ethanol
C. Acetic acid   D. Oxalic acid

26. What is the product of all the numbers in the dial of a telephone?
A. 362880   B. 388620
C. 366820   D. 0

27. Which of the following latitudes passes through India?
A. Equator
B. Tropic of Cancer
C. Tropic of Capricorn
D. Arctic Circle

28. Value of tan 45° is
A. 0   B. infinity
C. 1   D. $\dfrac{\sqrt{3}}{2}$

29. Which of the following is a rational number?
A. $\sqrt{2}$ B. $\sqrt{3}$
C. $\sqrt{4}$ D. $\sqrt{5}$

30. A man is walking at a speed of 9 kms/hr. After every km, he takes rest for 9 mins. How much time will he take to cover 27 kms?
A. 6 hrs   B. 6 hrs 45 mins
C. 6 hrs 54 mins   D. 6 hrs 35 mins

31. The tenure of a member of Rajya Sabha is:
A. 3 years   B. 4 years
C. 5 years   D. 6 years

32. Capital of Malaysia is:
A. Bangkok   B. Kuala Lumpur
C. Abu Dhabi   D. Doha

33. On which river is the Tehri dam built?
A. Alakananda   B. Bhagirathi
C. Ganga   D. Hooghly

34. Silk is obtained from cocoons and requires ________ trees.
A. Mulberry   B. Apple
C. Eucalyptus   D. Oak

35. With which country, India has the longest international boundary?
A. Nepal   B. Pakistan
C. China   D. Bangladesh

36. Earthquakes are caused by:
A. Denudation
B. Earth's Rotation
C. Movement of Tectonic Plates
D. Earth's Revolution

37. Which State in India has the largest coastline?
A. Tamil Nadu B. Andhra Pradesh
C. Gujrat D. West Bengal

38. Who composed the famous song "Sare Jahan se Achha"?
A. Jaidev
B. Mohammad Iqbal
C. Bankim Chandra Chatterjee
D. Rabindranath Tagore

39. Who is known as the Supreme Commander of the Indian Armed Forces?
A. President of India
B. Prime Minister of India
C. Defence Minister of India
D. Chief of the Army Staff of Indian Army

40. In which year was the Quit India Movement launched?
A. 1939 B. 1940
C. 1942 D. 1946

41. Volume of a cylinder of base with radius 'r' and height 'h' is

A. $\dfrac{1}{3}\pi r^2 h$ B. $\dfrac{2}{3}\pi r^2 h$

C. $\dfrac{4}{3}\pi r^2 h$ D. $\pi r^2 h$

42. If $x^2 - y^2 = 80$ and $x - y = 8$, then the average of x and y is:
A. 2 B. 3
C. 4 D. 5

43. Ankit started walking towards North. After walking 30 meters, he turned towards left and walked 40 meters. He then turned left and walked 30 meters. He again turned left and walked 50 meters. How far is he from his original position?
A. 50 meters B. 40 meters
C. 30 meters D. 10 meters

44. "Azad Hind Fauj" is associated with which of the following?
A. Jawaharlal Nehru
B. Chandrasekhar Azad
C. Bhagat Singh
D. Subhash Chandra Bose

45. Which of the following is correct?
A. $(a - b)(a + b) = a^2 - b^2$
B. $(a + b)^2 = a^2 + b^2 - 2ab$
C. $(a + b)^3 = a^3 + b^3$
D. $(a - b)^2 = a^2 + b^2 + 2ab$

46. Jog falls in Karnataka is located over which river?
A. Kaveri B. Godavari
C. Saraswati D. Krishna

47. Who is associated with "White Revolution"?
A. M.S. Swaminathan B. J.P. Narayan
C. V. Kurien D. Baba Amte

48. The United Nations Security Council has ____ Permanent members:
A. 3 B. 5
C. 7 D. 15

49. Telengana was carved out of which state?
A. Andhra Pradesh B. Bihar
C. Karnataka D. Tamil Nadu

50. Dronacharya Award is given to:
A. Scientists
B. Movie Actors and actresses
C. Sports Coaches
D. Sportspersons

51. Which of the following is the largest planet of the solar system?
A. Saturn B. Uranus
C. Neptune D. Jupiter

52. The largest fresh water lake in J&K is
A. Wullar B. Dal
C. Manasbal D. Anchar

53. Which of the following gases is primarily responsible for global warming?
A. Nitrogen B. Noble gases
C. Sulphates D. Carbon dioxide

54. Lok Sabha is also called:
A. Council of States B. Upper House
C. Lower House D. None of the above

55. A student got twice as many sums wrong as he got right. If he attempted 48 sums in all, how many did he solve correctly?
A. 32 B. 16
C. 18 D. 24

56. A train of 500 meters of length is moving at a speed of 90 kms/hr. How much time will it take to cross an electric pole located by the side of the railway track.
A. 10 seconds
B. 20 seconds
C. 30 seconds
D. 40 seconds

57. Which of the following state in India does not have a sea coast?
A. Maharashtra
B. Gujarat
C. Karnataka
D. Jharkhand

58. Choose the word with the correct spelling
A. Vahicle
B. Vehicle
C. Vahical
D. Vehicel

59. Professor Amartya Sen is famous in which of the fields?
A. Biochemistry
B. Electronics
C. Economics
D. Geology

60. The number of Lok Sabha seats from Jammu & Kashmir State is:
A. 4
B. 5
C. 6
D. 7

61. In which of the following market forms, a firm does not exercise control over price?
A. Monopoly
B. Perfect competition
C. Oligopoly
D. Monopolistic competition

62. Introducing a man, Shefali said, "He is the only son of the mother of my mother." How is Shefali related to the man?
A. Mother
B. Sister
C. Niece
D. Maternal Aunt

63. A dice is thrown once. Probability of getting an even number is:
A. 1/2
B. 1/3
C. 1/4
D. 1/6

64. Find what will be the simple interest on the Principal Amount of ₹ 1000 for 10 months at interest rate of 6% per annum.
A. ₹ 60
B. ₹ 30
C. ₹ 50
D. ₹ 10

65. In a right angle triangle, one angle is 15°, the other angle can be:
A. 15°
B. 75°
C. 115°
D. 65°

66. Unit of inheritance is called:
A. Nucleus
B. Gene
C. Cell
D. Tissue

67. Pashmina wool is obtained from:
A. Sheep
B. Yak
C. Goat
D. Camel

68. Loudness of sound is measured in
A. decibel (dB)
B. hertz (Hz)
C. metre (m)
D. metre/second (m/s)

69. Find the missing term:
ZA, YB, XC,____, VE, UF
A. WD
B. DW
C. UW
D. WU

70. Chemical formula for water is:
A. HO
B. H_2O
C. H_3O
D. H_2O_2

71. Blood group AB has
A. No antigen
B. No antibody
C. Neither antigen nor antibody
D. Both antigen and antibody

72. India shares longest international boundary with which of the following country?
A. Bangladesh
B. China
C. Nepal
D. Bhutan

73. A box contains 7 red balls, 8 green balls and 5 blue balls. When one ball is randomly drawn from the box, probability of its being a blue ball will be:
A. 1/2
B. 1/3
C. 1/4
D. 1/5

74. Malik is fourteen from right end in a row of 40 boys. What is his position from the left end?
A. 27th
B. 26th
C. 25th
D. 24th

75. The personality not connected with 1857 mutiny is:
A. Tantia Tope
B. Lakshmibai
C. Subhas Chandra Bose
D. Mangal Pandey

76. A bus for Delhi leaves every thirty minutes from a bus stand. An enquiry clerk told a passenger that the bus had already left ten minutes ago and the next bus will leave at 9:35 am. At what time did the enquiry clerk give this information to the passenger?
A. 9:15 am   B. 9:08 am
C. 8:55 am   D. 9:10 am

77. Who gave the slogan–"Swaraj is my birthright and I shall have it."?
A. Bhagat Singh
B. Sukhdev
C. Bal Gangadhar Tilak
D. Raj Guru

78. In an equilateral triangle:
A. all sides are equal
B. all angles are equal
C. both A & B are correct
D. both A & B are incorrect

79. Which Vitamins are those, if taken in excess can be dangerous as they are stored in the body?
A. B Complex   B. E and C
C. B and C   D. A and D

80. Find the right alternative in the given series: BEG, DGI, FIK, HKM, ___.
A. JMO   B. KMO
C. JML   D. JNP

81. Atomic explosion is triggered by:
A. thermo nuclear reaction
B. chemical reaction
C. controlled chain reaction
D. uncontrolled chain reaction

82. The phenomenon of change in direction of light when it passes from one medium to another is called:
A. Propagation   B. Reflection
C. Refraction   D. Dispersion

83. Rajatarangini, the famous chronology of Kashmir Kings was written by:
A. Parmanand
B. Kalhana
C. Zinda Kaul
D. Ghulam Ahmad Mahjoor

84. A circle is drawn inside a square having side as 'a' touching all the four sides of the square. Area of that circle will be:
A. πa^2 B. $\dfrac{\pi a^2}{2}$
C. $\dfrac{\pi a^2}{4}$ D. $4\,\pi a^2$

85. Choose the correct alternative:
Car : Garage as Aeroplane :
A. Port   B. Depot
C. Hangar   D. Harbour

86. If in a class of 37 students standing in a straight line, the place of Radha and Sita are 10th and 16th respectively, what are their places from the last?
A. 28th and 22nd   B. 27th and 21st
C. 28th and 20th   D. 27th and 22nd

87. Vitamin D deficient patient is recommended:
A. Sun bath
B. Sauna bath
C. Cold and Hot water bath
D. Massage

88. India is a "Secular" state. It means that the Indian State:
A. favours only selected religions
B. favours the religion of the majority community
C. favours the religion of the minority community
D. favours no particular religion

89. What is the currency of Bangladesh called?
A. Dinar   B. Rial
C. Taka   D. Rupees

90. Who has the right to decide whether a Bill is a money bill or not?
A. Speaker of Lok Sabha
B. Prime Minister
C. President
D. Finance Minister

91. Lack of __________ causes Diabetes.
A. Sugar   B. Insulin
C. Calcium   D. Vitamins

92. The discretionary powers of a Governor is limited in
A. Appointment of Chief Minister

   B. Dismissal of the Ministry
   C. Dissolution of the Legislative Assembly
   D. Assent to Bills

93. The force involved in falling of an apple from a tree is:
   A. Magnetic Force   B. Gravitational Force
   C. Contact Force   D. Electrostatic Force

94. Who is the first law officer of the country?
   A. Chief Justice of India
   B. Attorney General
   C. Law Minister
   D. Solicitor General

95. Which of the following is widely used as an anaesthetic?
   A. Chloroform   B. Methane
   C. Ammonia   D. Chlorine

96. FDI refers to:
   A. Fixed Deposit Interest
   B. Fixed Deposit Investment
   C. Future Derivative Investment
   D. Foreign Direct Investment

97. Which one of the following gases is given out during photosynthesis?
   A. Carbon dioxide   B. Nitrogen
   C. Hydrogen   D. Oxygen

98. Find the missing number:
25, 49, 81,___, 169, 225
   A. 100   B. 121
   C. 144   D. None of the above

99. Who was the first woman President of Indian National Congress?
   A. Sarojini Naidu   B. Annie Besant
   C. Sucheta Kriplani   D. Aruna Asaf Ali

100. Which is the capital of Arunachal Pradesh?
   A. Dispur   B. Gangtok
   C. Itanagar   D. Agartala

ANSWERS

1	2	3	4	5	6	7	8	9	10
A	B	C	D	C	B	C	B	B	D

11	12	13	14	15	16	17	18	19	20
D	B	D	C	D	B	A	C	D	A

21	22	23	24	25	26	27	28	29	30
A	B	C	A	A	D	B	C	C	C

31	32	33	34	35	36	37	38	39	40
D	B	B	A	D	C	C	B	A	C

41	42	43	44	45	46	47	48	49	50
D	D	D	D	A	C	C	B	A	C

51	52	53	54	55	56	57	58	59	60
D	A	D	C	B	B	D	B	C	C

61	62	63	64	65	66	67	68	69	70
B	C	A	C	B	B	C	A	A	B

71	72	73	74	75	76	77	78	79	80
B	A	C	A	C	A	C	C	D	A

81	82	83	84	85	86	87	88	89	90
D	C	B	C	C	A	A	D	C	A

91	92	93	94	95	96	97	98	99	100
B	D	B	B	A	D	D	B	B	C

EXPLANATORY ANSWERS

2. The minimum voting age in India is 18 years.

3. C A T is written as D B U

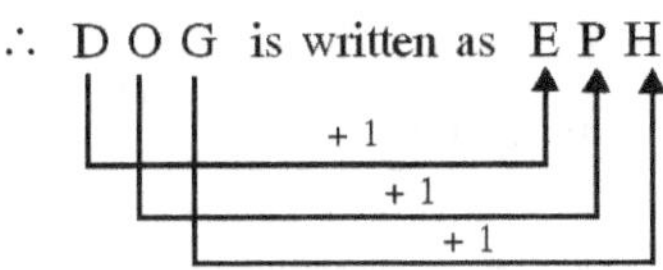

$\therefore$ D O G is written as E P H

5.
    1 to 10 = 1 (3)

11 to 20 = 1 (13)

21 to 30 = 2 (23, 30)

31 to 40 = 10 (31, 32, 33, 34, 35, 36, 37, 38, 39)

41 to 50 = 1 (43)

51 to 60 = 1 (53)

61 to 70 = 1 (63)

71 to 80 = 1 (73)

81 to 90 = 1 (83)

91 to 100 = 1 (93)

If we write down all the numbers from 1 to 100, then 20 times we can write 3.

7. The chemical name of table salt is sodium chloride.

8. 11   12   17   18   23   24   29

+ 1   + 5   + 1   + 5   + 1   + 5

Hence, the missing term is 29.

13. $\because$ + means $\div$

$\div$ means $-$

$-$ means $\times$

$\times$ means $+$

Then, $12 \div 6 - 3 \times 2 + 8$

$$= 2 - 6 + 8$$
$$= 10 - 6 = 4.$$

16.
$$x^2 + x - 12 = 0$$
$$\Rightarrow \quad x^2 + 4x - 3x - 12 = 0$$
$$\Rightarrow \quad x(x + 4) - 3(x + 4) = 0$$
$$\Rightarrow \quad (x + 4)(x - 3) = 0$$
$$\therefore \quad x = 3 \text{ or } x = -4$$

Hence, value of $x = 3, -4$.

20. Convex mirror is used by motorists to see road behind them.

23. Monkey climbs 10 feet in 1 hour (30 – 20)

Monkey climbs 90 feet in 9 hours

Monkey climbs 120 feet in 10 hours (90 + 30)

8 am + 10 hours = 6 pm

Hence, monkey will first touch the flag on the pole at 120 feet from the ground at 6 pm.

26. The product of all the numbers in the dial of a telephone is zero.

28. $\tan 45° = 1$.

29. $\sqrt{4} = \sqrt{2 \times 2} = 2$

which is rational number.

30. Time taken to cover 27 km at the speed of

$$9 \text{ km/hr} = \frac{27}{9} = 3 \text{ hours}$$

But every km he takes rest for 9 mins.

Time taken for rest

$$= 26 \times \frac{9}{60} = 26 \times \frac{3}{20} = \frac{78}{20}$$

$$= 3 \text{ hours } 54 \text{ mins.}$$

Total time taken = 3 hours + 3 hours 54 mins

$$= 6 \text{ hours } 54 \text{ mins.}$$

41. Volume of cylinder = $\pi r^2 h$.

42. $x^2 - y^2 = 80$ and $x - y = 8$

$$\because \quad x^2 - y^2 = 80$$
$$\Rightarrow \quad (x + y)(x - y) = 80$$
$$\Rightarrow \quad (x + y)(8) = 80$$

$$\Rightarrow \qquad (x + y) = \frac{80}{8} = 10$$

Now, $\qquad x + y = 10 \qquad$ ... (i)

$$x - y = 8 \qquad ...(ii)$$

Solving (i) and (ii) then we get,

$x = 9$ and $y = 1$

Average of x and $y = \dfrac{9+1}{2} = \dfrac{10}{2} = 5$.

43.

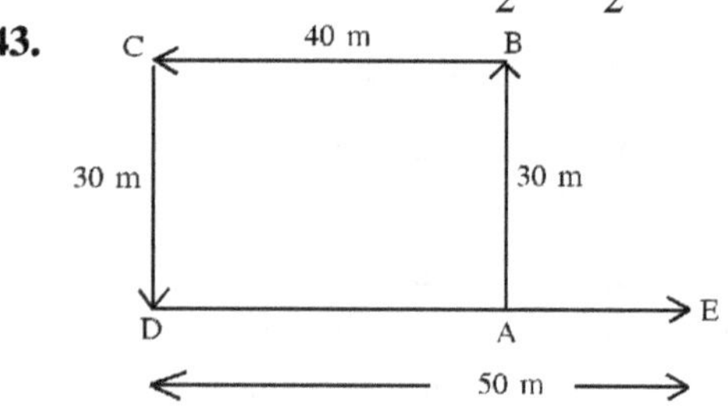

Hence, Ankit is 10 m away from the original position (50 m – 40 m = 10 m).

45. $\qquad (a - b)(a + b) = a^2 + ab - ab - b^2$

$$= a^2 - b^2$$

Hence, $(a - b)(a + b) = a^2 - b^2$.

55. Number of correct sums $= \dfrac{48}{3} = 16$.

56. Speed = 90 km/hr

$$= 90 \times \frac{5}{18} \text{ m/s} = 25 \text{ m/s}$$

Distance = 500 m

$$\text{Time} = \frac{500}{25} = 20 \text{ seconds.}$$

63. A dice has 1, 2, 3, 4, 5, 6 numbers = 6

Even number = 2, 4, 6 = 3

$$\text{Probability of even no.} = \frac{3}{6} = \frac{1}{2}.$$

64. Simple interest $= \dfrac{P \times r \times t}{100}$

$$= \frac{1000 \times 6 \times 10}{100 \times 12} = ₹ \ 50.$$

65. In a right angle triangle, one angle = 15°

$\therefore \qquad$ Other angle = 90° – 15° = 75°.

73. Total no. of balls = 7 + 8 + 5 = 20.

Probability of blue ball $= \dfrac{5}{20} = \dfrac{1}{4}$.

74. Required position = 40 – 13 = 27th.

76. The enquiry clerk gave this information to the passanger at 9 : 15 am.

80. BEG DGI FIK HKM JMO

+ 2   + 2   + 2   + 2

Hence, JMO will come in the given series.

84.

$\therefore$ Diameter of a circle = side of the square

$$= a$$

$\therefore \qquad$ Radius of circle $= \dfrac{a}{2}$

$$\text{Area of circle} = \pi r^2 = \pi \left(\frac{a}{2} \right)^2$$

$$= \frac{\pi a^2}{4}.$$

86. The place of Radha from the last

$$= 37 - 9 = 28\text{th}$$

The place of Sita from the last

$$= 37 - 15 = 22\text{th}$$

Hence, their places from the last

$$= 28\text{th and } 22\text{th.}$$

98.

25	49	81	121	169	225
5^2	7^2	9^2	11^2	13^2	15^2

Hence, 121 is the missing number.

Railway Recruitment Board (RRB)
GROUP 'D'
Recruitment Exam

1. Which one of the following is not a gland?
   A. Liver
   B. Kidney
   C. Stomach
   D. Pancreas

2. Which of the following statements is not true?
   A. Wheat is grown in Punjab
   B. Tea is produced in Assam
   C. Coffee is grown in Karnataka
   D. Saffron is produced in Himachal Pradesh

3. UN has how many principal organs?
   A. 6
   B. 8
   C. 10
   D. 12

4. The Supreme Commander of the Indian armed forces is
   A. The Chief of Army Staff
   B. Prime Minister of India
   C. The President of India
   D. Defence Minister

5. Which of the following is the Capital of Manipur?
   A. Kohima
   B. Imphal
   C. Guwahati
   D. Shillong

6. The difference between the simple interest and compound interest on ₹ 100 at 10% for 2 years is
   A. ₹ 10
   B. ₹ 1
   C. ₹ 5
   D. ₹ 15

7. The filament of electrical bulbs is made of
   A. Tungston
   B. Steel
   C. Silver
   D. Nickel

8. Which of the following is the name of a hormone?
   A. Aspirin
   B. LSD
   C. Cortex
   D. Insulin

9. To which Political party the present Chief Minister of Delhi belongs?
   A. INC
   B. NCP
   C. AAP
   D. BJP

10. Which of the following World famous event is held in Kerala to mark the Onam festivities?
    A. Bull race
    B. Snake boat race
    C. Cock fights
    D. All these

11. In which region of India did the dance form "Mohiniattam" develop?
    A. Odisha
    B. Tamil Nadu
    C. Manipur
    D. Kerala

12. The World famous Red Fort of Delhi was built by which of the following Mughal rulers?
    A. Akbar
    B. Aurangzeb
    C. Jahangir
    D. Shah Jahan

13. Who propounded the theory of natural selection?
    A. Mendel
    B. Lamark
    C. Darwin
    D. De Vries

14. What role does enzyme pepsin play?
    A. It converts fats into acids
    B. It converts fats into glycerol
    C. It converts proteins into peptones
    D. It converts starch into sugar

15. Which one among the following is responsible for formation of "Ozone Holes" in the atmosphere?
    A. Benzopyrene
    B. Hydrocarbons
    C. Chlorofluorocarbons
    D. UV radiation

16. A ray of white light strikes the surface of an object. If all the colours are reflected, the surface would appear:
A. Black   B. White
C. Grey   D. Opaque

17. Which Indian city is believed to have been founded by Karna, the eldest son of the Kunti in Mahabharata?
A. Dharwad   B. Karnal
C. Kannauj   D. Panipat

18. The area of a square is 64 sq.cm. Find its perimeter.
A. 16 cm   B. 8 cm
C. 32 cm   D. 10 sq.cm

19. Which Indian musician has recently been awarded the Lifetime Achievement Grammy Award?
A. A.R. Rahman
B. Pt. Ravi Shanker
C. Ustad Amjad Ali Khan
D. Lata Mangeshkar

20. Who among the following great Mughals, was also a first-rate poet?
A. Akbar   B. Babur
C. Jahangir   D. Shah Jahan

21. The Iron Pillar at Mehrauli in Delhi is believed to record the achievements of
A. Ashoka
B. Chandragupta Maurya
C. Samudragupta
D. Chandragupta II

22. The deficiency of which of the following vitamins is considered responsible for night-blindness?
A. B   B. E
C. K   D. A

23. Which of the following is not a stringed musical instrument?
A. Violin   B. Flute
C. Veena   D. Guitar

24. How many member states are there in the UNO?
A. 191   B. 102
C. 193   D. 105

25. Cotton fibres are made of
A. Cellulose   B. Starch
C. Proteins   D. Fats

26. The site of Harappa is located on the bank of river
A. Saraswati   B. Indus
C. Beas   D. Ravi

27. "Merdeka Cup" is associated with the game of
A. Badminton   B. Football
C. Hockey   D. Tennis

28. The normal body temperature of human beings is
A. 96.4°F   B. 97.4°F
C. 98.4°F   D. 99.4°F

29. How many letters of the English alphabet (capitals) appear same when looked at in a mirror?
A. 9   B. 10
C. 11   D. 12

30. A train is running at a speed of 72 km per hour. Find the distance it covers in 10 minutes.
A. 7.2 km   B. 10 km
C. 20 km   D. 12 km

31. $100° = ?$
A. 100   B. 10
C. 1   D. 0

32. Along with Master Blaster Sachin Tendulkar, who was the other to receive the India's highest civilian award, Bharat Ratna?
A. Prof. C.N.R. Rao B. Prof. P.N.R. Rao
C. Prof. E.N.R. Rao D. Prof. B.N.R. Rao

33. Area of circle having radius 7 cm is
A. 124 sq.cm   B. 154 sq.cm
C. 22 sq.cm   D. 19 sq.cm

34. German Silver is an alloy of
A. Copper, Silver and Zinc
B. Copper, Nickel and Zinc
C. Silver, Tin and Zinc
D. Silver, Nickel and Zinc

35. Which of the following is the hardest metal?
A. Gold   B. Iron
C. Platinum   D. Tungsten

36. The unit of currency, Dinar, is used in:
A. China
B. Iraq
C. Brazil
D. Thailand

37. Indian Constitution came into force on:
A. 15/8/1947
B. 30/1/1948
C. 26/11/1949
D. 26/1/1950

38. Present President of Indian Republic is:
A. Prathibha Patil
B. Manmohan Singh
C. Ram Nath Kovind
D. Rahul Gandhi

39. Expand U.P.S.C.
A. United Public Service Commission
B. Union of Private Service Commissions
C. Union Public Service Commission
D. United Private Service Commission

40. In India, one-rupee coins and notes and subsidiary 50-paisa coins are issued by:
A. Reserve Bank of India
B. Central Government
C. State Bank of India
D. The Unit Trust of India

41. If the letters in ACE are coded as 135 and in BAD are coded as 214, then how can BED be coded?
A. 215
B. 254
C. 245
D. 345

42. If in a code language AND is written as BOE and RENT is written as SFOU, then how is DEAF written in that code?
A. EFBG
B. FEBG
C. EGBF
D. PQRS

Directions (Qs. 43 to 46): *Find the missing numbers/ letters from the given responses.*

43. 5, 9 13, 17, ..., 25.
A. 27
B. 23
C. 21
D. 19

44. BMO, CNP, DOQ, ...
A. FAT
B. EPR
C. EOR
D. BNS

45. 410, 521, 632, ...
A. 645
B. 723
C. 854
D. 743

46. 1, 2, 3, 5, 8, 13, ...
A. 20
B. 17
C. 18
D. 21

47. Which one of the given responses would be meaningful order of the following?
1. Adult
2. Child
3. Infant
4. Boy
A. 2, 3, 1, 4
B. 3, 2, 4, 1
C. 1, 2, 3, 4
D. 3, 4, 2, 1

48. Which one of the given responses would be meaningful order of the following words?
1. Wall
2. Clay
3. House
4. Room
5. Bricks
A. 5, 2, 1, 4, 3
B. 2, 5, 4, 1, 3
C. 2, 5, 1, 4, 3
D. 1, 2, 3, 4, 5

Directions (Qs. 49 to 52): *Find the odd word/letters/ number from the given responses.*

49. A. refuse – accept
B. give – take
C. cold – cool
D. reward – punishment

50. A. 20
B. 64
C. 27
D. 125

51. A. 25, 41
B. 50, 66
C. 33, 48
D. 12, 28

52. A. DCFG
B. FEHI
C. HGJK
D. JHLM

Directions (Qs. 53 to 56): *Select the related letters/ word/number from the given alternatives.*

53. ABC : 123 : : BCD : ?
A. 456
B. 234
C. 345
D. 243

54. Physician : Treatment : : Judge : ?
A. Judgement
B. Lawyer
C. Court
D. Management

55. 12 : 15 : : 24 : ?
A. 36
B. 34
C. 30
D. 18

56. Long : length : : broad : ?
A. Breadth
B. Bread
C. Breed
D. Spread

57. Find the missing number from the given responses.

3	2	4	5
8	9	3	4
2	5	6	7
—	—	—	—
26	23	?	27

A. 20
B. 13
C. 18
D. 27

58. Find the missing number from the given responses.

4	3	5	4
7	6	9	3
1	2	6	6
—	—	—	—
10	7	?	1

A. 4
B. 6
C. 3
D. 8

59. Find the missing number.
594, 198, 66, _____
A. 33
B. 22
C. 44
D. 11

60. F is the brother of A and A is the daughter of B. How is F related to B?
A. Brother-in-law
B. Son
C. Uncle
D. Son-in-law

61. Arun travels 10 km towards North. From there he travels 7 km towards South. Explain his final position from the starting point A.
A. He is 3 km South of A
B. He is 4 km North of A
C. He is 3 km North of A
D. He is 1 km South of A

62. A word given in capital letters is followed by four answer words. Out of these, only one cannot be formed by using the letters of the given word. Find out the word.
INTERNATIONAL
A. NOTE
B. ALONE
C. LATER
D. RADIO

63. Keep the odd one out. (Identify that one which does not belong to the group)
A. Seek
B. Sang
C. Went
D. Came

64. Keep the odd one out.
A. Maharashtra
B. Chennai
C. Kerala
D. Punjab

Directions (Qs. 65 to 68): *Study the information given below and answer the given questions.*

In a certain code—

"facing problems with health" is coded as "mip hit ngi snk"

"health problem on rise" is coded as "hit sa rtv mip"

"rise with every challenge" is coded as "snk rtv lne riy"

"facing challenge each day" is coded as "ngi riy ncp hus"

65. What does the code "lne" stand for?
A. Facing
B. With
C. Every
D. Rise

66. What does the code "riy rtv snk" stand for?
A. Rise above challenge
B. Rise health challenge
C. Day rise challenge
D. With rise challenge

67. Which of the following is the code for "facing"?
A. ncp
B. rtv
C. ngi
D. snk

68. For which of the following "riy snk mip" could be a code?
A. Problem every day
B. Challenge with health
C. With health day
D. Every challenge facing

Directions (Qs. 69 to 72): *Study the following information and answer these questions.*

A, B, C, D, E, F are sitting around a circle facing at the centre. B who is sitting second to the left of A is in the middle of F and E who are facing C and A respectively. D is to the right of A.

69. Who is third to the right of A?
A. C
B. D
C. E
D. B

70. Who is facing B?
A. D
B. C
C. A
D. F

71. Who is to the right of D?
   A. A
   B. F
   C. E
   D. C

72. Who is fourth to the left of F?
   A. D
   B. C
   C. A
   D. E

Directions (Qs. 73 to 76): *In each of these questions, there are given three statements followed by four conclusions. You have to take the given statements as true even if they seem to be at variance from commonly known facts. Decide which of the conclusions logically follows from the given statements, disregarding commonly known facts.*

73. Statements: Some tables are chairs. No cupboard is table. Some chairs are cupboards.
   Conclusions:
   I. Some chairs are not tables.
   II. All chairs are either tables or cupboards.
   III. Some chairs are both tables and cupboards.
   IV. All chairs are tables.
   A. Only I and IV follow
   B. Only either II or III follows
   C. Only IV follows
   D. Only I follows

74. Statements: Some leaves are fruits. All branches are fruits. Some roots are branches.
   Conclusions:
   I. Some roots are fruits.
   II. Some branches are leaves.
   III. No leaf is branch.
   IV. Some leaves are roots.
   A. Only I follows
   B. Either II or III and I follow
   C. Only either II or III follows
   D. Only I or IV and III follow

75. Statements: All birds are animals. Some animals are humans. All humans are mammals.
   Conclusions:
   I. Some humans are not birds.
   II. Some birds are humans.
   III. Some animals are not mammals.
   IV. All animals are mamals.
   A. Only I and II follow

   B. Either III or IV follows
   C. Either I or II follows
   D. None of these

76. Statements: Some roads are lanes. Some streets are roads. Some lanes are highways.
   Conclusions:
   I. Some roads are streets.
   II. No highway is street.
   III. Some streets are not roads.
   IV. Some lanes are not roads.
   A. Only II follows
   B. Only III follows
   C. Only I follows
   D. Only IV and III follow

77. In a class, Sneha is 4th from the bottom. Harsha is 10th from the top. In between them there are 6 students with various ranks. How many students are there in the class?
   A. 25
   B. 20
   C. 30
   D. 28

78. Identify the one which does not belong to the group.
   A. Mend
   B. Rectify
   C. Trouble
   D. Repair

79. Identify the one which does not belong to the group.
   A. Syndicate Bank
   B. Corporation Bank
   C. South Indian Bank
   D. Canara Bank

80. Five students are sitting in a row. P is sitting between M and R. M is sitting next to B who is sitting on the extreme left and Q is sitting next to R. Who are sitting adjacent to M?
   A. B and P
   B. P and Q
   C. P and R
   D. R and Q

81. A man makes his upward journey at 16 kmp and downward journey at 24 kmp. What is his average speed in kmp?
   A. 19.5
   B. 19.2
   C. 19.4
   D. 20

82. A number is increased by 10% and then decreased by 10%. Then the number
   A. Does not change
   B. Increases by 1%
   C. Decreases by 1%
   D. None of these

83. A shop-keeper wants to sell his goods at cost price, but uses a weight of 800 gm instead of a kilogram weight. Thus he makes a gain of:
A. 2%
B. 8%
C. 20%
D. 25%

84. At what rate per cent per annum of simple interest will a certain sum of money become double in 5 years?
A. 20%   B. 25%
C. 30%   D. 10%

85. In selling an article of ₹ 55 there is a gain of 10%. The gain by selling that for ₹ 58 is:
A. 13%   B. 6%
C. 16%   D. 3%

86. By how much is the area of a square of side 6 cm increased when its side is increased by 2 cm?
A. 4 sq.cm   B. 16 sq.cm
C. 20 sq.cm   D. 28 sq.cm

87. If $x = 5$, $y = -2$, what is the value of $(2x^2 - 3y^2)$?
A. 62   B. 38
C. 50   D. 60

88. How many of the following numbers are divisible by 9?
1231, 2367, 6462, 5354, 7020, 1341
A. 3   B. 4
C. 5   D. 2

89. The difference between the place values of 7 and 3 in the number 527435 is :
A. 5   B. 4
C. 45   D. 6970

90. The three angles of a triangle are:
$(5x + 6)°$, $(3x - 3)°$ and $(x - 3)°$. Then $x = ?$
A. 30°   B. 40°
C. 20°   D. 10°

91. 40 men can dig a trench 32 metres long in 16 days. How many days will 60 men take to dig a trench 12 metres long?
A. 4   B. 16
C. 8   D. 20

92. $\dfrac{1}{4} + \dfrac{3}{8} + ? = \dfrac{13}{16}$
A. $\dfrac{5}{8}$ B. $\dfrac{3}{16}$
C. $\dfrac{2}{8}$ D. $\dfrac{5}{16}$

93. $\dfrac{4}{11}$ of $4\dfrac{1}{8}$ of ₹ 50 = ?
A. 75   B. 30
C. 40   D. 25

94. $\sqrt{\dfrac{49}{?}} = \dfrac{7}{15}$
A. 30   B. 25
C. 225   D. 105

95. Find the multiplier which will cause a number to increase it by 17%.
A. 17.7   B. 1.17
C. 117   D. 0.117

96. $\left(\sqrt{8} - \sqrt{3}\right)\left(\sqrt{8} + \sqrt{3}\right) = ?$
A. 5   B. 15
C. 25   D. None of these

97. 15 = 75% of ?
A. 10.25   B. 22.5
C. 25   D. 20

98. A trader sells 10 chairs and 2 tables for ₹ 7,000 to a customer and to another customer he sells 10 chairs and 3 tables at the same price for ₹ 8,000. Find the cost of a chair.
A. ₹ 600   B. ₹ 500
C. ₹ 400   D. ₹ 300

99. Mr. Singh invested ₹ 19,000 in a 5% stock at 95 and sold it when its price has fallen to 90. Thus he lost
A. ₹ 1,000   B. ₹ 100
C. ₹ 500   D. ₹ 900

100. Mr. Naveen invested ₹ 19,000 in a 6% stock at 95. Find the annual dividend he gets.
A. ₹ 600   B. ₹ 1,000
C. ₹ 1,200   D. ₹ 1,500

ANSWERS

1	2	3	4	5	6	7	8	9	10
C	D	A	C	B	B	A	D	C	B

11	12	13	14	15	16	17	18	19	20
D	D	C	C	C	B	B	C	B	B

21	22	23	24	25	26	27	28	29	30
D	D	B	C	A	D	B	C	C	D

31	32	33	34	35	36	37	38	39	40
C	A	B	B	D	B	D	C	C	A

41	42	43	44	45	46	47	48	49	50
B	A	C	B	D	D	B	C	C	A

51	52	53	54	55	56	57	58	59	60
C	D	B	A	C	A	C	D	B	B

61	62	63	64	65	66	67	68	69	70
C	D	A	B	C	D	C	B	C	A

71	72	73	74	75	76	77	78	79	80
D	A	D	B	D	C	B	C	C	A

81	82	83	84	85	86	87	88	89	90
B	C	D	A	C	D	B	B	D	C

91	92	93	94	95	96	97	98	99	100
A	B	A	C	B	A	D	B	A	C

EXPLANATORY ANSWERS

41. Letter : A C E   B A D
Code : 1 3 5   2 1 4
So, code of   B E D
             2 5 4

42.

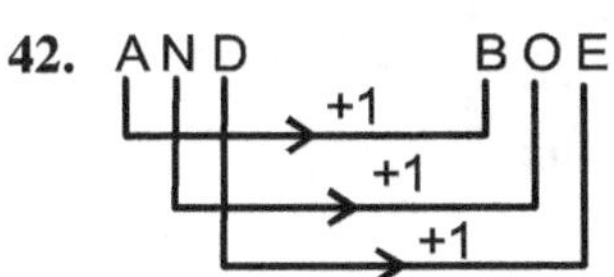

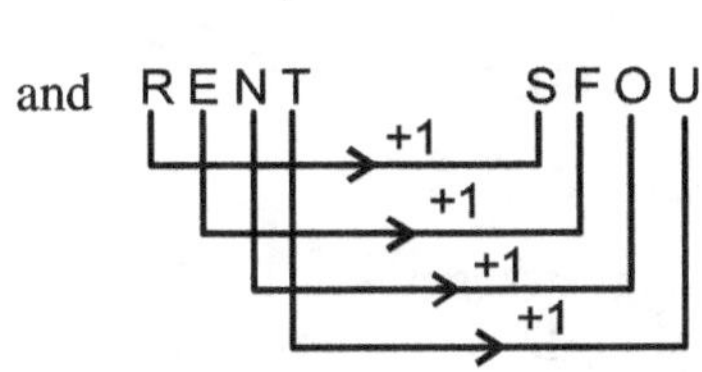

Similarly,

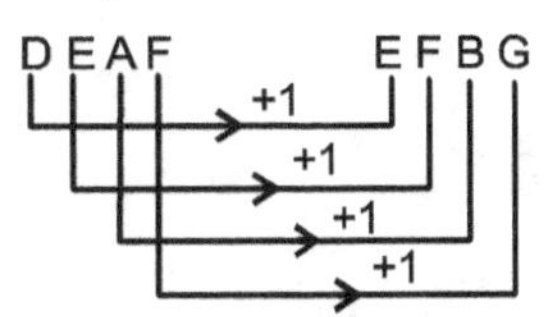

43.

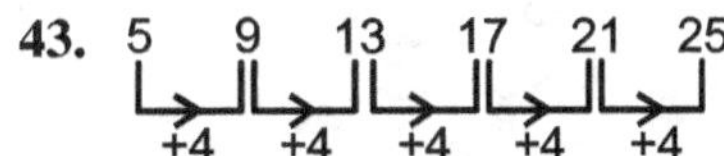

44.

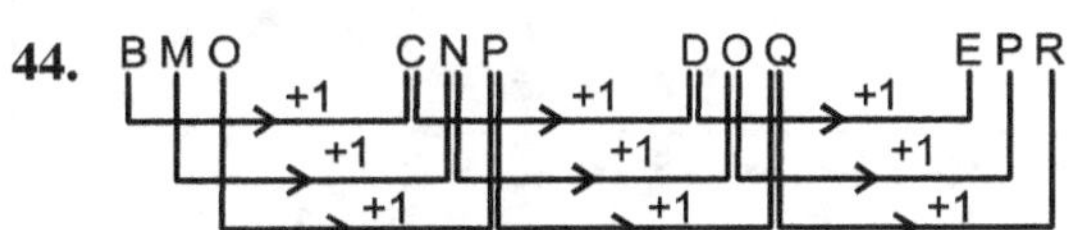

45. 410   521   632   743

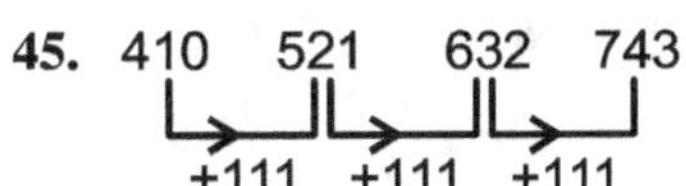

46. In this series n^{th} term ($n \geq 3$) is the sum of $(n-1)^{th}$ term and $(n-2)^{th}$ term.

$$3^{rd} \text{ term } 3 = 1 + 2$$
$$\underline{4^{th} \text{ term } 5 = 2 + 3}$$
$$7^{th} \text{ term } 21 = 8 + 13$$

47. Meaningful order is:

Infant, Child, Boy, Adult

48. Meaningful order is :

Clay, Bricks, Wall, Room, House.

49. Except 'cold-cool', other three pairs are antonymous words.

50. Except '20', other three are cube numbers.

51. $25, 41 \Rightarrow 41 - 25 = 16$
$50, 66 \Rightarrow 66 - 50 = 16$
$33, 48 \Rightarrow 48 - 33 = 15$
$12, 28 \Rightarrow 28 - 12 = 16.$

52. 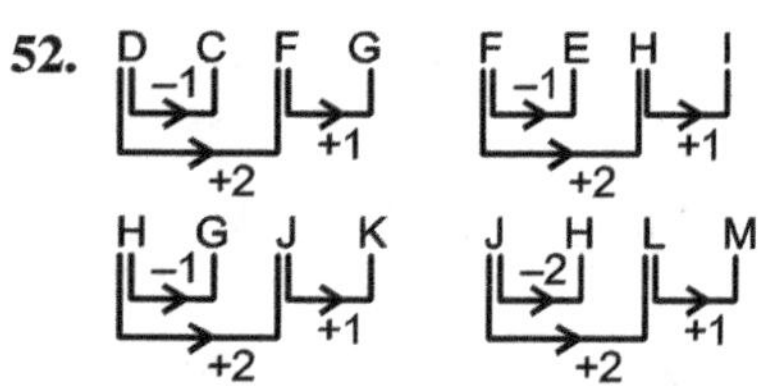

53. 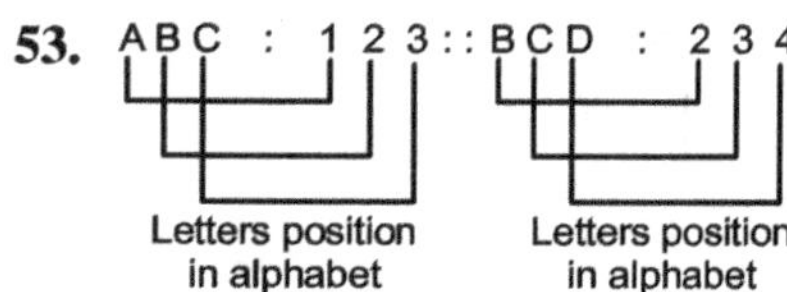

Letters position in alphabet

55. 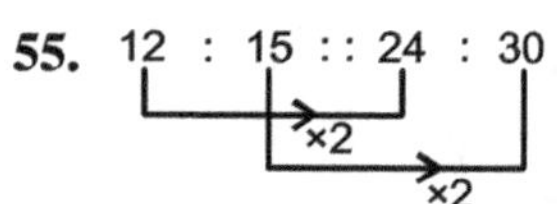

57.

3	2
8	9
2	5
$3 \times 8 + 2 = 26$	$2 \times 9 + 5 = 23$
4	5
3	4
6	7
$4 \times 3 + 6 = 18$	$5 \times 4 + 7 = 27$

58.

4	3
7	6
1	2
$4 + 7 - 1 = 10$	$3 + 6 - 2 = 7$

5	4
9	3
6	6
$5 + 9 - 6 = 8$	$4 + 3 - 6 = 1$

59. 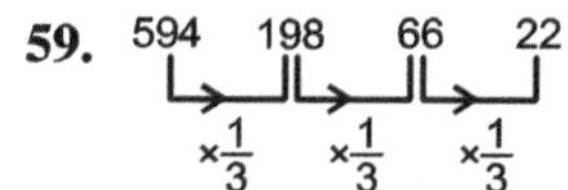

60. 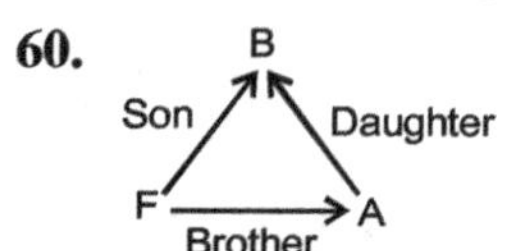

61. 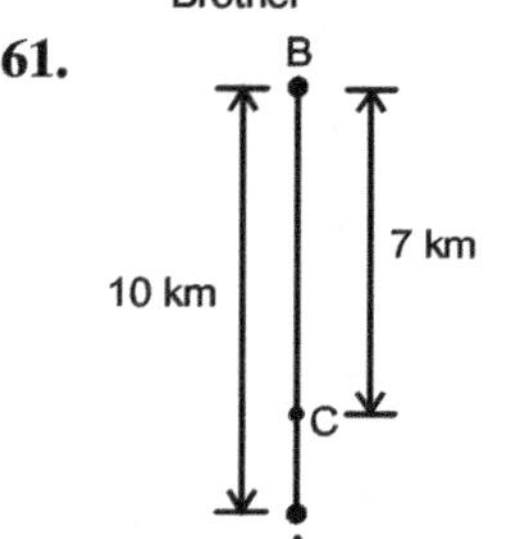

Let, final position of Arun is at point 'C'.

Then, $AC = AB - BC = 10 - 7 = 3$ km

And point 'C' is North of point 'A'.

62. Letter 'D' is not used in the given word 'INTERNATIONAL'. So, by using the letters of the given word, we can't make the word 'RADIO'.

64. 'Maharashtra', 'Kerala' and 'Punjab' are name of states, whereas 'Chennai' is the name of a city.

65-68. 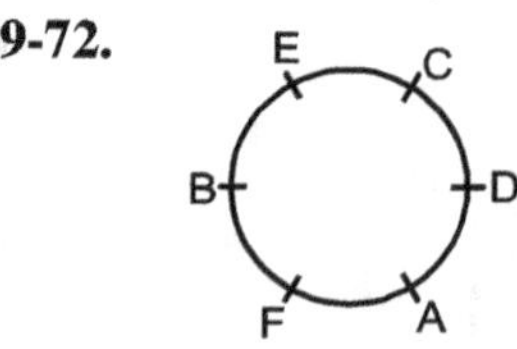

65. Code for 'every' is 'lne'.

69-72. 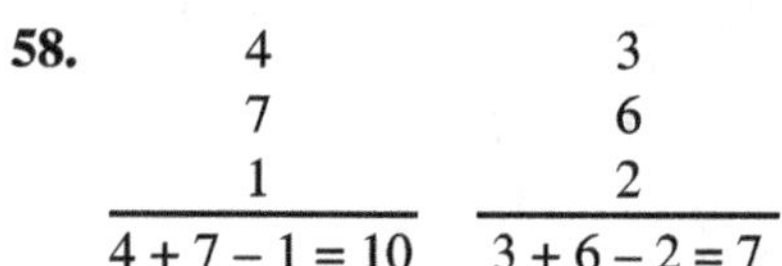

Circular sitting arrangement of six persons namely A, B, C, D, E and F.

73. 

No cupboard is table and some cupboards are chairs. So, some chairs are not tables.

74. 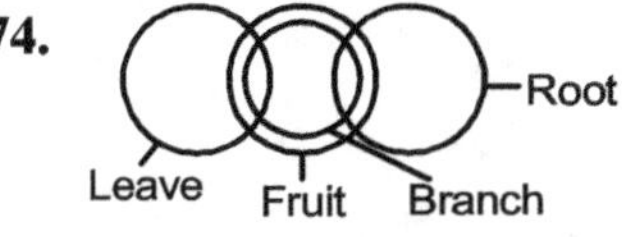

or 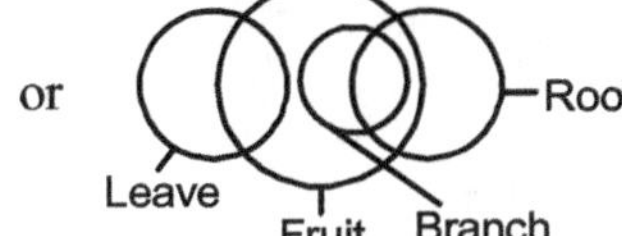

75. 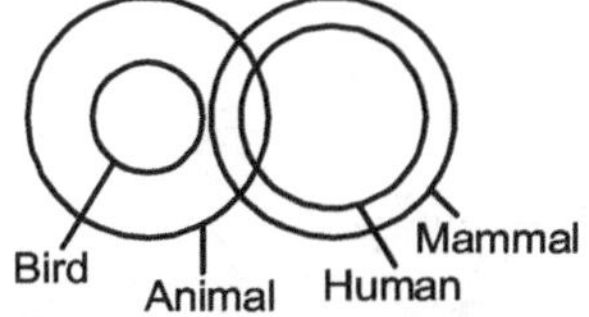

None of the conclusions follows.

76. 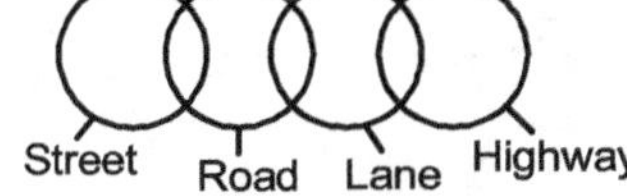

79. Syndicate Bank, Corporation Bank and Canara Bank are nationalised banks, whereas 'South Indian Bank' is a Private Bank.

80. Based on the given information, sitting arrangement of five students in a row is like this.

$$B \quad M \quad P \quad R \quad Q$$

So, adjacent to 'M' is B and P.

81. Average speed $= \dfrac{2xy}{x+y}$

$$= \dfrac{2 \times 16 \times 24}{16 + 24}$$

$$= \dfrac{2 \times 16 \times 24}{40}$$

$$= \dfrac{96}{5} = 19.2 \text{ km/hr}$$

82. If a number or amount increases by $x\%$ again decreases by $x\%$, then in that case:

The number or amount always decreases by

$$\left(\dfrac{x^2}{100}\right)\%$$

Hence, required decrease

$$= \left(\dfrac{10^2}{100}\right)\%$$

$$= \left(\dfrac{100}{100}\right)\% = 1\%.$$

83. If a trader professes to sell his goods at cost price, but uses false weights, then

Gain%

$$= \left(\dfrac{\text{Error}}{\text{True Value} - \text{Error}} \times 100\right)\%$$

$$= \left(\dfrac{1000 - 800}{1000 - 200}\right) \times 100$$

$$= \dfrac{200}{800} \times 100 = 25\%.$$

84. Let, $p = ₹\, x$

$$A = ₹\, 2x$$

$$\therefore \quad SI = 2x - x = x$$

$$r = \dfrac{SI \times 100}{p \times t}$$

$$= \dfrac{x \times 100}{x \times 5} = 20\%.$$

85. Let, $CP = ₹\, x$

$$\dfrac{x + 10}{100}x = 55$$

$$110x = 55 \times 100$$

$$x = \dfrac{55 \times 100}{110} = 50$$

Profit $= 58 - 50 = 8$

Profit % $= \dfrac{8}{50} \times 100 = 16\%.$

86. $\because$ Side of square $= 6$ cm

$\therefore$ Area of square $= 36$ cm^2

New side of square

$$= 6 \text{ cm} + 2 \text{ cm} = 8 \text{ cm}$$

$\therefore$ Area $= (8)^2 = 64$ cm^2

Area increased $= 64 - 36$

$= 28$ cm^2.

87. $\because$ $x = 5$ and $y = -2$

The value of $(2x^2 - 3y^2)$

$= 2(5)^2 - 3(-2)^2$

$= 50 - 12 = 38.$

88. $1231 = 1 + 2 + 3 + 1 = 7$

which is not divisible by 9

$2367 = 2 + 3 + 6 + 7 = 18$

which is divisible by 9

$6462 = 6 + 4 + 6 + 2 = 18$ divisible by 9

$5354 = 5 + 3 + 5 + 4 = 17$

not divisible by 9

$7020 = 7 + 0 + 2 + 0 = 9$ divisible by 9

$1341 = 1 + 3 + 4 + 1 = 9$ divisible by 9

$\therefore$ There are 4 numbers divisible by 9.

89. In 527435

Place value of $7 = 7000$

Place Value of $3 = 30$

Required difference $= 7000 - 30$

$= 6970.$

90. $\because$ The sum of three angles of a triangle $= 180°$

$\therefore$ $(5x + 6)° + (3x - 3)° + (x - 3)° = 180°$

$\Rightarrow 9x + 6 - 3 - 3 = 180°$

$\Rightarrow$ $9x = 180°$

$\Rightarrow$ $x = \dfrac{180}{9} = 20°.$

91. $\dfrac{m_1 d_1}{w_1} = \dfrac{m_2 d_2}{w_2}$

$\Rightarrow \dfrac{40 \times 16}{32} = \dfrac{60 \times d_2}{12}$

$\therefore$ $d_2 = \dfrac{40 \times 16 \times 12}{32 \times 60} = 4$

Hence, required no. of days = 4 days.

92. $\dfrac{1}{4} + \dfrac{3}{8} + x = \dfrac{13}{16}$

$\Rightarrow$ $x = \dfrac{13}{16} - \dfrac{1}{4} - \dfrac{3}{8}$

$= \dfrac{13 - 4 - 6}{16} = \dfrac{3}{16}$

93. $\dfrac{4}{11} \times \dfrac{33}{8} \times ₹\, 50 = ₹\, 75.$

94. $\sqrt{\dfrac{49}{x}} = \dfrac{7}{15}$

Squaring both sides, we get

$\dfrac{49}{x} = \dfrac{49}{225}$ $\Rightarrow$ $x = 225.$

96. $\left(\sqrt{8} - \sqrt{3}\right)\left(\sqrt{8} + \sqrt{3}\right) = 8 - 3 = 5.$

97. $15 = 75\%$ of x

$\Rightarrow$ $15 = \dfrac{75}{100} \times x$

$\Rightarrow$ $x = \dfrac{15 \times 100}{75} = 20.$

98. $10x + 2y = 7000$ ...(i)

$10x + 3y = 8000$ ...(ii)

$y = 1000$

Putting the value of y in (i)

$10x + 2 \times 1000 = 7000$

$\Rightarrow$ $10x = 5000$

$\Rightarrow$ $x = 500$

$\therefore$ Cost of a chair $= ₹\, 500.$

Railway Recruitment Board (RRB)
GROUP 'D'
Recruitment Exam

1. Which of the following languages is NOT included in the Eighth Schedule of the Indian Constitution?
   A. English   B. Sindhi
   C. Sanskrit   D. Hindi

2. Who appoints the Comptroller and Auditor General of India?
   A. Union Public Service Commission
   B. President of India
   C. Union Law Minister
   D. Prime Minister

3. A and B start together from the same place in the same direction to go round a circular path. If A takes 10 minutes and B takes 15 minutes to make one complete round, they will meet after
   A. 30 minutes
   B. 33 minutes
   C. 40 minutes
   D. 45 minutes

4. Two trains of equal length, running in opposite directions, pass a pole in 18 and 12 seconds. The trains will cross each other in
   A. 16.6 secs.   B. 15.5 secs.
   C. 14.4 secs.   D. 17.7 secs.

5. Capital of Mizoram is
   A. Imphal   B. Aizawal
   C. Dispur   D. Agartalal

6. Two iron shots each of diameter 6 cm are immersed in the water contained in a cylindrical vessel of radius 6 cm. The level of the water in the vessel will be raised by
   A. 1 cm   B. 3 cm
   C. 6 cm   D. 2 cm

7. Which one among the following pairs is NOT correctly matched?
   A. Union List: Banking
   B. State List: Agriculture
   C. Concurrent List: Marriage
   D. Residuary List: Education

8. The names of Yamanaka and Gurdon are related to
   A. Induced stem cell technique
   B. Cell cycle regulation studies
   C. Genome sequencing of virus
   D. Protein engineering

9. Who among the following Governor-Generals formed the Triple Alliance against Tippu Sultan?
   A. Warren Hastings
   B. Lord Cornwallis
   C. Lord Wellesley
   D. Lord William Bentinck

10. Which of the following lakes is the oldest in the world and it is the deepest fresh water lake?
   A. Lake Titicaca   B. Lake Baikal
   C. Lake Chilika   D. Lake Superior

11. Which of the following diseases is NOT a vector-borne disease?
   A. Polio   B. Malaria
   C. Leishmaniasis   D. Filaria

12. Low levels of HDL and high levels of LDL increase the risk of
   A. Cancers
   B. Blood pressure
   C. Diabetes
   D. Coronary artery disease

13. Who among the following freedom fighters was associated with the foundation of Bharatiya Vidya Bhavan?
A. Madan Mohan Malviya
B. Acharya Narendra Dev
C. K.M. Munshi
D. J.B. Kripalani

14. To further cement business ties between both the countries, South Africa will grant visas to Indian businessmen within .... of submitting an application.
A. four days   B. four weeks
C. three months   D. six weeks

15. Speed of light is maximum in the following (out of 4 given media):
A. water   B. glass
C. diaomond   D. air

16. The first woman Chief Minister of Gujarat who has replaced Mr. Narendra Modi is
A. Sumitra Mahajan   B. Vasundara Raje
C. Anandiben Patel   D. Kamla Beniwal

17. The autobiography of which prominent Indian is sub-titled "My Music, My Life" and has an introduction by Yehudi Menuhin?
A. Balamurali Krishna   B. Yesudas
C. Amjad Khan   D. Ravi Shankar

18. Which six hundred years old temple in Deshnoke is well known for the large number of rats who are called "Kabas" and routinely venerated?
A. Pathni Mata Temple
B. Karni Mata Temple
C. Rajni Mata Temple
D. None of these

19. The boundary line demarcating India and China is known as:
A. McMahon Line
B. Mt. Everest Line
C. Nehru-Chou Enli Line
D. Gandhi-Chou Line

20. Pure gold is:
A. 1 carat gold   B. 18 carat gold
C. 22 carat gold   D. 24 carat gold

21. Which of the following is NOT a cause for the present global warming and climate change?
A. Carbon dioxide   B. CFC emission
C. Devaluation   D. Methane emission

22. Right to information in India is a part of
A. Fundamental Right
B. Legal Right
C. Neither Fundamental nor Legal Right
D. None of these

23. Uttar Kashi is situated on the banks of the river
A. Alaknanda   B. Bhagirathi
C. Ganga   D. Mandakini

24. Which of the following is known as the Morning Star?
A. Jupiter   B. Mars
C. Mercury   D. Venus

25. How many bright stars are there in the constellation named 'Ursa Major' or the 'Great Bear'?
A. 7   B. 8
C. 9   D. 10

26. Which one of the following Articles has declared untouchability in any form as unconstitutional?
A. Article 14   B. Article 17
C. Article 44   D. Article 45

27. Dada Saheb Phalke Award is given for outstanding contribution in the field of:
A. Cinema   B. Sports
C. Social Service   D. Science

28. A certain amount was to be distributed among A, B and C in the ratio $2 : 3 : 4$ respectively, but was erroneously distributed in the ratio $7 : 2 : 5$ respectively. As a result of this, B got ₹ 40 less. What is the amount?
A. ₹ 210   B. ₹ 270
C. ₹ 230   D. ₹ 280

29. What is the difference between the simple and compound interest on ₹ 7,000 at the rate of 6% p.a. in 2 years?
A. ₹ 21.50   B. ₹ 25.20
C. ₹ 22   D. ₹ 20

30. There are 10 teachers including the Head Master. How many committees of 5 teachers with Head Master as the chairman can be made?
A. 136 B. 252
C. 126 D. 200

31. Dandia is the folk dance of
A. Punjab B. Gujarat
C. Haryana D. Maharashtra

32. India's national game is:
A. Football B. Cricket
C. Tennis D. Hockey

33. Sathya Nadella is the C.E.O. of
A. IBM B. WIPRO
C. MICROSOFT D. CITY BANK

34. The concept of Anuvratha was advocated by
A. Mahayana Buddhism
B. Hinayana Buddhism
C. Jainism
D. The Lokayata School

35. The Bronze icons of Nataraja cast during the Chola period invariably show the deity with
A. eight hands B. six hands
C. four hands D. two hands

36. Large scale warfare is going on in .... between the supporters of Shia led government and Sunni Militants.
A. Pakistan B. Iran
C. Iraq D. Saudi Arabia

37. In which state was Panchayat Raj first introduced?
A. Gujarat B. Rajasthan
C. Bihar D. Andhra Pradesh

38. Bhagavad Gita consists of .... verses.
A. 700 B. 670
C. 650 D. 600

39. Which is the oldest known computation tool used by mankind?
A. Calculator B. Compute
C. Abacus D. Transistor

40. From the digits 5, 6, 7, 4, 1, how many 3 digits even numbers can be formed (without repetition of digits)?
A. 24 B. 10
C. 20 D. 60

41. Which is the one that does not belong to the group?
A. Dinar B. Door
C. Doller D. Rupee

42. Three of the following four are alike in a certain way and so form a group. Which is the one that does NOT belong to that group?
A. 125 B. 27
C. 100 D. 64

43. "GUN" is related to "Bullet" in the same way as "CHIMNEY" is related to
A. House B. Roof
C. Smoke D. Ground

44. In a certain code "ROUTE" is written as "47289" and "GEAR" is written as "5914". How is "GATE" written in that code?
A. 5187 B. 5189
C. 5289 D. 5429

45. How many meaningful english words can be made with the letters TMEA using each letter only once in each word?
A. 4 B. 3
C. 2 D. 6

46. Which is the one that does NOT belong to the group?
A. Saucer B. Mug
C. Jar D. Jug

47. ABC : BCD : : PQR : ....
A. QRS B. RST
C. RSQ D. STU

48. 'Medicine' is to 'sickness' as 'Book' is to
A. Story B. Ignorance
C. Author D. Brake

49. 'Dumb' is to 'speech' as .... is to 'sight'.
A. Deaf B. Hearing
C. Blind D. Lame

50. Court : Justice : : School : ?
A. Education B. Building
C. Ground D. Plan

Directions (Qs. 51 to 55): *Select the related word/number/letters from the given alternatives.*

51. 8 : 64 : : 17 : ?
- A. 118
- B. 289
- C. 288
- D. 324

52. INTIMATE : UNFAMILIAR : : ?
- A. Interior : Internal
- B. Interested : Indifference
- C. Forbear : Patience
- D. Popular : Friendly

53. PIN : NIP : : TRIP : ?
- A. TOUR
- B. RACE
- C. PIRT
- D. RIPT

54. CDE : ZXY : : ECD : ?
- A. YZX
- B. XYZ
- C. ZYX
- D. YXZ

55. FRUIT : JUICE : : COCONUT : ?
- A. TREE
- B. OIL
- C. BRANCH
- D. TEMPLE

Directions (Qs. 56 to 58): *Which one of the given responses would be a meaningful order of the following words in ascending order?*

56.
1. Grand father
2. Son
3. Father
4. Grandson

- A. 4, 2, 1, 3
- B. 3, 4, 2, 1
- C. 4, 2, 3, 1
- D. 1, 2, 3, 4

57.
1. Doctor
2. Disease
3. Cure
4. Medicine
5. Diagnosis

- A. 2, 3, 1, 5, 4
- B. 2, 1, 5, 4, 3
- C. 4, 3, 5, 1, 2
- D. 2, 3, 5, 1, 4

58.
1. Study
2. Admission
3. Job
4. Result
5. Examination

- A. 1, 5, 4, 2, 3
- B. 2, 3, 4, 5, 1
- C. 3, 4, 5, 2, 1
- D. 2, 1, 5, 4, 3

59. Which of the following words will appear fourth in the dictionary?
- A. Negotiate
- B. Neighbour
- C. Neither
- D. Negative

60. Which of the following words will appear first in the dictionary?
- A. Sanskrit
- B. Sanctity
- C. Sanction
- D. Sanatorium

61. Which one set of letters when sequentially placed at the gaps in the given letter series shall complete it?

r – rs – srr – ss –
- A. rsrs
- B. rrss
- C. ssrr
- D. srsr

62. Find the missing number from the given response.

9	8	7
5	6	8
3	5	?
11	9	13

- A. 3
- B. 2
- C. 1
- D. 4

63.

18	16	14	7
9	8	7	10
45	40	?	24

- A. 30
- B. 21
- C. 35
- D. 28

64. Naveen travelled from point P to point Q which is at a distance of 7 feet from P. He then travelled 6 feet to his right and then turned to left and went 4 feet. Finally he again went 6 feet to his left. How far is he from the point Q now?
- A. 6 feet
- B. 4 feet
- C. 7 feet
- D. 10 feet

65. Select the correct combination of mathematical signs to replace * signs and to balance the given equation.

17 * 8 * 2 * 1 * 20
- A. + ÷ – =
- B. ÷ + = –
- C. + – ÷ =
- D. – + ÷ =

66. Some equations are solved on the basis of a certain system. On the same basis find out the correct answer for the unsolved equation.
If 7 × 3 = 12; 6 × 5 = 03, what is 8 × 10 = ?
- A. 80
- B. 01
- C. 08
- D. 81

67. Y is 4 km to the East of X which is to the North of Z. If P is 6 km to the East of Z, then in which direction of Y is P?
A. South
B. South-East
C. South-West
D. West

68. Lekhana is shorter than Charithra but taller than Namitha. Amritha is the tallest. Rekha is a little shorter than Charithra and little taller than Lekhana. If they stand in the order of increasing heights who will be the second?
A. Rekha   B. Charithra
C. Namitha D. Lekhana

69. If M stands for "multiplication", D for "division", A for "addition", G for "greater than", and L for "less than", then which of the following will be logically correct?
A. 20 A 4 D 4 L 4 A 6 D 2
B. 20 D 5 A 4 L 4 A 2 M 3
C. 20 D 5 G 8 D 4 A 6 M 2
D. 20 A 2 G 10 M 3 A 12 D 2

70. Five people were climbing up a hill. John was following Ahmed. Ram was ahead of Govind. Naveen was between Govind and Ahmed. If they were climbing up in a column, with John at the lowest, who was second from the highest?
A. Govind   B. Ram
C. Naveen   D. Ahmed

71. Sakshi remembers that Amith's birthday is after 10th but before 13th March, whereas Rekha remembers that Amith's birthday is after 11th but before 15th March. If both are correct, on which day is Amith's birthday?
A. 14th March B. 11th March
C. 12th March D. 13th March

72. Of the six towns, A is bigger than B, C is bigger than D, E is NOT as big as C but bigger than B and B is smaller than D but bigger than F. Which is the smallest?
A. C   B. D
C. B   D. F

73. In a certain code, 'ble nee see' means 'where are you' and 'nee tim see' means 'who are you', what is the code for 'where'?
A. nee   B. ble
C. tim   D. see

74. Find the word which cannot be made from the letters of the given word ANDROCLES?
A. ROADS   B. ROSELAND
C. LANDER D. DREAMS

75. In a certain coding system EDUCATION is coded as 531278946. How will you code NOTICE in that system?
A. 648935   B. 649825
C. 648925   D. 643965

Directions (Qs. 76 to 78): *Read the following statements and answer the questions that follow.*

Nine friends are sitting together in a theatre in one row. They are J, K, L, M, N, O, P, Q and R, L is at the right of 'M' and at the third place at the right of 'N', 'K' is one end of the row. 'Q' is immediately next to 'O' and 'P'. 'Q' is at third place at the left of 'K'. 'J' is right next to the left of 'O'.

76. Who is sitting in the centre among these friends?
A. L   B. J
C. O   D. M

77. Friends sitting on the right of 'O' are
A. JPK   B. JQK
C. QPK   D. KRP

78. Who is at the other end of this row of friends?
A. R   B. M
C. L   D. N

79. If VICTORY is coded as YLFWRUB, how can SUCCESS be coded in that system?
A. VXFFHVV B. VXEEHVV
C. VYEEHVV D. VYEFIVV

80. A is the father of B, C is the brother of A and D is the sister of B. If E is the father of A, then describe the relationship between D and C.
A. Daughter and Father
B. Niece and Uncle
C. Sister and Brother
D. Wife and Husband

81. If 8 men or 12 boys can do a piece of work in 16 days, the number of days required to complete the work by 20 men and 6 boys is:

A. $5\dfrac{1}{3}$ B. $6\dfrac{1}{3}$

C. $8\dfrac{1}{3}$ D. $7\dfrac{1}{3}$

82. A person covers half of his journey at 6 km/hr. and the remaining half at 3 km/hr. His average speed is

A. 4.5 km/hr   B. 4 km/hr
C. 3.5 km/hr   D. 9 km/hr

83. The length of a rectangle is increased by 10% and breadth is decreased by 10%. Then the area of the new rectangle is

A. Neither decreased nor increased
B. Increased by 1%
C. Decreased by 1%
D. Decreased by 10%

84. ₹ 395 are divided among P, Q and R in such a way that Q gets 25% more than P and 20% more than R. The share of P will be

A. ₹ 180   B. ₹ 195
C. ₹ 120   D. ₹ 98

85. Out of 7 given numbers, the average of the first four numbers is 21 and that of last four numbers is also 21. If the average of all the seven numbers is 20, the fourth number is

A. 30   B. 28
C. 32   D. 21

86. When an article was sold, there was a loss of 10%. If its selling price was increased by ₹ 30, there would have been a profit of 10%. Find its cost price.

A. ₹ 150   B. ₹ 130
C. ₹ 110   D. ₹ 200

87. $\sqrt{5\left(2\dfrac{3}{4}-\dfrac{3}{10}\right)} = ?$

A. $2\dfrac{1}{2}$ B. 3

C. $3\dfrac{1}{2}$ D. $4\dfrac{1}{4}$

88. The smallest number which when divided by 42 and 54 leaves the remainders 34 and 46 respectively is

A. 378   B. 388
C. 384   D. 370

89. The greatest number which when divides 590, 908 and 1014 leaves the same remainder each time is

A. 106   B. 104
C. 108   D. 102

90. Four bells are ringing at intervals of 12, 16, 24 and 36 minutes. They start ringing simultaneously at 12 O'clock. When will they again ring together?

A. 2.28 P.M.   B. 2.48 P.M.
C. 2.24 P.M.   D. 2.44 P.M.

91. $7 - 5 \times 2 \text{ of } 3 + \left(19 - \overline{7-4}\right) \div 4 = ?$

A. 16   B. –19
C. 22   D. 19

92. A passenger train, 150 m long, passes a railway platform, 200 m long, in 35 seconds. Time taken by this train to pass a stationary man is

A. 36 sec.   B. 20 sec.
C. 18 sec.   D. 15 sec.

93. If $A : B = 8 : 9$, $B : C = 15 : 16$, $A : C = ?$

A. 6 : 7   B. 3 : 4
C. 1 : 2   D. 5 : 6

94. 108 kg of ration is sufficient for 18 students for 15 days. For how many students will 70 kg of ration be sufficient for 25 days?

A. 7   B. 8
C. 9   D. 10

95. 3 men and 4 boys can complete a certain work in 28 days, where as 4 men and 6 boys can complete the same work in 20 days. According to the amount of work done, one man is equivalent to how many boys?

A. $1\dfrac{1}{2}$ B. 2

C. $2\dfrac{1}{2}$ D. 3

96. A man is 24 years older than his son, in 2 years, his age will be twice the age of his son. What is the present age of the son?
A. 20 yrs.   B. 25 yrs.
C. 22 yrs.   D. 24 yrs.

97. The ratio of incomes of A and B is 5 : 6. If A gets ₹ 1,100 less than B, their total income in rupees is
A. 9,900   B. 12,100
C. 14,400   D. 10,000

98. The ratio in which tea costing ₹ 192 per kg is to be mixed with tea costing ₹ 150 per kg so that the mixed tea, when sold for ₹ 194.40 per kg, gives a profit of 20% is

A. 2 : 5   B. 3 : 5
C. 5 : 3   D. 5 : 2

99. The ratio of the volume of a cube to that of a sphere, which will exactly fit inside the cube, is
A. $4 : \pi$ B. $5 : 3\pi$
C. $6 : \pi$ D. 4 : 3

100. Gangamma and Paravva, working separately can mow a field in 8 and 12 hours separately. If they work in stretches of one hour alternately, Gangamma beginning at 9 A.M., when will the mowing be completed?
A. 6 P.M.   B. 6.30 P.M.
C. 5 P.M.   D. 5.30 P.M.

ANSWERS

1	2	3	4	5	6	7	8	9	10
A	B	A	C	B	D	D	A	C	B

11	12	13	14	15	16	17	18	19	20
A	D	C	A	D	C	D	B	A	D

21	22	23	24	25	26	27	28	29	30
C	A	B	D	A	B	A	A	B	C

31	32	33	34	35	36	37	38	39	40
B	D	C	C	C	C	B	A	C	A

41	42	43	44	45	46	47	48	49	50
B	C	C	B	A	A	A	B	C	A

51	52	53	54	55	56	57	58	59	60
B	B	C	A	B	C	B	D	C	D

61	62	63	64	65	66	67	68	69	70
A	B	C	B	A	C	B	D	B	A

71	72	73	74	75	76	77	78	79	80
C	D	B	D	C	B	C	D	A	B

81	82	83	84	85	86	87	88	89	90
A	B	C	C	B	A	C	D	A	C

91	92	93	94	95	96	97	98	99	100
B	D	D	A	B	C	B	A	C	B

EXPLANATORY ANSWERS

41. Dollar, Dinar and Rupee are currency of different countries.

42. $125 \rightarrow (5)^3$ $27 \rightarrow (3)^3$
$100 \rightarrow (10)^2$ $64 \rightarrow (4)^3$

43. Bullet is fired from Gun, like that smoke comes out from chimney.

45. For meaningfull words are TEAM, TAME, MEAT, MATE.

47. 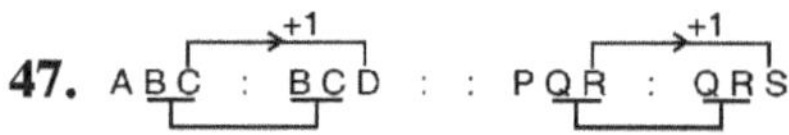

49. As Dumb person can't speak, like that Blind one can't see.

51. $8 : (8)^2 : : 17 : (17)^2$

and $(17)^2 = 289$.

52. Intimate and unfamiliar are antonym words similarly interested and indifference are antonyms.

53. 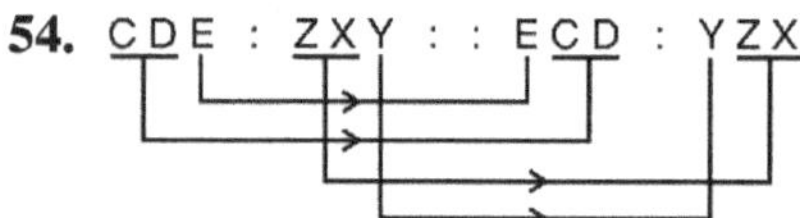

54. 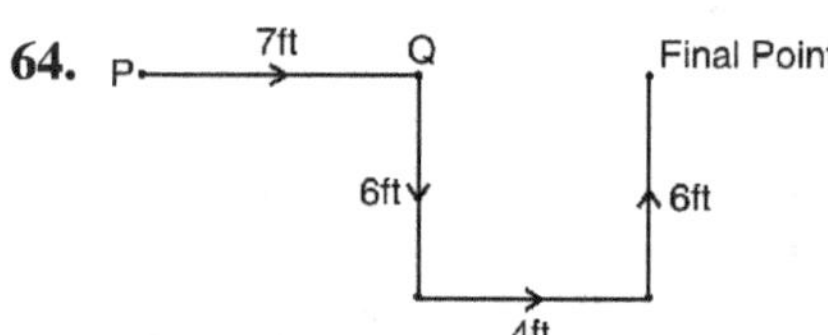

55. FRUIT : JUICE : : COCONUT : OIL.
Juice is extracted from fruits like that oil is extracted from coconut.

56. Grand father < father < son < grandson

57. Disease < Doctor < Diagnosis < Medicine < Cure

58. Admission < Study < Examination < Result < Job.

59. Negative, Negotiate, Neighbour, Neither.

60. Sanatorium, Sanction, Sanctity, Sanskrit.

61. The series is rrr, sss, rrr, sss.

62.

9	8	7
5	6	8
3	5	2
$9+5-3$	$8+6-5$	$7+8-2$
$=11$	$=9$	$=13$

63.

18	16	14
$9\left(=\dfrac{18}{2}\right)$	$8\left(=\dfrac{16}{2}\right)$	$7\left(=\dfrac{14}{2}\right)$
$45(=9\times5)$	$40(=8\times5)$	$35(=7\times5)$

64. 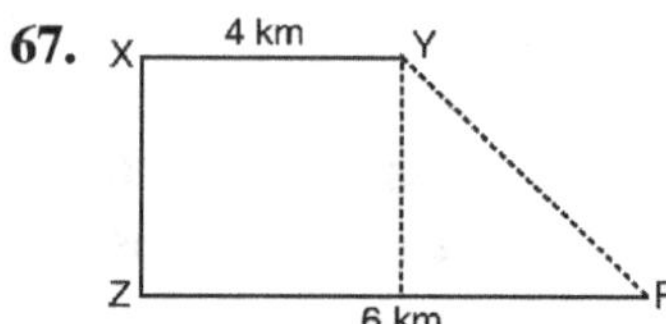

Hence, distance from starting point = 4fts.

65. $17 + 8 \div 2 - 1 = 20$

$17 + 4 - 1 = 20$

$20 = 20$

67.

Hence, P is in South-East with respect to Y.

68. Namitha < Lekhana < Rekha <
↑ (Shortest)   Charithra < Amritha
                                    ↑ (Tallest)

69. A. $20 + 4 \div 4 < 4 + 6 \div 2$

$20 + 1 < 4 + 3$

$21 < 7$ False

B. $20 \div 5 + 4 < 4 + 2 \times 3$

$4 + 4 < 4 + 6$

$8 < 10$ True

C. $20 \div 5 > 8 \div 4 + 6 \times 2$

$4 > 2 + 12$

$4 > 14$ False

D. $20 + 2 > 10 \times 3 + 12 \div 2$

$22 > 30 + 6$

$22 > 36$ False

70.

RAM	— Highest
GOVIND	
NAVEEN	
AHMED	
JOHN	— Lowest

Hence, Govind is second from highest.

71. According to Sakshi, Amith's birthday is either on 11th or 12th March, whereas as per Rekha's memory birthday is on either 12th, 13th, or 14th March.

As both are correct on their points, so, Amith's birthday is on 12th March.

72. Based on the given data six towns in decreasing order of their size, F is smallest.

73. where ⓐⓡⓔ △you → ble ⓝⓔⓔ △see

who ⓐⓡⓔ △you → ⓝⓔⓔ tim △see

Hence, code for where is 'ble'.

75.

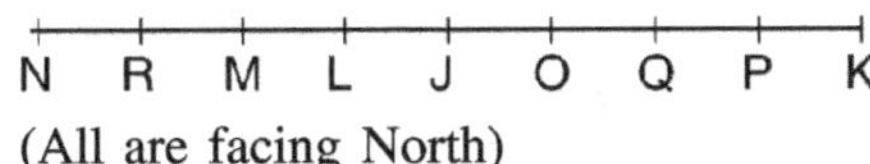

Hence code for NOTICE is 648925.

76-78.

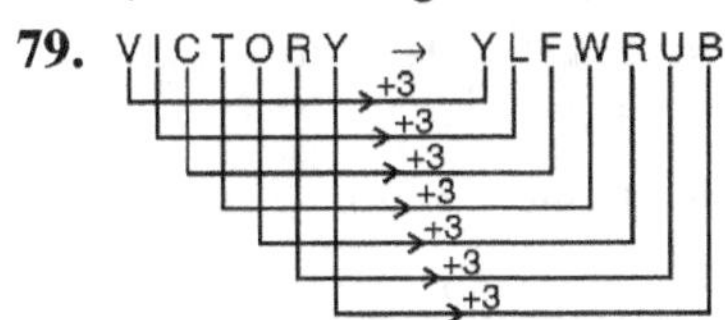

(All are facing North)

79. VICTORY → YLFWRUB

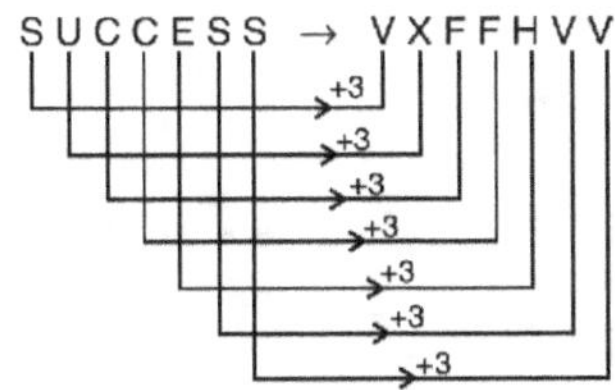

Similarly,

SUCCESS → VXFFHVV

81. 8 men = 12 boys

$$1 \text{ man} = \frac{12}{8} = \frac{3}{2} \text{ boys}$$

$$20 \text{ men} + 6 \text{ boys} = 20 \times \frac{3}{2} + 6 = 30 + 6$$
$$= 36 \text{ boys}$$

12 boys can do a work in 16 days

36 boys can do this work in $\dfrac{16 \times 12}{36}$

$$= \frac{16}{3} = 5\frac{1}{3} \text{ days}$$

Hence, required days = $5\dfrac{1}{3}$ days.

82. Average speed

$$= \frac{\text{total distance covered}}{\text{total time taken}}$$

$$= \frac{d}{\dfrac{d/2}{6} + \dfrac{d/2}{3}}$$

(here d = total distance to cover)

$$= \frac{d}{\dfrac{d/12} + \dfrac{d/6}} = \frac{d}{\dfrac{d}{4}} = 4 \text{ km/hr.}$$

83. Area of rectangle A = length (ℓ) × breadth (b)

i.e.,   A = ℓb

when length increases by 20%

$$\ell' = \ell\left(1 + \frac{10}{100}\right) = 1.1\ell$$

when breadth decreases by 10%

$$b' = b\left(1 - \frac{10}{100}\right) = 0.9b$$

New Area A′ = $\ell' b'$

$$= 1.1\ell \times 0.9b$$
$$= 0.99 \ \ell b = 0.99 \text{ A}$$

$$A' = A\left(1 - \frac{1}{100}\right) = A - 1\%A$$

Hence, New Area is decreases by 1%.

85. Sum of all 7 numbers
$$= 20 \times 7 = 140$$
Sum of first four numbers
$$= 21 \times 4 = 84$$
Sum of last four numbers
$$= 21 \times 4 = 84$$
Hence, fourth number
$$= 84 + 84 - 140$$
$$= 168 - 140 = 28.$$

87.

$$\sqrt{5\left(\frac{11}{4} - \frac{3}{10}\right)} = \sqrt{5\left(\frac{55-6}{20}\right)}$$

$$= \sqrt{\frac{5 \times 49}{20}} = \sqrt{\frac{49}{4}} = \frac{7}{2} = 3\frac{1}{2}.$$

90. L.C.M. of 12, 16, 24 and 36 = 144 minutes

So, in interval of 144 minutes all bell are ringing together.

Hence, they will ring together at $\dfrac{144}{60}$ hours

or, 2:24 P.M.

91. $7 - 5 \times 2 \text{ of } 3 + (19 - \overline{7 - 4}) \div 4$

$$= 7 - 5 \times 2 \text{ of } 3 + (19 - 3) \div 4$$
$$= 7 - 5 \times 2 \text{ of } 3 + 16 \div 4$$
$$= 7 - 5 \times 6 + 16 \div 4$$
$$= 7 - 5 \times 6 + 4$$
$$= 7 - 30 + 4 = -19.$$

92. Speed of the train $= \dfrac{150+200}{35} = 10$ m/sec.

Time taken to pass the stationary man
= time taken to pass its length

$= \dfrac{150}{10} = 15$ sec.

93. $\dfrac{A}{B} = \dfrac{8}{9} \Rightarrow B = \dfrac{9}{8}A$

again, $\dfrac{B}{C} = \dfrac{15}{16} \Rightarrow B = \dfrac{15}{16}C$

therefore, $\dfrac{9}{8}A = \dfrac{15}{16}C$

or, $\dfrac{A}{C} = \dfrac{15}{16} \times \dfrac{8}{9} = \dfrac{5}{6}$.

94. 108 kg of ration is sufficient for 15 days for 18 students

108 kg of ration is sufficient for 1 day for 18×15 student

1 kg of ration is sufficient for $\dfrac{18 \times 15}{108}$ student

$\therefore$ 70 kg of ration is sufficient for 25 days

$\dfrac{18 \times 15}{108} \times \dfrac{70}{25} = 7$ students.

96. Let present age of his son is x years.
then father's age $= (x + 24)$ years.
According to the question,
$(x + 24 + 2) = 2(x + 2)$
$\qquad x + 26 = 2x + 4$
or, $\qquad x = 22$
Hence, Present age of the son = 22 years.

97. According to the question,
$6x - 5x = 1100 \Rightarrow x = 1100$
$\therefore 6x + 5x = 11x = 12100$.

98. Let ratio in which two types of tea mixed is in $x : y$.
So, Cost price $= (192x + 150y)$
From question,
$$\left\{ \dfrac{(194.40)(x+y) - (192x+150y)}{(192x+150y)} \right\} = \dfrac{20}{100}$$

$2.4x + 44.4y = \dfrac{1}{5}\{192x + 150y\}$

$12x + 222y = 192x + 150y$
$\qquad 180x = 72y$

$\dfrac{x}{y} = \dfrac{72}{180} = \dfrac{2}{5}$.

99. When a sphere exactly fit into a cube,
Diameter of the sphere
= Side length of the cube = a (say).

$$\dfrac{\text{Volume of Cube}}{\text{Volume of Sphere}} = \dfrac{a^3}{\dfrac{4}{3} \times \left(\dfrac{a}{2}\right)^3} = \dfrac{1}{\dfrac{\pi}{6}} = \dfrac{6}{\pi}$$

$= 6 : \pi$.

100. Work done in one hour by Gangamma $= \dfrac{1}{8}$

Paravva $= \dfrac{1}{12}$

If they work alternately for one hour, work done in two hours

$= \left(\dfrac{1}{8} + \dfrac{1}{12}\right) = \dfrac{5}{24}$

In next 8 hours they will finish $\dfrac{10}{12}$ work

Remaining work $= \dfrac{1}{6}$ work

Work remaining after working Gangamma for one hour.

$= \dfrac{1}{6} - \dfrac{1}{8} = \dfrac{1}{24}$ work.

Paravva finish $\dfrac{1}{24}$ work in

$= \dfrac{\dfrac{1}{124}}{\dfrac{1}{12}} = 30$ minutes

Total time taken = 9:30 hours
Hence, time when work completed would be 6:30 P.M.